Kenneth Gardnier was born on the
former French and English colony
His father was a successful hotelier
hotel chefs, after being taught to c
eight. He has worked in England as
as a member of the Royal Shakespe
with the Northumberland Theatre Company. He played a major role in two London restaurants, Borshtch 'n' Tears and the Creole Caribbean restaurant Le Caraïbe, which was voted restaurant of the year in 1981. He has contributed to several food magazines and to the *Sunday Times Colour Supplement*. He is now based at Osbourne's delicatessen in Fulham Broadway and is evolving plans for a new Creole restaurant venture.

By the same author

Creole Caribbean Cookery

KENNETH GARDNIER

Creole Vegetarian Cookery

Photographs by Chris Crofton
Line illustrations by Sarah Saville

'Some *Bookes are to be Tasted,
others to be Swallowed, and
Some Few to be Chewed and Digested'

Francis Bacon

* For 'Bookes' read 'cooks'

GRAFTON BOOKS
A Division of the Collins Publishing Group

LONDON GLASGOW
TORONTO SYDNEY AUCKLAND

Grafton Books
A Division of the Collins Publishing Group
8 Grafton Street, London W1X 3LA

A Grafton Paperback Original 1989

A CIP catalogue record for this book
is available from the British Library

ISBN 0-586-20504-7

Printed and bound in Great Britain by
Collins, Glasgow

Set in Plantin

To my friend, Gary Bogard.
Without whom many things to come
would not have been possible.
My thanks always.

Contents

Acknowledgements

I wish to show my gratitude to the following people for their kind help (and extreme endurance in some cases) in many different ways – typing, tasting and fearful advice, all that goes with producing a cookery book: Diana Beatty, Alexander Bentley, Carole Bentley, John Brookesmith, Krysia Campbell, Diane Harkness, Jacqueline Malcolm, Kirsty Malcolm, George Skipper, The Fresh Fruit and Vegetable Information Bureau, M & M of New Covent Garden Market, Nine Elms, Buy-Rite Fruit Stores Ltd, Bute Street, South Kensington, Michael P. Agrippa, Hildreth Street Market, Balham and Matahari Impex, Hogarth Place, Earl's Court. For her invaluable help throughout the book, and especially in the preparation of the photographs, I am deeply indebted to Sarah Saville. To those who feel they have been left out – it was not intentional: my thanks.

Introduction

I am truly privileged to have been born on the island of Dominica, one of the most fertile islands in the Caribbean, with its lush rainforests where the heat-drenched soil allows any seed to germinate and fallen branches will root within days. Dominica is noted for its wide variety of yams, taros and other root vegetables, including sweet potatoes. Our grapefruits and limes are distinctive, as are our mangoes, of which there are over two dozen varieties. On several of the Caribbean islands there is such an abundance of fruit and vegetables that we still use small coconuts, unripened avocados and green mangoes as cricket balls (no better training for fast bowlers!). This is typical of the West Indian attitude to life – adaptability.

In my childhood we had to adapt; we could rarely afford meat or fish. The same can be said for today: with the advent and expansion of tourism and the demand created by the large hotels, our rivers no longer teem with mullet and crayfish, and even the price of land crabs has scuttled beyond the reach of most local inhabitants. So through economic necessity, the poorer peoples have learnt to survive. Yet, regardless of circumstances, we of the Caribbean enjoy life and take nothing for granted. Through our creative use of a multitude of herbs, spices, fruits and vegetables, we have made a unique contribution to vegetarian cuisine.

In Europe and North America exotic vegetables are becoming more widely available at all times of the year: yams, cassava, tannias, dasheen, sweet potatoes, and the famous breadfruit, which has made its way into English history through Captain William 'Breadfruit' Bligh and the mutiny on the *Bounty*. It is also possible to buy okra, pigeon peas, christophenes, bananas and plantains, and even the banana flower can be found in oriental emporiums.

The list of exotic fruits is just as impressive: sugar apples and custard apples, soursops, pawpaws and scented guavas, kiwi fruits, mangoes, avocados and juicy pineapples. The lesser-known ones are now rapidly growing in popularity too, fruits such as the mangosteen, sapodilla and tamarillo from South-East Asia, the Caribbean and the South-American mainland.

The cuisine of the Caribbean has been contributed to not only by Carib Indians and Africans, but also by the peoples of India, China and, to a great extent, Europe. I have adapted a few European recipes to make use of the more familiar vegetables cultivated in even the smallest of kitchen gardens. I am most fortunate at my cottage in Northumberland to be able to grow my own organic herbs and vegetables, which I used when testing these recipes. Not all of the dishes are spicy hot and therefore they should satisfy the majority of tastes. There is a wide choice of delicious and aromatically seductive dishes which will give you a different experience in flavours.

The colourful soups can be meals in themselves: sopa de frijole negro from Cuba is a black bean soup with tomato sauce, sweet peppers, coriander leaves, garlic, onions, herbs and spices. Callaloo soup from the Eastern Caribbean is perhaps the most famous of all West Indian soups and is made from the young leaves of the dasheen or taro plant with coconut cream, okra, fresh hot pepper and spices. From the French-speaking islands comes Fedilia's green gumbo soup, made from leaf vegetables and okra. There is pumpkin soup and red bean and sweet potato soup, and for the heat of the summer the cooks of the Spanish-American mainland have given us cream of watercress soup and chilled avocado soup. For those who enjoy a peppery hors d'oeuvre, I have included avocado Dominique – avocado halves with a rich, steaming filling – and for the more delicate palate there are dishes such as mushrooms in coconut cream, creole aubergine and guacamole with rum.

The sumptuous main courses boast Keshy Yena, from the old Dutch colony of Curaçao, where a whole Edam cheese is hollowed out and stuffed with a delicious filling then baked (a good dish for a formal dinner party); curried green bananas from Martinique; breadfruit, cheese and onion flan from Barbados; creole rice mould with bananas and avocado from the Eastern Caribbean; stuffed yam from Dominica; and, from all parts of the Caribbean, onion and sweet pepper casserole, breadfruit and cashew pie and stuffed ripe plantains. There are several dishes which make use of spinach, nuts and beans, and last, but not least, the infamous rice and peas!

To complete, there is a range of cooling sorbets, ice-creams and tempting fruit desserts. Before, during and after the meal, try some of the titillating rum punches or non-alcoholic beverages.

Most vegetarians are all too aware of the importance of dietary requirements, but they may not be familiar with the nutritional values of exotic fruits and vegetables. To this end, included in this book are tables listing the composition of some of the fruits and vegetables I have used in the recipes.

Some of the most memorable and enjoyable meals that I have ever eaten were prepared with simple care and planning by vegetarians. It is my sincere wish that all vegetarians and non-vegetarians who enjoy good food will find some pleasure in this book. The recipes I have chosen are ones that suit my taste; may they prove to be as tempting to you too.

Glossary

Accra, Akkra, Accras A fritter which is originally from West Africa and made with black-eyed peas. It is very popular throughout the Caribbean, where it usually consists of a heavy batter with herbs, spices and flaked fish. Accra made from vegetables, such as aubergine, is also very good.

Achee, Ackee (*Blighia sapida*) The fruit of an evergreen tree from West Africa and now widely cultivated in Jamaica. The plant was introduced into the West Indies by Captain William Bligh of *Bounty* fame. Cooked with salted cod it has become known as Jamaica's national dish. Achee has a scarlet pod and shiny black seeds, and the edible flesh is pale cream in colour with a texture and flavour similar to scrambled eggs. Until the fruit is fully grown, matured and ripened it is poisonous. It is available tinned in Asian and West Indian shops and in open markets which specialize in exotic and tropical produce.

Arrowroot (*Maranta arundinacea*) The starch obtained from a plant originating in the West Indies and later introduced into India by the English. It is an ideal agent for thickening stews, sauces and soups, as it leaves no taste. It should be added to a dish at the last minute or two, as if it is cooked for too long the liquid will thin down again. The best arrowroot comes from St Vincent in the West Indies, but it is also grown in Madagascar. A less-refined form of arrowroot is used as a feed for infants, young children and invalids, as it is easily digestible. The texture when cooked with sugar and water, with sometimes a stick of cinnamon, is that of a thick jelly. In days past, it was used for starching the national costumes (*la robe creole* and *wob dwiyet*) of the French- and Patois-speaking peoples of the Antilles.

Aubergine, Eggplant, Melongene, Morelle (*Solanum melongena*) Originating from India, this vegetable is very popular in creole cookery. It can be fried, baked, stuffed, puréed as an hors-d'oeuvre or dip, or used in stews and casseroles. There are many different-coloured varieties of aubergine, the most common being purple. The flower of the shrub is very similar to that of deadly nightshade and is a member of the same family. Available all the year round, even in the smallest of shops.

Avocado, Alligator Pear, Zaboca, Avocat (*Persea americana*) A native tree of tropical America, hence the Latin name, but extensively cultivated throughout the Caribbean and many parts of the world today. Consequently the fruit is available all the year round. A well-matured and ripe avocado, regardless of where it is from, should peel as easily as a banana (see Techniques). It is excellent on its own, in salads, stuffed with a spicy filling or even in ice-cream. Great in sandwiches. The fruit of the avocado can weigh anything from 25 g to 1.25 kg (1 oz–2½ lb) and sometimes even more. Avocados are a good source of vitamin E.

Bakes A doughy dumpling, made with baking powder, flour, water and sometimes lard, then fried in oil. Very popular throughout the West Indies. A quick and easy substitute for bread.

Banana, Bluggoe, Cocoy, Fig, Plantain, Matabooro, Mafube, Fig Sucrier (the *musa* family) All members of this very large family are green when unripe, except for one of the cocoys, or matabooro, a stumpy first cousin which is purple-red and remains that colour even when ripe. All the other *musas* ripen to a rich yellow. Whether ripe or green, the plantain, cocoy, bluggoe or matabooro can only be eaten when cooked. When green, all edible *musas* are used as a starchy vegetable. Ripe plantains and cocoys can be fried, stuffed or boiled (see Techniques). Green bananas and plantains are not as high in iron as is commonly believed throughout the West Indian islands – though they do contain traces of certain vitamins and minerals.

Beans, Peas, Pulses On many Caribbean islands the terms peas and beans are used interchangeably. They are very popular on the islands, and form a part of most meals, especially cooked with rice. The most commonly used are red kidney beans, pigeon peas, black beans (*frijole negro*), black-eyed peas, white beans, haricot beans and green peas. All are used either fresh or dried (see Techniques).

Breadfruit, Yam Pain, Pain Bois (***Artocarpus communis***) The tree most associated with Captain Bligh, and originally a native of the South Pacific islands. It is a large green fruit, the size of a small football, which can only be eaten when cooked. It can be boiled, fried, stuffed or roasted, either in the oven or on a charcoal fire. After cooking it can also be pounded in a mortar and pestle to make breadfruit foo-foo. After the ill-fated voyage of the *Bounty* in 1787, Captain Bligh made a second and successful attempt to get the breadfruit and other plants to the 'New World' in 1793 when he sailed on the HMS *Providence* from the island of Otahiti in the South Pacific to St Vincent in the Caribbean. It is said that the original breadfruit tree which he planted on St Vincent is still thriving.

When buying breadfruits make certain that they are well matured but not ripe, firm but not soft, although a slightly ripe breadfruit is ideal for stuffing and roasting. Breadfruits are available throughout the year from most West Indian and Asian shops, and from markets dealing in tropical produce. They are also available tinned, but these can only be boiled or fried. A gum excreted from the trunk is still used today by the Carib Indians for sealing holes in fishing canoes.

Calabaza, West Indian Pumpkin Paler in colour than most other pumpkins, very delicate in flavour and ideal in soups and stews. It is one of the largest pumpkins, weighing anything up to 10 kg (22 lb). Available in markets specializing in tropical produce.

Callaloo, Callilu, Calaloo The Creole and Caribbean name for the young leaves of the dasheen or tannia plant, very similar in texture and taste to spinach. It is used in the most famous of Caribbean soups, to which it has given its name. Like spinach it can be used in soufflés and many other recipes. Callaloo leaves must not be eaten raw and should be cooked according to the directions given in the recipes, otherwise they may cause irritation to the mouth. They can be purchased almost all year round in markets dealing in tropical produce, and are a good source of vitamin A.

Cashew Nut (***Anacardium occidental***) The cashew is an evergreen tree native to many parts of the tropics. It used to be widely cultivated throughout the Caribbean but was replaced long ago on some islands by bananas and other crops. A few trees are still to be found here and there, and it is a shame that there are not many more. The tart, red, pear-shaped fruit is edible and is used in jams and jellies, but the kidney-shaped shell which grows at the bottom of the fruit and contains the nut is poisonous and can cause severe burns and skin irritation; it must be roasted before it is cracked open to reveal the nut. Cashew nuts are a good source of nutrients, including the minerals magnesium and potassium.

Cassava, Manioc (*Manihot utilissima*) The tapered root of a tropical plant native to the West Indies, South and Central America and some North American states. It once formed the staple diet of the Carib Indians and the Arawaks before them. There is both a sweet cassava and a bitter cassava. The sap of the bitter cassava is poisonous, but is eradicated by cooking or fermentation. The sweet cassava, which is non-poisonous, is the only cassava allowed into Europe for consumption. When grated, cassava can be made into bread (see Farine). The juice extracted from grated cassava can be boiled on a moderate heat, stirring constantly until it thickens. It will then keep for a few days in the fridge and can be used to thicken sauces. Cassava is also the base for tapioca, and is used to make starch or refined to glucose. Available in most markets dealing in West Indian fruits and vegetables.

Cherimoya, Custard Apple (*Annona cherimola*) Has either a pale-green or light-pink skin according to where in the tropics it is grown. The skin is either dull or has a slight sheen and a leathery feel with scalelike patterns. The edible flesh is pale white to cream, surrounding dark, brown-black seeds, and can be very sweet and not unlike custard in texture. Ideal in ice-creams, drinks or eaten on its own. Sold in markets dealing in tropical produce, Chinese shops in the Soho district of London and in up-market delicatessens.

Chillies See Peppers.

Christophene, Chayote, Cho-cho (*Sechium edule*) A tropical, pear-shaped squash of a climbing vine belonging to the marrow family. It can be boiled, baked or stuffed, and in the Caribbean it is widely used in stews. On sale in shops and open markets dealing in tropical produce, and also available in many of the larger supermarkets.

Coconut (***Cocos nucifera***) Think of the tropics and one thinks of golden beaches lined with the coconut palm. But to the inhabitants of the islands the coconut tree is more than purely decorative; it is life itself – 'the tree of life' – for it is the most valuable and versatile of all palms. From the coconut comes oil, water, milk, cream and even sugar; wine is made from it, and it produces fibre for ropes, mats and mattresses. The heart is cooked as a vegetable or used raw in salads, and the trunk itself is valued as building material. There are many recipes calling for coconut in this book – soups, savoury dishes, curries, cakes, drinks and sweets. (See Techniques on how to choose a coconut and how to make coconut milk and cream.)

Cornmeal The ground grains of the maize corn, used extensively in West Indian cooking in sweets, breads, puddings and savoury dishes. Its most popular use is in coo-coo (recipe on page 154). Cornmeal has traces of vitamins A, B and C and also traces of minerals.

Curaçao A liqueur made from bitter oranges on the island of Curaçao, which lies near to the mainland of Venezuela.

Cush Cush The smallest member of the yam family which, like the yam, is the root of the vine. May be boiled, baked or fried, and really can be treated as one would an Irish or English potato. When cooked it has a texture that can only be described as dry and silky (see Techniques). Like dasheen, other members of the taro family, and yams, the cush cush is high in carbohydrates with traces of vitamins and minerals.

Dasheen One of the taro group of root vegetables, which includes the eddo, tannia, malanga, yantia and several others. This member of the *arum* family has a rough brown skin and varies in size from that of an avocado to a very large, oval melon. Its young leaves are used like spinach and are one of the most important ingredients in the famous callaloo soup. The flesh of the dasheen can be white, cream or very pale, almost blue-grey. It must be peeled before cooking, and can be boiled, roasted, fried or creamed (see Techniques).

Eddo See Tannia.

Farine A rough, coarse meal made from grated cassava which is then dried, usually in the sun. It can be used in soups, dumplings, puddings, cakes and bread. Pulped together with avocado it is delicious served with a hot sauce. Farine is available in packets from Asian and West Indian shops.

Floats A yeasted or unleavened flat bread which is either baked or fried.

Frijole negro A shiny black bean related to the red kidney bean. It is very popular throughout the Caribbean and even more so on the mainland of South America, where it forms part of many a national dish, such as *gallo pinto* from Costa Rica – a fried black bean dish with rice. Re-fried black beans are also very popular in many places on the South American mainland. Black beans are good and nutritious, containing protein, vitamins and most minerals.

Funchi, Fungee A sweet pudding made from cornmeal. More or less a sweet version of the coo-coo made from cornmeal and okra.

Guava, Goyave (*Psidium guajava*) The heavily scented fruit of an evergreen tree which grows wild on many islands in the Tropics. There are several species of this fruit, with pale green or yellow soft skins, and when ripe it can be eaten whole – skin, seeds and all. The flesh of the guava can be very pale yellow or pink in colour, and can be eaten as a fruit, or made into jams, jellies, pies, ice-creams and other sweet dessert dishes. Available all the year round, fresh or canned. Guavas, of all fruits, contain the highest amount of vitamin C.

Gunga, Gungo, Gongo See Pigeon Peas.

Keshy Yena A whole Edam cheese, hollowed out then stuffed with mushrooms, sweet peppers, olives, a mixture of other vegetables, herbs, spices and some of the cheese. A Dutch speciality of the islands (recipe on page 129).

Kiwi Fruit (*Actinidia sinensis*) Certainly not native to the Caribbean, but it is exotic and rapidly growing in popularity. Grown mostly in New Zealand, it can be eaten on its own or in fruit salads, and makes a great sorbet.

Mango (*Mangifera indica*) The fruit of an evergreen tree which can reach a height of twenty feet or more. There is a very wide variety of this most delicious of all fruits, which originated in India and was introduced into the West Indies about 200 years ago. The best are the Julie from the Caribbean and the Alphonse from India. The sweeter the mango the stronger the aromatic scent. Just because a mango is large and brightly coloured does not necessarily mean that it is deliciously tasty and full of that wonderful exotic flavour. I have seen many mangoes on sale in Europe at the most exorbitant prices that are only fit for animal feed. Mangoes can be eaten by themselves or used in jams, chutneys, mousses, ice-creams, fruit salads, pies and drinks. Available fresh from most greengrocers, supermarkets, corner shops and open markets. They are a rich source of vitamin A.

Mangosteen (*Garcinia mangostana*) Originating from and widely cultivated in East Asia, this fruit is really one of the true exotics and very delicious. It is also now grown in South America and there are a few trees scattered around the Caribbean; I personally know of several in Dominica. The trees, which are evergreen, can reach a height of over twenty-five feet. It is now possible to buy mangosteens in Europe, and in London they are available from any of the Chinese shops in Soho, Earl's Court or Westbourne Grove and some of the better supermarkets. They are very expensive but worth it. Great on their own, in ice-creams, sorbets, or fruit salads.

Molasses A thick, black syrup which is a by-product of sugar refining and can be used instead of sugar in drinks, cakes, puddings and even savoury dishes. Molasses is rich in minerals, especially calcium, iron, potassium and phosphorus. Available canned from most grocers and supermarkets.

Naseberry See Sapodilla.

Okra, Okroes, Bindhi, Ladies' Fingers, Gumbo (*Hibiscus esculentus*) A member of the *hibiscus* family, which was introduced into the West Indies from Africa – also cultivated in India and other parts of Asia. Okra are very popular in creole cooking and are used in stews and served simply as a vegetable. They are also the principal ingredient in coo-coo, a dish made with cornmeal, which is very popular on the island of Barbados. Okra can now be obtained from almost any greengrocer, Asian or West Indian shops and supermarkets.

Otaheiti Apple, Pomerac Red, pear-shaped fruit originating in Tahiti. It can be eaten by itself or used in pies, fruit salads, puddings and jams. It can be found occasionally in specialist shops and markets.

Pain Mey A cornmeal, pumpkin and coconut savoury or sweet dish, mixed with herbs and spices and cooked wrapped in banana leaves. Sold by street vendors and open markets in the Caribbean.

Passion Fruit, Granadilla, Grenadilla, Barbadeen (*Passiflora edulis*) So named by Spanish missionaries, to whom the cross of the open flower represented Christ's passion and his crucifixion. There are over 250 varieties of this climbing plant, though they do not all produce edible fruit. The plants most certainly originated in South America and the Caribbean, and were cultivated by the Indians long before Columbus's encounter with the New World. Passion Fruit vary in size, the largest being the barbadeen, or granadilla, which is oblong in shape and can be as long as 30 cm (12 inches). The most readily available variety in Europe is the purple, eggshaped one, which can be bought in almost any greengrocer's, open market or supermarket. Other fruit vary in colour from pale green to yellow and orange when ripe. The purple fruit crinkles very quickly when ripe and should not be left for too long before being used. The skin of the yellow fruit is very smooth and shiny. The flowers, which are pollinated either by insects or by hand, open during the morning and close in the late evening when it is dark. It is a wonderful experience to watch the flowers open before your very eyes. The taste and aroma of the fruit is very exotic and lends a unique flavour to any dish. The fruit can be sliced in half and the inside spooned out and eaten as is, or it can be used in ice-creams, sorbets, soufflés, cakes and many luxurious drinks. It makes a great rum punch. Passion fruit contain a fair amount of protein and fibre.

Pawpaw, Papaya (***Carica papaya***) The fruit of a tree native to the Caribbean and tropical America. Cultivated in many other tropical parts as well. A pawpaw can weigh anything from 225 g (8 oz) to 5 kg (11 lb). When green, the fruit is served cooked as a vegetable or parboiled and stuffed with cheese and other savoury fillings; it can then be baked or grilled according to its size. Green pawpaw is also used in chutneys and relishes. Thinly sliced and cooked in a syrup with spices it makes a very good sweet. Pawpaw is also believed to contain a medicinal agent which is very powerful in the healing of the most difficult sores. The white enzyme (papain) excreted from the pawpaw is used in many countries as a tenderizer; it can at the same time cause skin irritation, so should not be brought into contact with the eyes. When ripe, pawpaw can be eaten on its own with or without lime or lemon juice. It is ideal in fruit salads, in rum punches and other drinks. It is a very good source of vitamins A and C.

Pepper, Chilli (***Capsicum annuum***) A member of the same family as the bell pepper (sweet pepper or pimiento), the chilli pepper is widely grown in Latin America, Mexico, the West Indies, Africa, India and many parts of Asia. The sweet or bell peppers, which are the biggest, are used in salads, stews and sauces. They can also be stuffed and then grilled or roasted. Like hot chillies they vary in colour from green to different shades of red and yellow and to an almost-black purple. Hot peppers vary considerably in size and strength; from half the size of a tapered matchstick (in Patois, *pima zozio*; in English, bird pepper) to a very large walnut (*Bom de Ma Jacques* in Patois; in English, Mrs Jake's Bottom or Scots Bonnet). The latter has the best flavour and is recommended for the recipes in this book. The seeds are the hottest part and should not be used unless called for in the recipe (see Techniques). Fresh peppers are available all the year round, and pepper sauces from all parts of the world can be found in even the smallest corner shops. It is best to try and use a West Indian pepper sauce in the recipes where such is called for. Red chilli peppers are high in protein and in carotene.

Pigeon Peas, Gongo Peas, Gunga Peas, Tuvar Peas (*Cajanus cajan*) Very popular in Caribbean cooking, on their own or in soups, stews and rice dishes. The trees can reach a height of over eight feet, with pods of about 7.5 cm (3 inches) in length which are curved like a scimitar. Each pod contains an average of between six and eight peas. The pods are either pale green, variegated with purple, or rich purple. The peas themselves vary in colour from green, cream, light brown, soft red or deep purple, but they all dry to the same beige shade. Pigeon peas imported fresh from the Caribbean are available in Europe from November until March or April. But they are also available throughout the year, as other tropical countries yield crops at different times. Pigeon peas can be purchased tinned, dried or frozen. If using tinned it is best to drain before using. I sometimes rinse them. Pigeon peas are rich in protein.

Pineapple, Ananas (*Ananas comosus*) Very little need be said about this well-known fruit, which originated in South America and the Caribbean islands. It can be eaten on its own, or used in jams, ice-creams, cakes, compôtes, fritters and many other desserts. Pineapple has a very high sugar content, but also a large amount of vitamins A and B. Today pineapples are grown in many other countries, especially Asia and Africa, which ensures their availability all year round.

Plantain (*musa*) See Banana.

Rum, rhum A by-product of sugar cane refining, rum is possibly one of the best spirits that can be used in cooking. Though it suffers from the old reputation of being the drink of the devil, it remains one of the most celebrated of alcoholic drinks with a proof of anything from 50–200 per cent. The word 'rum' is supposed to have derived from the old Devon word 'rumbullion', meaning 'to create a rumpus'. The best rums are still made in the Caribbean and each island boasts its own, with those from the French island of Martinique being in the forefront. In all recipes calling for rum in this book, and most certainly the rum punches, I recommend that a rum from the Caribbean is used, preferably a light brown one. The dark navy rums will drastically alter the flavour of any dish or drink, which in these recipes certainly will not do. White rums from the islands may be substituted, but I personally would not recommend Bacardi. It may be a good drinking rum, but used in cooking it is not in keeping with the true flavour and characteristics of other Caribbean rums. A few good brands to look for are Cockspur, Mount Gay, Lemon Hart, Appleton and Vat 19. The best ones are the famous St James and Rhum Clément from Martinique; buy some next time you are in France.

Sapodilla, Sapota, Zapoti, Chapoti, Naseberry (*Zapota achras*) This delicious fruit, which has a slightly rough, brown skin and yellowish flesh, is about the size and shape of a kiwi fruit. It originated in Central America but is now to be found throughout the Caribbean and many other parts of the world. It must be fully matured and ripe before it is eaten. Goes well in most sweet dishes, including fruit salads, sorbets and ice-cream. Available from Asian and West Indian shops, and from markets dealing in tropical produce.

Sorrel, Rosella A member of the *hibiscus* family, this is grown throughout the West Indies for its bright red sepals, which are used to make drinks, jams and jellies. It is harvested during December and January, and is very popular as a Christmas drink. It is available during the months of December and early January in most shops and markets selling exotic produce.

Soursop (*Annona muricata*) Fruit of a tropical tree, with a spiky skin which remains green even when ripe. The fruit, which can be very large, has a pure white, heavily scented pulp which is very juicy with a sharp-sweet creamy flavour. It can be used in drinks, sorbets, sherbets and ice-creams or eaten as a fruit. Available fresh from open markets. The juice is also available in cans.

Sugar Apple Sometimes called 'sweet sop', this has a raised, green, scale-like lumpy skin. It belongs to the same family as the custard apple and soursop (*annona*). It is deliciously sweet, with a whitish flesh and a cluster of small tentacles enclosing black seeds. Available in markets and specialist shops.

Sugar Cane Resembles a thick reed similar to a reed once used by the Carib Indians and the Arawaks before them, for building material, basket weaving and a hundred and one other things; even the leaves were used – and still are – to make thatch, mats and hats. Sugar cane was introduced into the Caribbean from Gomera in the Canaries by Christopher Columbus on his second voyage in 1493. From sugar cane comes over half of the sugar consumed in the world, as well as several by-products, including molasses and rum. Sugar cane is available fresh, either in whole lengths or short pieces, from markets, shops and supermarkets selling tropical produce. Avoid buying pieces that are too dry at the ends, especially the shorter bits.

Sweet Potato, Patate, Boniato Native to tropical America, the West Indies and the Pacific. They are the edible tubers of a vine that crawls along the ground. Their skin can be pink, cream, yellow or reddish brown. The flesh itself is varied in colour too, from white to different shades of yellow, orange and even pink. Some tubers, regardless of colour, are sweeter than others and softer or firmer in texture when cooked. Sweet potatoes can be boiled, fried, roasted, baked or stuffed; they can also be used in sweets, cakes and breads. A sweet potato which has been parboiled, then peeled, thinly sliced and glazed in a syrup of cane sugar flavoured with cinnamon, lemon zest and nutmeg, makes a pudding worth trying. Sweet potatoes are now available from the smallest of greengrocers and corner shops. The yellower they are, the richer in vitamin A they become, but they all have traces.

Tamarillo, Tree Tomato A native of South America, this is now cultivated in many parts of the world. The fruit is egg-shaped, with a deep, reddish-orange skin, which is bitter and so should not be eaten. The flesh is slightly sharp and may not be pleasing to some but it is ideal in fruit salads, ice-creams and sorbets. Makes an excellent jam, rich in flavour and colour. The fruit is very rich in vitamins.

Tannia, Eddo, Coco, Taro A member of the *arum* family, to which the dasheen also belongs. The tannia is smaller than the dasheen, though of similar skin texture, and is drier when cooked. It is rather more pear-shaped than any other member of the family. The leaves are used for callaloo, and are rich in vitamin A.

Taro See Dasheen and Tannia.

Yams, Igname The edible tubers of a large family of climbing vines which includes the cush cush. Yams come in all shapes and sizes and can weigh anything from 225 g (½ lb) to 50 kg (110 lb). The skins of yams are brown, except for the cush cush which can have a slightly purple colour. Yams are a starchy vegetable and should be treated like dasheen (see Techniques). They can be boiled, baked, roasted, stuffed or creamed, and are available in shops, supermarkets and open markets dealing in tropical produce. Like the taro family, they are high in carbohydrates.

Herbs, Spices and Other Condiments

The following is a list of herbs, spices and flavourings used in the recipes in this book and in creole cooking in general.

Although spices can be bought already ground it is best to buy them whole whenever possible and grind them yourself when needed. A coffee grinder or pestle and mortar are ideal for this purpose. Alternatively, tie the spices in a clean cloth, such as a corner of a kitchen towel doubled in two, and pound gently with a heavy instrument on a hard surface. Always store spices in airtight jars away from direct sunlight, and buy only a little at a time. I try to use up all my spices within three to four months. Cinnamon sticks and whole nutmegs will keep much longer. Use your spices sparingly until you are familiar with each individual flavour; a little can transform a dish into a unique experience to be savoured with pleasure.

Like freshly ground spices, fresh herbs can greatly enhance your cooking and each herb will add its own character and flavour to your dish. Use a little at a time until you are familiar with a particular herb. Though fresh herbs can be frozen, they are best kept with their stems in a jar of water, and the water should be changed about every three days. Avoid buying too much at a time; if they are in large bunches, split the difference with friends. Fresh herbs also make a very attractive garnish.

Allspice, Jamaican Pepper, Pimento, Toute Épice The dried berries of an evergreen tree native to the Caribbean. They are similar in appearance to peppercorns and have a taste and scent reminiscent of a combination of cloves, cinnamon and nutmeg. They are used widely in creole and West Indian cooking in soups, stews, savoury dishes, cakes, puddings and pies.

Almond extract For flavouring cakes, ice-cream and other sweet dishes. It is always best to use a natural essence rather than a synthetically produced one.

Angostura Produced in Trinidad and used to flavour rum cocktails, ice-cream, fruit salads, lime and lemon squash, sauces and savoury dishes. It is made from the bark of a tree, Galipea, and blended with nutmeg, cinnamon and other spices. It is expensive but worth having in store. A bottle will last for years.

Anise, Nannee A spice with a distinctive liquorice flavour, which can be used in puddings, cakes, curries, vegetable dishes, confectionery and drinks. Both the fresh leaves and the seeds are used. I have grown the plant myself, very successfully, in Northumberland. In the Caribbean fresh sprigs are immersed in bottles of white rum and left to steep for weeks, after which the rum tastes like Greek Ouzo or the French liqueur, Anisette. Use only a small quantity of anise when cooking as it has a very strong flavour.

Annatto, Anato, Achote (*Bixa orellana*) The prickly fruit and seed of a tree native to tropical America, but also found in other areas of the Caribbean and South-East Asia. The seed is ground and used as a spice. The orange pulp surrounding the seed is principally used as a colouring agent in cooking oils, butter and lard. The dye was used by the South-American Indians and Caribs on their bodies, clothes and in decorative work. Both the seed and liquid are available from some oriental shops.

Bay The bay leaves used in West Indian cooking are much stronger in flavour than the ones available in Europe. Bay leaves can be used to flavour soups, sauces, casseroles and spicy dishes, including curries. It is best to use whole leaves and remove them just before serving. They are one of the three herbs used in the traditional bouquet garni of French cuisine, the other two being thyme and parsley.

Cardamon There are three varieties of this pod – black, green and white – with a number of small seeds. Both the pods and seeds are available in this country. Cardamon is a very aromatic and expensive spice so should be used sparingly. Used in curries and rice dishes.

Chives A member of the onion family. Used extensively in creole cooking, especially on the French- and Patois-speaking islands. The chives grown in the Caribbean are much stronger in scent and flavour than their European cousins. Ideal in salads, egg dishes, sauces, soups and hors d'oeuvres. Fresh chives are best and can be grown in a pot on the window ledge or in any small garden. Spring onions can be used as a substitute. Avoid dried or frozen chives.

Cinnamon, Canel, Canela Reputed to be one of the oldest known spices, with a reputation for medicinal properties, such as relief of flatulence and internal haemorrhages. The cinnamon, an evergreen tree, is a member of the laurels, like the bay, and can reach a height of thirty feet or more. It is cultivated in India, Madagascar, the Seychelles and the Caribbean. Cinnamon is chiefly used as a flavouring in cakes and sweet desserts but does well in sauces, especially curries. In the Caribbean both the peeled bark and the leaves are used in cooking. It also plays a very great part in drinks and syrups. Cinnamon sticks boiled in some water then sweetened with brown sugar with a little milk added makes a very pleasant drink. Try adding a piece of ginger as well.

Cloves, Clous de Girofle A native of the West Indies, India, Tanzania and Madagascar. It is an evergreen tree which can reach a height of over thirty feet or more. The clove itself is the deep red bud of the unopened flower. They are heavily scented and hang in clusters from the branches of the tree. Ground cloves are excellent in cakes, sweets and puddings, and give an unmistakable flavour to soups, sauces, stews and other spicy dishes. Great in mulled wine.

Coriander Both the leaves and seeds are used. This is another plant I have been successful in growing. The leaves are used as a herb and the seeds are used as a spice, mostly in curried dishes. Both are very potent in flavour and should be added sparingly. The leaves are available from Asian and Mediterranean shops, and from supermarkets and open markets. Coriander has a very similar appearance to a large-leaf parsley, so be careful not to pick the wrong one. The leaves are best kept with their stems immersed in a jar of water. They can also be stored in plastic bags in the refrigerator.

Cumin, Geera There are two varieties of this spice: a very dark one, and the better-known, lighter-coloured seed. Both can be used in breads, curries, stews and cheese dishes.

Fennel A spice with a slightly similar taste to anise. The plant originated in the Mediterranean but now grows throughout the world. Almost all of the plant can be used in cooking: the leaves in salads, the seeds in stews and vegetable dishes, especially cabbage, and the stems cooked as a vegetable. Fennel stems simmered in butter with a little salt and pepper, then covered with lots of grated cheese and baked until brown, makes a wonderful side dish.

Garlic A member of the lily family, cultivated for its bulb. It can be used in most savoury dishes, soups, stews, casseroles, dips, salads and dressings, sauces and even on bread. Use fresh whole cloves either finely chopped or crushed with a flat implement. A garlic press should be part of your kitchen equipment.

Ginger This plant, which belongs to the same family as the turmeric, is a rhizome and a native of Asia and the Caribbean. It is used in cakes, sauces, curries and drinks. The skin should be peeled off before the root is used in cooking. Ginger will keep for months if planted in a light potting compost, where it will germinate and grow with its pointed leaves; you simply dig the plant up when needed, cut or break a piece and replant it in the pot. The plant can be kept on the window sill of your kitchen. The root is not only available fresh, but can be bought preserved in syrup, crystallized or glazed, for cakes, sorbets, mousses and ice-creams. It is also available dried or powdered. When buying fresh ginger avoid wrinkled roots; they should be as firm and plump as possible.

Lemon Peel In the Caribbean the skin of the lemon is peeled off very carefully, in a long strip, with a sharp vegetable knife, leaving behind the white spongy part. It is then hung up indoors to dry. When dry, pieces can be broken off to use in cakes, breads, stews, and hot drinks. Dried lemon peel boiled for a few minutes in a cup or two of water, on its own or with fresh ginger added, is believed to soothe stomach aches, indigestion and even colds. It is also ideal as a refreshing drink, sweetened or unsweetened.

Lime Peel Treat as lemon peel. Can be used in spiced hot drinks, mulled wines, or ground for cakes and sweets.

Mace The deep red 'blade' surrounding the hard brown shell of the nutmeg. The mace turns to a yellow-brown when dried. When ground, the blades have a similar aroma to the grated nut, and can be used not only in savoury dishes but sweet ones as well, especially puddings. Like all dried spices it is best bought whole and ground when needed.

Nutmeg, Muscade, Moscado An indigenous tree of the East Indian islands which was introduced into the Caribbean in either the late sixteenth or early eighteenth century and is extensively cultivated on many Caribbean islands, especially Grenada, the 'spice island' of the West Indies. It is an evergreen tree, which can attain a height of thirty feet or more. It also produces mace (see above), which is the deep-red, Art Nouveau-patterned peel that covers the hard shell holding the actual nut. The nutmeg also has an outer yellow skin which resembles an apricot – when matured this outer skin splits into two perfect halves to reveal the mace and brown shell. The mace is peeled off, and the brown shell cracked to extract the nut. Use grated in drinks, sweets, cakes and savoury dishes.

Orange Peel Treat as lemon peel. The dried peel is used in sweets, cakes, puddings and hot drinks. Try a deliciously refreshing orange-peel tea, with or without milk.

Parsley There are several varieties of this wonderful herb, which can be found in virtually every country in the world in one form or another. The three most commonly known varieties are Italian parsley, broad-leaf parsley and curly-leaf parsley. Parsley is one of the three herbs in the French bouquet garni. It can also be used in soups, stews, vegetable dishes, sauces and salads. Try a salad with nothing else but a few bunches of parsley, served with a French dressing to which a little wine mayonnaise has been added. Parsley lends itself very well as a garnish.

Peppercorns Possibly one of the most popular spices. Both black and white berries come from a vine-like shrub, and they are not related to the capsicum family. Black peppercorns are picked from the vine while still green and then dried in the sun. White peppercorns are the fully matured and ripened seeds, which are picked, skinned and left to dry in the sun. Black corns are much stronger in flavour. Today it is also possible to buy green and red peppercorns. Although fairly aromatic they are best used for decorative presentation. Peppercorns lose their flavour and aroma when ground so should not be ground until needed.

Pepper Sauce There are many brands of hot sauces on the market today, which can be obtained from any small shop. But the recipes in this book call for distinctively West Indian sauces. Why not make your own? There is a recipe on page 182.

Saffron The stigmas of a crocus, grown in Asia and Southern Europe, and once extensively cultivated in Saffron Walden, England. It can be purchased either in powdered form or as stigmas. It produces a very bright yellow dye with a distinct flavour which can be used in cakes, curries, rice dishes, breads, sweets, soups and other savoury dishes. Saffron is the world's most expensive spice, for which there really is no substitute, though turmeric can be used in its stead as a colouring agent.

Salt I have always strongly believed that it is important to use salt to bring out the flavour of most foods; the amount depends on your particular taste. Caribbean cooks have always preferred to use rock sea salt, and I do recommend that you make use of sea salt in all your cooking, whether coarse salt, fine salt or rock salt.

Tamarind The pod of a large tropical tree cultivated in India, East Africa, the Caribbean and many tropical parts of the world. The name comes from Persia and means 'the fruit of India'. The trees are massive, growing to over twenty-five feet with a spread almost as wide. They line many a coast of the Caribbean islands, and grow where it is relatively dry. The brown pods are very brittle, and the edible flesh inside encases shiny black seeds. Tamarind can be used in most curried dishes and in drinks, cakes, sweets, sorbets and other desserts. Available in Asian and West Indian shops and in markets dealing in tropical produce.

Thyme Certainly the best known of herbs, and one in whose honour songs have been written. I know of several varieties not only in Europe but also in the Caribbean and Central America. The best in

Europe for culinary use is either wild thyme or Mediterranean thyme, though English or lemon thyme can be excellent substitutes. Use in soups, stews, vegetable and egg dishes, for stuffings and in salad dressings. Always use fresh when possible. I dry my own by putting a bunch of fresh thyme in a brown paper bag and leaving it until dry. I then shake it and use the leaves as needed, keeping the remainder stored in the paper bag in a dry cupboard.

Turmeric Like the ginger, to which it is related, it is a rhizome. The root is similar in appearance to ginger, though when peeled it is bright orange in colour. Used frequently, in Caribbean cookery, it imparts colour and a distinct flavour and aroma all of its own. It can be used to colour foods as a substitute for saffron, but of course will alter the taste of the dish. Powdered turmeric can be bought almost anywhere, and occasionally the fresh roots can be found in oriental and Asian shops in Europe.

Vanilla The long pod of a climbing vine related to the orchid. Vanilla is native to tropical America and was once cultivated extensively in the Caribbean. Used in cakes, ice-cream, puddings, sweet desserts and drinks. Vanilla is also used to flavour perfumes and tobacco. Use the pods whenever you can, even make your own vanilla sugar (see Techniques). The pods can be used more than once. Avoid vanilla flavouring which is made from coal tar and waste paper pulp with added chemicals. Pure vanilla extract or essence of vanilla is available from most health food shops and good delicatessens.

The following is a list of other condiments and flavourings used in this book and in creole cookery in general: capers, olives, coconut oil, honey, nuts, soya sauce, Worcestershire sauce, rum, sherry, brandy, tomato ketchup, olive oil, and a variety of vinegars.

A further note: evaporated milk or condensed milk is used in many instances in place of fresh cream or milk because of the climate.

Equipment

To me, the kitchen is the most important room in the house, and possibly the room where a family spends the most time. Not only must it be attractive and comfortable, but it must also be functional and well equipped, so that you can produce the best for the table without too much fuss and bother. Assuming that you have the basic equipment – a cooker, a refrigerator, and maybe a freezer to help with this busy and hectic modern life – the following items are recommended: a set of heavy pots, in varying sizes, with tight-fitting lids (including a large one for the preparation of stews, soups and rice dishes); at least three frying pans, again in varying sizes, and an omelette pan which can also be used for pancakes and for dough breads such as roti; wire whisks, a collection of robust sieves, and a colander; a steamer and a double boiler; a four-sided grater for grating by hand anything from cheese to nutmeg or dry coconut and for slicing cucumbers, carrots, etc.; a coffee grinder which can also be used for spices; a measuring jug; a set of funnels for straining drinks and sauces; and a strong set of kitchen scales, capable of weighing anything from tiny quantities of spices to large vegetables. Many kitchens now boast a food processor for chopping, puréeing, blending, grating and shredding vegetables. All sorts of electrical and other gadgets are available, but remember, the equipment is only as good as the cook.

It is useful to possess at least two chopping boards, as well as a large, well-polished marble slab for making bread and pastry. For baking you will need a rolling pin, mixing bowls, and a range of baking tins for cakes, breads, cookies and so on. One or two should certainly be non-stick. The list of kitchen cutlery always seems endless: wooden spoons, spatulas, perforated spoons, ladles, long kitchen forks, scissors, measuring spoons, a garlic press, a knife sharpener, a can opener, and, of course, a set of kitchen knives. How many times have I been invited to cook in someone else's kitchen only to find that I have to struggle with the dullest and most useless knives imaginable? It is essential to possess a set of strong and very sharp knives, including a 30 cm (12 inch) cook's knife and a stainless-steel fruit and vegetable knife. Finally, do not forget muslin or cheesecloth, an apron and oven gloves – after all, you do not want to drop that earthenware casserole lifted straight out of a hot oven, or soil that beautiful dress or suit just before your guests arrive.

A few special items are required for making drinks: small buckets for mixing large quantities of party drinks, not only for adults but for children as well; cocktail shakers, a fine strainer, a nutmeg grater, a juice extractor or citrus squeezer; and last but not least, a blender or strong wire sieve for puréeing tropical fruits such as mangoes, pawpaws, guavas, tamarillos and bananas. Spend as much as you can afford on your kitchen and invest in the best-quality equipment; you won't regret it.

Techniques

It is essential when preparing vegetables that the vitamins and mineral salts they contain should not be destroyed in the cooking process. Vegetables should not, as we say on the French Caribbean islands, 'bore trope kleau', meaning 'drink too much water', as they often do in England. Avoid that awful smell of over-cooked cabbage and sprouts. However, most vegetables should be cooked sufficiently to soften the fibres, which makes them more digestible.

When choosing vegetables, particularly the leafy ones, pick out those that are firm and crisp. Do not be fobbed off with stale, cheap and limp specimens. A stale, half-dead vegetable is like stale sweat and won't be sweetened no matter how many herbs, spices and other condiments are used. It is a waste of valuable time and money. As a rule, always try and buy most vegetables just when you need them, and do not store them for too long.

AVOCADOS

These are one of the exceptions to the rule. Do not wait until the day that they are needed. The chances are that you may not be able to find any ripe ones, particularly during the winter months. Try and buy them a few days in advance, then wrap them in newspapers, brown paper, cloths or old jumpers, and leave in a warm cupboard to ripen. Do not handle and squeeze them too much, you will only end up with bruised, blackened fruit. Everyone has his or her own theories on how to ripen fruit, but I have found the above method quite reliable. I was once kindly advised by a greengrocer to put some half-ripe tomatoes in a plastic bag with the avocado pears to help shorten the ripening time. Growing my own tomatoes, and having a few to spare, I did as I was told, only to end up with a plastic bag of fermenting tomato purée and still very hard avocados. Not all methods work for everyone.

BEANS, PEAS AND PULSES

All pulses should be washed well and soaked in cold water; this saves both cooking time and gas or electricity. As with dried herbs and spices, never buy too much at any one time. Unless they are well cooked, pulses are not readily digestible and tend to cause flatulence. All beans or peas should be boiled at a very high temperature for the first ten to twelve minutes to remove the toxic substances which can affect the stomach. Salt should never be added to beans of any kind until they are tender. If cooking your beans in stock, use unsalted stock. There are further directions given in most of the recipes where pulses are called for.

BREADFRUIT

These can be cut into segments, washed and then boiled in their skins, unless the recipe directs otherwise. Again, wash with lime and lemon before cooking. Cooking breadfruit with the skin on prevents it 'drinking' too much water and losing its nutritional value. When cool enough to handle, peel and core before serving.

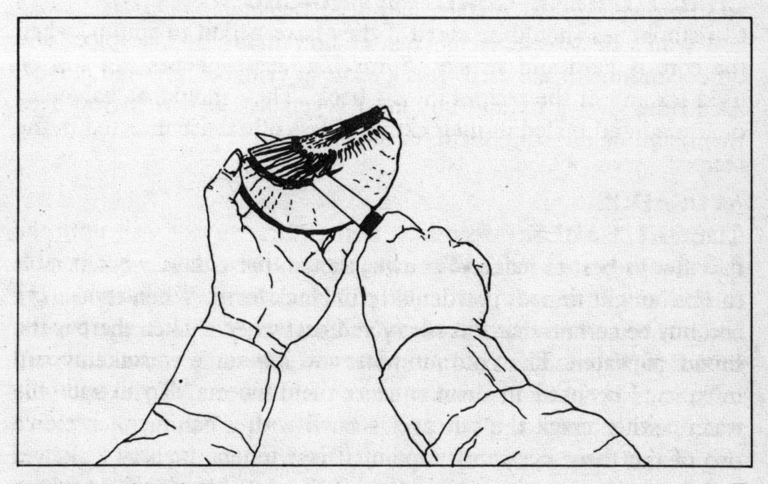

How to core a breadfruit

CARAMEL *colouring or browning*

To give a natural colour to your cakes, stews, sauces, breads, sweets or any savoury dish why not add your own colouring?

225 g (8 oz) soft brown or demerara sugar
water

1 Mix 2 tablespoons of water with the sugar in a heavy-bottomed pan.

2 Cook over a moderate heat until it begins to smoke and turns a dark rich brown. Stir constantly to prevent burning.
3 Add about 450 ml (¾ pint) boiling water, a little at a time, stirring continuously. Continue to boil, stirring, until the caramel becomes slightly syrupy.
4. Remove from the heat and allow to cool before storing in a sterilized bottle or jar.

The caramel must not be allowed to burn or it will be too bitter, but at the same time, if it is undercooked it will be too sweet. Never, whatever you do, pour cold water into the hot caramel. The temperature of the syrup is so high that this could cause severe eruptions, leading to accidents and burns. The caramel will keep for months in a cool place.

CHRISTOPHENE, CHAYOTE, CHO-CHO

Christophenes should be cored if they have begun to sprout, when the core is hard and stringy. Sprouting christophenes can still be used for any of the recipes in this book. They should be halved or quartered and boiled in their skins, unless otherwise directed in the recipe.

COCONUT MILK

It is always best to make your own, though these days coconut milk can be bought tinned, powdered or in block form. When choosing a coconut be certain that it is heavy and that when shaken there is the sound of water. The coconut water, which some mistakenly call milk, can be used in drinks, sauces and sweets. To extract the water, either crack the nut over a bowl with a hammer, or pierce two of the three eyes with a pointed instrument such as a skewer and drain the water into a jug. One of the eyes, the one from where a seedling will eventually germinate, is much easier to pierce than the other two. After draining off the water, break the coconut by tapping with a hammer or other heavy instrument a few times then place it on a hard surface and give a final blow to break the nut into pieces. Use a blunt knife, never a sharp vegetable knife, to lever off the coconut flesh as illustrated. Now using a sharp knife, cut the flesh into smaller pieces about 2 cm (¾ inch) square. Place these in a blender with about 600 ml (1 pint) warm water (some advise boiling water – I say that is totally unnecessary) and blend at high

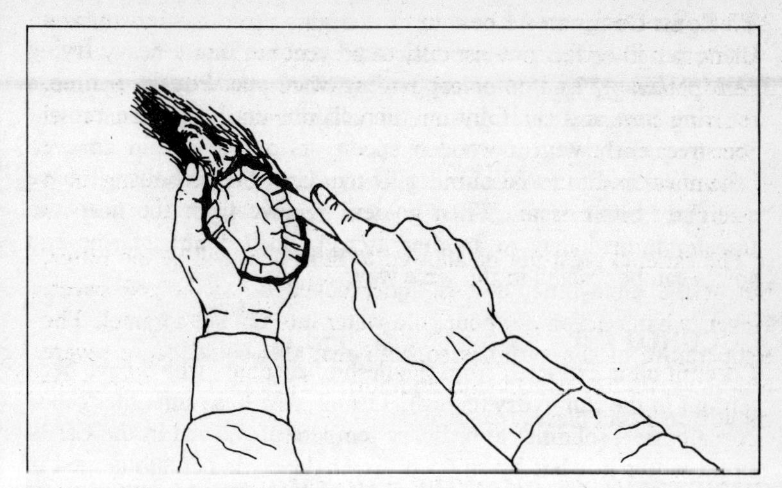

Removing the flesh from a coconut

speed until the coconut is puréed. From time to time switch off the machine and scrape any bits clinging to the sides back into the main mixture. Strain through a very fine muslin cloth or a clean kitchen towel into a bowl. The ends of the cloth must be brought together and wrung very tightly. Discard the pulp.

The coconut can also be grated by hand then the water poured over and squeezed through a cloth, as is still done on the islands. In fact the coconut must be grated by hand when making sweets, coconut cakes, jams and pralines. Though I know some cooks recommend it, it is not always necessary to peel the brown inner skin off the flesh even when making coconut milk, unless you want a particularly white milk.

To make coconut cream, simply follow the instructions for coconut milk but pour the milk into a glass container, such as a wide-necked jar or a bowl, set aside and allow the cream to rise to the top until it reaches the consistency you require. Skim off the cream into another container and retain the lighter liquid to add to the cream if it needs thinning slightly. For a very much richer cream, especially for serving with fruits or fruit salads, the coconut flesh may be blended with milk instead of water.

Coconut milk or cream will keep for about 3 days in a refrigerator. After that it becomes rancid. It will keep in a freezer for several months.

To Roast Desiccated Coconut

Using no oil or fat, put the desiccated coconut into a heavy frying pan, preferably an iron or copper-bottomed one. Put the pan on a medium heat and carefully fry the coconut until a golden brown. Stir frequently with a wooden spoon or fork to obtain an even brownness and to avoid burning. If too dark, the coconut will have a slightly bitter taste. When golden, remove from the heat and transfer immediately to another utensil. Shelled nuts, farine and spices can be roasted in the same way.

COCONUT OIL

Coconut oil is extracted from the flesh of coconuts which have been left out in the sun to dry (copra). The oil, which is sometimes called cocoa butter, solidifies at ordinary temperatures, even in the Caribbean, where it is left by an open fire or the container submerged in hot water before it can be used. It is a very easily digestible oil and ideal for vegetarian cookery. Available from West Indian and Indian shops.

CURRY POWDER

I must confess that through sheer laziness I have on the odd occasion bought tinned curry powder. There is no excuse for this as I always have in store a variety of ingredients with which to make curries – and I am certain most people do.

Think of the pleasure of pounding, grinding or roasting your own spices as the aromatic smells drift through your kitchen. It not only stimulates the taste buds and the sensual nerves (many spices used in the making of curry are considered to be aphrodisiacs), but the end result gives one the pleasure of knowing that any commercially made curry powder is surely a poor substitute.

The following three recipes from the Caribbean have been very much influenced by the East Indians who first arrived there as indentured labour.

Poudre de Colombo

This classic recipe comes from the island of Martinique. It is extremely mild and therefore is ideal for any of the curried dishes in this book. I do believe that vegetables need a delicate curry and should not be too spicy. This curry powder is best made fresh when needed. The amount of hot pepper you use is to your taste.

3 cloves garlic
1 teaspoon turmeric
1 teaspoon mustard seeds
1 teaspoon coriander seeds
1 teaspoon annatto seeds
Deseeded and chopped hot pepper (strictly to taste, see p. 33)
2 cm (¾ inch) fresh ginger, peeled
½–1 teaspoon salt

Pound all the ingredients to a fine paste with a pestle and mortar, and use in the recipes as directed.

Curry Powder

25 g (1 oz) coriander seeds
25 g (1 oz) dried ginger
4 cm (1½ inch) cinnamon stick
8 allspice
8 cloves
1–2 dried chilli peppers (or to taste)
Seeds 2 cardamon pods
8 whole black peppercorns
½ teaspoon dried lemon peel (see Herbs, Spices and Other Condiments)
75 g (3 oz) turmeric

1 Pound all the whole ingredients separately in a pestle and mortar, i.e. the coriander seeds, ginger, cinnamon, lemon peel, allspice, cloves, chilli peppers, cardamon seeds and peppercorns. Every last bit should be scraped off the sides of the mortar.
2 Thoroughly mix together all the ingredients. Store in an airtight jar.

Makes about 150 g (6 oz)

Mild Curry Powder

20 green cardamon pods
5 teaspoons coriander seeds
2 teaspoons cumin seeds
1 teaspoon fennel seeds
¾ teaspoon freshly ground dried chillies
18 whole cloves
1 rounded teaspoon black peppercorns

1 teaspoon freshly ground dry ginger
1 level teaspoon whole allspice
3 tablespoons ground turmeric

1 In a dry, shallow frying pan roast the cardamons until lightly brown – about 1½–2 minutes. Transfer to a dish or mortar.
2 In the same frying pan roast the coriander, cumin and fennel seeds for about 1–1½ minutes.
3 Place all the ingredients in a mortar and pound into a powder. Store in an airtight jar for up to 2½ months.

Makes approximately 75 g (3 oz)

DASHEEN, YAM, EDDO, TANNIA, CUSH CUSH

Peel with a sharp knife then cut into pieces for cooking. If the dasheen or yam is too large, cut it into pieces before peeling. Wash all starchy vegetables, scrubbing with lime or lemon cut in half, and changing the water three or four times; as with the green *musas* (bananas) squeeze a little lime or lemon juice in the water in which they are to be boiled. Cook in boiling, salted water until tender. Test with a sharp knife or skewer. Immediately the vegetables are cooked remove from the heat and drain. Do not leave cooked vegetables sitting in water.

FRUIT

To ripen custard apples, sugar apples, mangoes, pawpaws, soursops, plantains, bananas and any other tropical fruits, especially in the winter months, wrap them in old cloths, newspapers, or an old jumper and place them in a warm airing cupboard, or any other warm place. Check them every day. Do not store unripened fruit with any of the citruses, especially limes and lemons, as they prevent the other fruits from ripening properly; sometimes they may not ripen at all.

GHEE

Ghee is clarified butter or margarine, and is available from Indian, West Indian and other specialist shops. Vegetable ghee can also be bought. You can make your own ghee by simmering on a low heat 450 g (1 lb) of the best unsalted butter or margarine for 1–1¼ hours. Do *not* allow it to boil. Skim off any impurities rising to the surface but do not disturb it too much. Strain through several layers

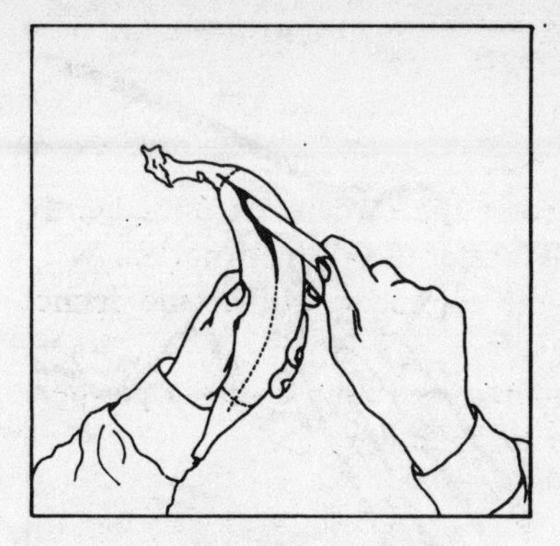

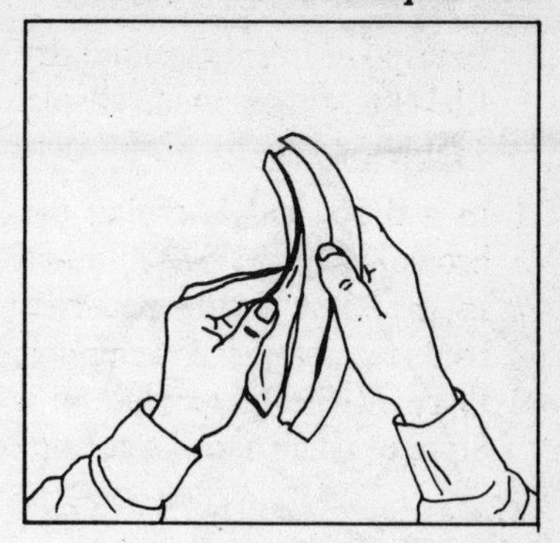

How to peel a green banana or plantain

of cheesecloth into a sterilized jar. Store in a refrigerator, where it will keep for months.

GREEN BANANAS, BLUGGOE and PLANTAIN

For cooking, unless otherwise directed in the recipes, peel by cutting off both ends with a sharp knife (large plantains may be cut across the middle unless they are to be stuffed). Then make two or three slits lengthways in the skin down to the flesh (be careful not to cut too deep). Place the tip of the knife into each slit and lever the skin up. Then using your thumb and finger peel off the skin completely. If there are any green bits left clinging to the flesh scrape off with a sharp knife. Wash thoroughly in cold water, scrubbing with either lime or lemon. A little lime or lemon juice added to the cooking water prevents discoloration. Like potatoes, *musas* should be boiled until tender. The milk or enzyme secreted from all green *musas* can stain, so avoid bringing them into contact with your clothes or any other materials.

HOT PEPPERS

Do not buy too many at any one time unless you need them for making hot pepper sauces and chutneys. After a while most peppers, especially the *Bom de Ma Jacques* or Scots bonnet (so named because it resembles a large Tam o'Shanter) tend to lose their aroma. The Scots Bonnet is recommended for recipes in this book but others can be substituted. Adjust the amount according to the type used, remembering that the Scots Bonnet is one of the hottest. Use all peppers sparingly or to taste, and unless otherwise stated never use

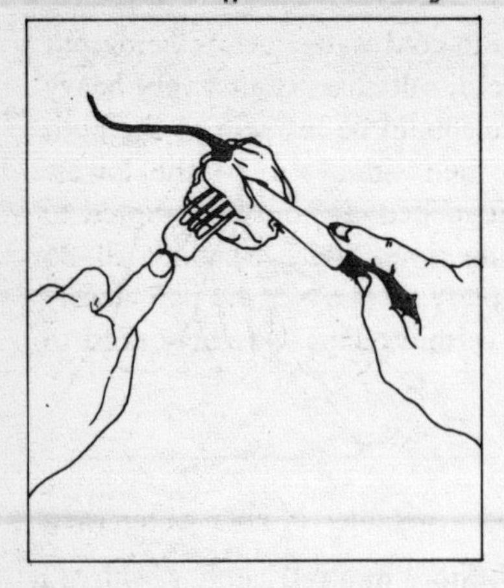
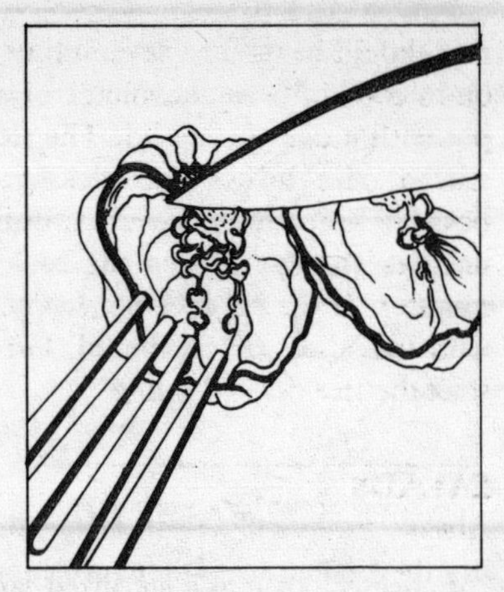

How to handle a hot pepper

the seeds (see illustration). Avoid touching hot peppers with your bare hands. If by chance you do touch a chopped hot pepper, rub your hands with either lime or lemon juice and wash them with milk or in cold running water.

PASSION FRUIT

To extract the juice, cut the fruit in half and scoop out the pulp and seeds into a fine sieve placed over a bowl. Using your fingers, squeeze the pulp and seeds and rub them round the sieve until all of the juices have been extracted and only the seeds are left. Pour a very little water over the seeds and rub again. If you are preparing a large quantity of passion fruit the process with the water can be repeated two or three times but it is advisable to use as little water as possible, unless you are making a passion fruit drink with water as one of the ingredients.

PUMPKINS

These are best boiled in their skin, then peeled when cooked, unless they are being used in pies, stews and soups, in which case prepare as directed in the recipe. Always discard the seeds and fibrous parts before cooking.

RICE

There are many ways of preparing rice and each country has its own method. Unless otherwise stated in the directions on the packet all rice should be washed several times in cold water, before being put on to cook in twice its volume of cold, salted water in a very heavy pot with a tight-fitting lid. The rice should be brought to the boil, stirred once to prevent sticking, then simmered on the lowest possible heat, tightly covered, until cooked. Do not be tempted to uncover the rice during the cooking time, which is about 20–25 minutes. If the lid does not fit properly, first cover the pan closely with foil, then put on the lid. For certain recipes you may need to soak the rice before boiling.

SALADS

Always thoroughly clean leafy salad vegetables in cold water then dry them carefully without crushing or damaging the delicate leaves. Remember that most dressings will not blend with wet vegetables. Salads should not be dressed until just before they are needed, otherwise the leaves will lose their crispness. Certain fruits, such as avocados and ripe bananas, should be added to salads at the very last minute as they change colour if they are peeled and cut in advance. Another point to keep in mind is that to serve an attractive salad you should always mix the ingredients lightly and retain a few leaves or pieces of fruit for garnishing the top.

STOCK

Try to make your own whenever possible (see page 179), but if using vegetable cubes or any other manufactured stock, choose a light-coloured one. Dark stocks contain too much artificial colouring and may ruin the flavour of your dish.

SWEET POTATOES

Prepare and cook as you would ordinary potatoes, but remember that they are best boiled in their skins and then peeled once they are cooked. Add a little lime or lemon juice to the cooking water. The Louisiana yam, which is in fact a sweet potato, should always be boiled in its skin; it needs less cooking than other varieties.

VANILLA SUGAR

Do make your own, for it is always useful to have some in store for cakes, sweets, drinks and iced desserts.

900 g (2 lb) caster sugar (brown or white; there is now a brown caster sugar on the market made from sugar cane)
3 vanilla pods

1 Make a slit lengthways down each pod and place in an airtight jar. Pour in the sugar, cover and shake well.
2 After a week or so you can start using the sugar. Top up each time with fresh sugar and shake well. The vanilla pods should retain their flavour for at least 3–4 months.

Soups and Hors d'Oeuvres

CHILLED AVOCADO SOUP

75 g (3 oz) margarine
1 medium onion, chopped
1 clove garlic, chopped
1 stick celery with leaves, chopped
900 ml (1½ pints) vegetable stock (see page 179)
4 ripe avocados weighing 225–300 g (8–10 oz) each
1½ tablespoons lemon juice
Freshly ground white pepper to taste
Sea salt to taste
West Indian hot pepper sauce to taste
300 ml (½ pint) single cream
2 tablespoons chopped fresh chives to garnish

1 Melt the margarine in a pot and sauté the onion until translucent but not brown.
2 Add the garlic, chopped celery and stock, bring to the boil and simmer covered for about 8 minutes.
3 Remove from the heat and allow to cool, then blend or pass through a sieve.
4 Peel and stone the avocados, and pass through a fine sieve into a bowl. Mix in the lemon juice immediately.
5 Add the white pepper and sea salt to taste to the avocado purée. Blend well.
6 Thoroughly combine the avocado mixture with the stock. Add pepper sauce to taste and stir in the cream.
7 Chill for about 30 minutes before serving, garnished with the chopped chives. This soup should not be prepared too far in advance, or it might discolour.

Serves 4–6

RIPE BANANA AND COCONUT MILK SOUP

75 g (3 oz) unsalted butter
1 tablespoon wholemeal flour

½ teaspoon freshly grated nutmeg
1.25 litres (2 pints) coconut milk (see Techniques)
Deseeded and chopped hot pepper to taste (see Techniques)
Sea salt to taste
3 large ripe bananas
1 tablespoon chopped fresh chives

1 Melt the butter in a heavy saucepan then gradually stir in the flour. Blend well.
2 Add the nutmeg and slowly pour in the coconut milk, stirring constantly to avoid any lumps. Simmer for about 20 minutes.
3 Remove from the heat and add the hot pepper and salt to taste.
4 Mash the bananas and add to the soup with the chives. (The bananas must not be mashed beforehand or they will turn brown.)
5 Return to the heat and simmer until hot, stirring occasionally. Taste for seasoning and serve immediately.

This really is a hot, spicy soup and should be served with freshly chopped hot peppers or pepper sauce.

Serves 4–5

BLACK BEAN SOUP

A black bean soup from South America that can be served with rice or root vegetables.

450 g (1 lb) black beans, soaked overnight
2 medium onions, chopped
3 cloves garlic, chopped
Deseeded and chopped hot pepper to taste (see Techniques)
2 tomatoes, chopped
2 celery sticks, chopped
2 carrots, chopped
1 sweet pepper, deseeded and chopped
4 whole cloves
½ teaspoon demerara sugar
½ teaspoon freshly ground allspice
Juice ½ lime or lemon
1 sprig fresh parsley
Sea salt to taste

3 tablespoons island rum – preferably Cuban
300 ml (½ pint) thick coconut cream (optional – see Techniques)

1 Drain the beans and rinse in cold water, then bring to the boil in enough water to cover by about 7.5 cm (3 inches). Boil rapidly for 10 minutes, scooping away any scum that forms. Lower the heat and cook covered for about one hour.
2 Add all the other ingredients except the rum, salt and coconut cream and simmer gently for another 1½ hours. Add the salt halfway through that cooking period. You may also need to top up with more boiling water. The soup must not be too thick nor too watery.
3 Taste for seasoning, adding more hot pepper if you wish. Stir in the rum, and coconut cream if using, and cook for a further 10 minutes. Serve when just slightly cooled.

Serves 6–8

CALLALOO SOUP

Possibly the most famous soup of the Caribbean.

2 tablespoons oil
75 g (3 oz) butter
2 onions, chopped
3 cloves garlic, chopped
¼–½ hot pepper (or to taste), deseeded and chopped (see Techniques)
1.75 litres (3 pints) vegetable stock (see page 179)
1.5 kg (3 lb) taro leaves, washed and chopped
225 g (½ lb) okra, trimmed and sliced
½ teaspoon freshly ground allspice
1 green sweet pepper, deseeded and chopped
1 sprig fresh thyme
1 sprig fresh parsley
Sea salt to taste
Freshly ground black pepper to taste
300 ml (½ pint) coconut cream (see Techniques)

1 In a large heavy pot, heat the oil and butter and sauté the onions until translucent.
2 Add all the remaining ingredients except the coconut cream and

seasoning, and bring to the boil. Season with salt and pepper. Lower the heat and simmer covered for 30 minutes.
3 Add the coconut cream, taste for seasoning and simmer for a further 10 minutes before serving.

Callaloo can be served as a main course with boiled green bananas or green plantains; these are sometimes added to the soup just before serving.

Serves 6–8

CARROT AND MANGO SOUP

Unusual but very tasty.

450 g (1 lb) carrots, scraped, washed and chopped
340 g (¾ lb) ripe mangoes (peeled and stoned weight), chopped
1 large onion, chopped
225 g (½ lb) tomatoes, skinned, deseeded and chopped
3 cloves garlic, chopped
1.5 litres (2½ pints) vegetable stock (see page 179)
Pinch of cayenne pepper
2 teaspoons fresh marjoram or 1 teaspoon dried
Freshly ground black pepper to taste
Sea salt to taste
150 ml (5 fl oz) natural yoghurt
2 egg yolks, beaten
1 generous glass Madeira
Chopped chives to garnish

1 Place all the ingredients except the yoghurt, egg yolks, Madeira and chives, into a large pot, bring to the boil, lower the heat and simmer covered for 10 minutes.
2 Remove from the heat and liquidize.
3 Return to the heat, warm through if necessary, keeping the heat low, then slowly blend in the yoghurt and egg yolks, stirring continuously. Add the Madeira.
4 Remove from the heat and taste for seasoning. Add salt or pepper if necessary and return to the heat for no more than 1 minute. Serve immediately, garnished with the chopped chives.

Serves 6

CARROT AND ORANGE SOUP

450 g (1 lb) carrots, peeled and grated
1 medium onion, grated
450 ml (¾ pint) vegetable stock (see page 179)
Small piece cinnamon
600 ml (1 pint) fresh orange juice
Freshly ground white pepper to taste
1–2 teaspoons demerara sugar
Sea salt to taste
150 ml (5 fl oz) Madeira
Rind 1 orange, finely chopped

1 Place the carrots in a saucepan with the onion, vegetable stock and cinnamon and bring to the boil.
2 Turn down the heat and simmer gently for 5 minutes. Discard the cinnamon and liquidize the soup in a blender.
3 Return to the heat, add the orange juice, white pepper and sugar and bring to the boil.
4 Lower the heat and simmer for about 6–8 minutes. Taste for seasoning and stir in the Madeira.
5 Pour into a warm serving bowl, sprinkle with the orange rind and serve.

Serves 4–6

CAULIFLOWER AND AVOCADO SOUP

Simple, quick and delicious.

560 g (1¼ lb) cauliflower florets
1 leek, 225 g (½ lb) trimmed weight, chopped
1 clear vegetable stock cube
1 clove garlic, crushed
½ teaspoon fennel seeds
1 generous sprig fresh parsley
Freshly ground white pepper to taste
Sea salt to taste
600 ml (1 pint) water
300 ml (½ pint) milk
50 g (2 oz) butter
1 large avocado
300 ml (½ pint) single cream

1 heaped tablespoon finely chopped fresh chives
1 tablespoon sherry
Croûtons to garnish

1 Place the cauliflower, leek, vegetable cube, garlic, fennel seeds, parsley, pepper and salt in a heavy pot. Pour in the water and bring to the boil.
2 Lower the heat and simmer covered for 20 minutes.
3 Remove from the heat and liquidize with the milk (if you have the time, pass the soup through a fine sieve as well).
4 Return to the pan with the butter and heat thoroughly until the butter has melted.
5 Meanwhile, peel and stone the avocado then purée it in a bowl. Mix in the cream and chives and add salt to taste.
6 Off the heat stir the sherry into the soup and taste for seasoning.
7 Divide the avocado mixture between 4 warm soup bowls. Pour the soup over and serve immediately, garnished with the croûtons.

Crushed, salted mixed nuts can be used instead of the croûtons.

Serves 4

CHRISTOPHENE SOUP

450 g (1 lb) christophenes
50 g (2 oz) margarine
2 medium onions, finely chopped
900 ml (1½ pints) vegetable stock (see page 179), or 2 stock cubes in the same quantity of water
300 ml (½ pint) single cream
Freshly ground white pepper to taste
Sea salt to taste (optional if using salted stock cubes)
Chopped fresh chives or parsley to garnish

1 Peel the christophenes and chop them into small pieces (see Techniques).
2 Melt the margarine in a heavy pot and fry the onions until translucent but not brown.
3 Add the christophenes and stock, bring to the boil, then simmer for 30 minutes.
4 Remove from the heat, then either liquidize or pass through a fine sieve.

5 Add the cream, stir in well, and season with pepper and salt to taste.
6 Reheat thoroughly and serve sprinkled with the chopped chives or parsley.

Serves 4

FEDILIA'S GREEN GUMBO SOUP

Gumbo always brings back memories of my early childhood in Dominica, when piles of macadam stood in front of people's homes before the roads were tarred and asphalted, and when oxen drew heavily laden carts of lime cordial to the bay to be shipped to London, Paris and the great cities of Europe. Then gumbo referred to rich, green soups and stews, spicy and peppery hot, made with okra and other greens, callaloo leaves, cabbage, watercress, celery and fresh herbs. Today almost any soup or stew with greens, seasoned and thickened with file (a thickening agent made from sassafras) seems to be called gumbo. I do not believe anything without okra can honestly be called gumbo, which is the Creole name for okra.

2 tablespoons olive oil (or substitute vegetable oil)
50 g (2 oz) butter
2 medium onions, finely chopped
4 cloves garlic, finely chopped
1 sweet green pepper, deseeded and chopped
450 g (1 lb) taro leaves (or substitute spinach)
2 celery stalks with leaves, chopped
1.6 litres (2¾ pints) vegetable stock (or 2–3 vegetable stock cubes in the same quantity of hot water)
1 bunch watercress, chopped
1 head lettuce, cleaned and chopped
8 chives, chopped (or substitute spring onions)
½ green hot pepper, or to taste, deseeded and chopped (see Techniques)
2 teaspoons fresh thyme
3 tablespoons fresh chopped parsley
340 g (¾ lb) okra, topped and diced
10 peppercorns, freshly ground
3 bay leaves, pounded or finely crushed

2 glasses French dry white wine
Sea salt to taste

1 In a large, heavy pot, heat the oil and butter and sauté the onions until translucent but not brown.
2 Add the garlic, sweet green pepper, taro leaves and celery with about 300 ml (½ pint) of the stock and bring to the boil. Lower the heat and simmer covered for 10 minutes.
3 Add all the other ingredients plus the remaining stock and simmer covered for 15 minutes.
4 Taste for seasoning, then simmer uncovered for a further 15–20 minutes.
5 Remove from the heat and liquidize, but not to too fine a purée. Reheat if necessary before serving.

Serves 8

PARSNIP AND COCONUT SOUP

50 g (2 oz) butter
2 medium onions, chopped
675 g (1½ lb) parsnips, peeled and chopped
50 g (2 oz) desiccated coconut
½ teaspoon ground ginger
½ teaspoon freshly ground coriander seeds
½ teaspoon freshly ground allspice
½ teaspoon freshly ground cinnamon
900 ml (1½ pints) vegetable stock (see page 179), or 1½ bouillon cubes plus the same quantity of hot water
450 ml (¾ pint) coconut milk (see Techniques)
Sea salt to taste
Freshly ground black pepper to taste
Freshly grated nutmeg

1 Melt the butter in a heavy pot. Sauté the onions until translucent but not brown.
2 Add the parsnips and cook for a further 6 minutes.
3 Add all the other ingredients except the nutmeg and continue to cook for about 45 minutes.
4 Remove from the heat and liquidize. Taste for seasoning and reheat if necessary. Serve sprinkled with grated nutmeg.

Serves 4–6

PUMPKIN SOUP

This is a delicious soup, very simple to prepare with everything thrown in at once. You can serve it either as it is or puréed. It can also be served as a main course with a few dumplings, and with one or two green bananas or tannias added and cooked together with the rest of the ingredients; but then lime or lemon juice must be included.

675 g (1½ lb) calabaza, peeled, deseeded and chopped (or substitute any other pumpkin)
1 large onion, finely chopped
2 cloves garlic, finely chopped
1 sprig fresh parsley
1 sprig fresh thyme
1 tablespoon chopped fresh dill leaves (or 1 teaspoon dried)
Deseeded and chopped hot pepper to taste (see Techniques)
4 whole cloves
Pinch turmeric
Freshly ground black pepper to taste
2 vegetable stock cubes
1.3 litres (2¼ pints) water
Sea salt to taste (this may not be necessary because of the stock cubes)

1 Place all the ingredients into one large pot and bring to the boil.
2 Lower the heat and simmer covered for 45–50 minutes, or until the calabaza is tender.
4 Taste for seasoning and serve.

Serves 6–8

RED BEAN AND EGG DUMPLING SOUP

The dumplings in this recipe are very similar to ones I first tasted in my childhood, which my stepmother prepared on my first visit to the island of Guadeloupe to spend Easter holidays with my father.

This soup makes a meal on its own.

450 g (1 lb) red beans, soaked overnight
1.75 litres (3 pints) water
340 g (¾ lb) wholemeal flour

1 teaspoon fine sea salt
2 eggs
2 medium onions, sliced
2 cloves garlic, finely chopped
6 whole cloves
1 sprig fresh thyme
1 sprig fresh parsley
Freshly ground black pepper to taste
Sea salt to taste
2 tablespoons olive oil or butter

1. Drain and rinse the soaked red beans and bring to the boil with the water. Boil on a high heat for 10–12 minutes then lower the heat and simmer, adding more boiling water if necessary.
2. Meanwhile make a stiff dough with the flour, the fine salt and the eggs, adding a little cold water. Knead well.
3. Flour a work surface and roll out the dough to about 1 cm (½ inch) thick. It should resemble a long thick macaroni.
4. Cut into 1 cm (½ inch) strips. Do not flatten or shape.
5. When the beans are fairly tender (after about 45 minutes) add the dumplings, onions, garlic, cloves, thyme, parsley, black pepper and salt to taste.
6. Continue to simmer gently for about another 30 minutes or until the beans are completely cooked. Add the oil or butter and serve.

Hot, freshly made bread or a breadfruit coo-coo (see page 147) is an ideal accompaniment, if serving as a main course.

Serves 6–8

RED BEAN AND SWEET POTATO SOUP

225 g (½ lb) red kidney beans, soaked overnight
1.5 litres (2½ pints) water
1 large onion, finely chopped
3 cloves garlic, finely chopped or crushed
8 whole cloves
1 large sprig fresh thyme
2 bay leaves
1 sprig fresh parsley
1 teaspoon brown cane sugar

2 vegetable stock cubes
Freshly ground black pepper to taste
Sea salt to taste
450 g (1 lb) sweet potatoes, peeled, scrubbed with some lemon and cut into small cubes
2 tablespoons olive oil

1. Drain the beans and rinse in cold water, then place in a large pot with the 1.5 litres (2½ pints) water. Bring to the boil and cook rapidly on a high heat for 10–12 minutes.
2. Lower the heat and simmer covered until the beans are fairly tender (about 45 minutes). Do not allow the liquid to reduce too much; add more boiling water if necessary.
3. When the beans are fairly tender add all the remaining ingredients except the sweet potatoes and olive oil and cook covered for about 15 minutes.
4. Now add the cubed potatoes and continue to cook until the potato pieces are tender. Again, remember to keep the level of the liquid up.
5. Taste for seasoning and check that the beans are well cooked. Add the olive oil.

Serves 6 as a starter, 4 as a main course

RIVER CLAIRE SOUP WITH TURMERIC

This soup is based on a similar one I once concocted using fresh turmeric. River Claire runs through one of Dominica's most beautiful valleys, which is totally unspoilt as there is no road.

5 cm (2 inch) piece fresh turmeric (or substitute 1 teaspoon ground turmeric)
3 cloves garlic
2 medium onions, chopped
6 cloves
2 dried bay leaves, crushed
Deseeded and chopped hot pepper to taste (see Techniques)
3 tablespoons coconut oil
2 green bananas, peeled and diced
1 christophene, peeled and diced
110 g (4 oz) cabbage, chopped
3 carrots, diced

1 tannia, diced
110 g (4 oz) fresh peas (shelled weight)
1 green sweet pepper, deseeded and diced
Small sprig fresh parsley
Juice 1 small lime
1.5 litres (2½ pints) coconut milk, using 2 coconuts (see Techniques)
Sea salt to taste
Freshly ground black pepper to taste
Pepper sauce (see page 182) to serve

1 Pound together in a mortar and pestle the turmeric, garlic, onions, cloves, bay leaves and hot pepper.
2 In a heavy pot heat the oil and sauté the pounded mixture for no more than 2 minutes.
3 Add all the other ingredients except the pepper sauce, and simmer covered until the vegetables are tender.
4 Taste for seasoning and serve with pepper sauce, a must with this soup, and bakes (see p. 217) instead of bread.

Serves 4–6

SOFRITO BEAN SOUP

The following recipe is as inexpensive as you can get, and as full of protein, aromatic and delicious as any meat dish. The soup here varies only slightly from the original which contains ham. It can be served either as a starter or as a main meal with rice or freshly baked wholemeal bread.

450 g (1 lb) beans (haricot, black-eyed or cannellini), soaked overnight
2 litres (3½ pints) water
100 ml (4 fl oz) olive oil
1 medium-to-large onion, neatly chopped
3 cloves garlic, finely chopped
2 small carrots, scraped and chopped
1 sweet pepper, deseeded and chopped
1 small leek, chopped
1 sprig fresh parsley, chopped
1 teaspoon fresh oregano
4 cloves, freshly ground

Freshly ground black pepper to taste
Sea salt to taste
2 tablespoons chopped fresh coriander leaves
3–4 tablespoons tomato purée
2 teaspoons liquid annatto
Chopped chives to garnish

1 Drain and rinse the beans and bring to the boil in the water. Boil on a high heat for 10 minutes.
2 Lower the heat and simmer covered until almost tender (about 45 minutes). Do not add salt.
3 Meanwhile, heat the olive oil in a saucepan and sauté the onion, garlic, carrots, sweet pepper, leek, parsley, and oregano for about 4 minutes.
4 Mix in the cloves, black pepper and salt to taste, coriander leaves, tomato purée and annatto. Sauté for another 3 minutes.
5 Add the mixture to the beans and mix well. Continue to simmer for about 20 minutes or until the beans are well cooked, then taste for seasoning. Sprinkle with the chives and serve.

Serves 6–8

SOPA DE FRIJOLE NEGRO

A Spanish creole dish, which can be served as a first course or as a main meal with fried breadfruit, plain boiled rice and a salad.

450 g (1 lb) black beans, soaked overnight
1.75 litres (3 pints) unsalted vegetable stock (see page 179)
2 onions, chopped
2 tomatoes, peeled and chopped
1 small sweet pepper, chopped
4 cloves garlic, chopped
Deseeded and chopped hot pepper to taste (see Techniques)
6 cloves, freshly ground
1 tablespoon olives, chopped
1 heaped teaspoonful fresh thyme
Freshly ground black pepper to taste
2 vegetable stock cubes
Sea salt to taste (if using salted vegetable cubes be careful)
2 tablespoons olive oil, or to taste

1 Wash the beans a few times and boil with the stock at a high heat for 10–12 minutes.
2 Reduce the heat and add the onions, tomatoes, sweet pepper, garlic, hot pepper, ground cloves, olives and thyme. Do not add salt.
3 Simmer covered for 50–60 minutes or until the beans are tender. Remove from the heat and liquidize in a blender.
4 Return to the heat with black pepper, stock cubes and a little salt added. Heat through, stirring occasionally to prevent burning.
5 Taste for seasoning (beans need quite a lot of salt and pepper), pour in the olive oil and serve.

Serves 8 as a first course, 4 as a main course

SPINACH, LEEK AND HARICOT BEAN SOUP

I am very fortunate to be able to grow my own vegetables, and this is one of my own recipes using leaf spinach and leeks from my vegetable garden.

170 g (6 oz) haricot beans, soaked overnight
225 g (½ lb) spinach, washed and chopped
2 leeks, cleaned and chopped
225 g (½ lb) potatoes, peeled and cubed
½ teaspoon dill seeds (optional)
Freshly ground black pepper to taste
Sea salt to taste
100 ml (4 fl oz) fresh cream
75 g (3 oz) unsalted butter or margarine

1 Drain and rinse the beans and then bring them to the boil in enough cold water to cover by about 5 cm (2 inches). Lower the heat and cook until tender.
2 Drain and measure the liquid from the beans. Make up with boiling water to 1.5 litres (2½ pints).
3 Put the spinach, leeks, potatoes, dill seeds if using, and seasoning into a pot. Pour in the liquid, bring to the boil and simmer for 15 minutes.
4 Add the beans, cream and butter or margarine and simmer gently for another 15 minutes. Taste for seasoning and serve.

Serves 4–5

TANNIA AND WATERCRESS SOUP

675 g (1½ lb) tannia (potatoes can be substituted but they are not as tasty)
1 lemon or lime, cut in half
1.25 litres (2 pints) vegetable stock (use stock cubes)
1 onion, finely chopped
Freshly ground black pepper to taste
Sea salt to taste
25 g (1 oz) unsalted butter
300 ml (½ pint) single cream
3 egg yolks, beaten
1 bunch of watercress, washed and trimmed
A little grated cheese to taste
Few blades chives, chopped

1. Peel and wash the tannias, scrubbing with the citrus. Then chop into small pieces to lessen the cooking time. Rinse.
2. In a heavy pot bring the stock to the boil together with the tannia and onion. Simmer for about 20–25 minutes or until tender.
3. Pass through a fine sieve or blend in a liquidizer, return to the heat and season with pepper. Taste for salt and keep on a low heat.
4. Warm a soup tureen so that the butter will melt when placed in it. Heat the cream in a saucepan. Drop the egg yolks into the buttered tureen and pour in the heated cream. Mix thoroughly and keep warm.
5. Add the watercress to the soup, which should be very gently simmering. Simmer for a further minute or two.
6. Pour the soup into the tureen over the egg and cream mixture. Serve immediately, sprinkled with a little grated cheese and the chives.

Serves 4–6

TOMATO AND GUMBO SOUP

The following recipe is based on the gumbo of New Orleans. The word gumbo, meaning okra, is used on the French- and Patois-speaking islands of the Caribbean and by the Creoles of New Orleans.

75 g (3 oz) butter
2 onions, chopped
450 g (1 lb) tomatoes, chopped
225 g (½ lb) callaloo or spinach, washed and chopped
110 g (4 oz) cabbage, shredded
1 bunch watercress, washed and trimmed
2 celery stalks with leaves, chopped
½ hot pepper, or to taste, deseeded and chopped (see Techniques)
1 sprig fresh parsley, chopped
1 sprig fresh thyme
2 bay leaves
Juice 1 lemon
1.75 litres (3 pints) vegetable stock (see page 179)
Freshly ground black pepper to taste
2 teaspoons yeast extract (optional)
Sea salt to taste
450 g (1 lb) okra, topped (or substitute tinned)

1 Melt the butter in a deep heavy pot and sauté the onions for about 2 minutes.
2 Add the tomatoes and continue to cook for a further 2–3 minutes.
3 Add the callaloo or spinach, cabbage, watercress, celery, hot pepper, parsley, thyme, bay leaves and lemon juice. Pour in the stock and quickly bring to the boil.
4 Lower the heat and season with black pepper, yeast extract if using, and salt to taste. Simmer covered for 10 minutes.
5 Add the okra to the pot and simmer for 30 minutes. Taste for seasoning. Discard the bay leaves and thyme before serving.

For a main course serve with breadfruit coo-coo (see page 147) or plantain foo-foo (see page 158).

Serves 6–8 as a first course, 4 as a main course

TRINIDAD CURRIED LENTIL SOUP

This can be a meal on its own, served with freshly baked bread or bakes (see page 217), and a salad.

3 tablespoons ghee (see Techniques)
2 medium onions, chopped
2 cloves garlic, finely chopped

340 g (¾ lb) green lentils, soaked for 3 hours and drained
3 small tannias, peeled, washed and diced (see Techniques)
2 green bananas, peeled, washed and diced (see Techniques)
Juice 1 small lime or ½ lemon
1.5 litres (2½ pints) unsalted vegetable stock (see page 179)
2 tablespoons curry powder (see Techniques)
Freshly ground black pepper to taste
Sea salt to taste
2 tablespoons chopped fresh coriander or parsley

1 Melt the ghee in a heavy pot and sauté the onions and garlic until golden brown. (Browning the onions gives a special flavour to the lentils.)
2 Add all the other ingredients except the salt and the coriander. Bring to the boil, then simmer covered for 1 hour. After the first 30 minutes add salt to taste.
3 Serve garnished with the coriander or parsley.

Serves 4

CREAM OF WATERCRESS SOUP

50 g (2 oz) butter
1 medium onion, chopped
225 g (½ lb) tannia, peeled, washed and chopped (or substitute potatoes)
2 leeks, washed and chopped
900 ml (1½ pints) vegetable stock (see page 179)
Deseeded and chopped hot pepper to taste (see Techniques)
½ teaspoon freshly ground nutmeg
Freshly ground black pepper to taste
Sea salt to taste
3 bunches watercress, washed and chopped
300 ml (½ pint) single cream
2 tablespoons chopped fresh chives

1 Heat the butter in a heavy pot and sauté the onions until soft but not brown.
2 Add the tannia, leeks, vegetable stock, hot pepper, nutmeg, black pepper and salt. Bring to the boil, then lower the heat and simmer covered until the tannias are tender (about 20 minutes).

3 Add the watercress and cook on a moderate heat for a further 3–4 minutes.
4 Remove from the heat and allow to cool slightly, then liquidize or pass through a sieve. Taste for seasoning.
5 If serving chilled, allow to cool completely before mixing in the cream, then chill for about 30–40 minutes. If serving hot, stir in the cream then return to the heat and heat through without boiling.
6 Serve garnished with chopped chives. You may sprinkle on a little extra grated nutmeg if you wish.

Serves 6

AUBERGINE PÂTÉ

Very simple, very delicious.

2 large aubergines
2 tablespoons olive oil
1–2 cloves garlic (to taste)
½ hot pepper, or to taste, deseeded and chopped (see Techniques)
Juice ½ lemon
Freshly ground black pepper to taste
Sea salt to taste

1 Peel and slice the aubergines, sprinkle with salt and lay evenly on a towel. Leave to sweat for 1 hour then pat dry.
2 Heat the oil in a frying pan and fry the aubergine until soft, but only slightly brown.
3 Put into a mortar with all the other ingredients and pound to a smooth paste, or use a food processor or blender. Serve with hot bakes (see page 217), floats (see page 219) or buttered toast.

Serves 4–6

DEEP-FRIED AUBERGINE

3 tablespoons water
2 vegetable stock cubes
Juice ½ lemon
1 tablespoon yellow pepper sauce
2 cloves garlic, very finely chopped
2 teaspoons grated fresh ginger

1 whole egg and 2 egg yolks, beaten
4 tablespoons flour
4 aubergines
Oil for deep frying
Sea salt to taste

1. Heat the water and dissolve the vegetable cubes. Transfer to a mixing bowl and allow to cool slightly.
2. Blend in the lemon juice, pepper sauce, garlic and ginger, then beat in the eggs.
3. Add the flour to make a smooth batter. Taste for seasoning. If the batter is too heavy, add a little extra stock or water.
4. Wash the aubergines and cut them into cubes about 3 cm (1¼ inches) square.
5. Completely coat the aubergine cubes in the batter, and deep fry in hot oil until golden brown. Drain on kitchen paper and serve.

Serves 6–8

AVOCADO DOMINIQUE

My own special avocado dish from my favourite island – Dominica. This dish can be served either as a first course or as a main course with seasoned rice and a salad. It is best as a hot spicy dish, but the amount of pepper used is left entirely to your taste and that of your guests.

1 tablespoon extra virgin olive oil
75 g (3 oz) butter
8 shallots, coarsely chopped
3 cloves garlic, chopped
6 allspice berries, freshly ground
1 tablespoon tomato purée
Deseeded and chopped hot pepper to taste (see Techniques)
1 small green sweet pepper, deseeded and chopped
1 small red sweet pepper, deseeded and chopped
Juice ½ lemon (or to taste – I prefer a little more)
1 vegetable stock cube
2 tablespoons chopped fresh coriander leaves
2 tomatoes, peeled and chopped
Sea salt to taste (if using salted vegetable stock cubes be careful)

Freshly ground black pepper to taste
4 avocados
Watercress or lettuce leaves
Chopped parsley to garnish

1 Heat the oil and butter in a large, shallow frying pan and sauté the shallots until translucent but not brown.
2 Add the garlic, allspice, tomato purée, hot pepper, sweet peppers, lemon juice and stock cube. Simmer uncovered for 3 minutes, stirring occasionally.
3 Now add the coriander and tomatoes. Season with salt and pepper to taste. Simmer uncovered until most, but not all, of the cooking juices have reduced (if intended as a main course reduce only by about a quarter).
4 Cut each avocado in half lengthways, discard the stone, but do not peel.
5 Arrange a bed of watercress or lettuce leaves on eight individual dishes or a large serving platter. Place the avocado halves on the leaves, fill each one with an equal amount of the mixture, garnish with parsley and serve immediately.

A slice of lemon with each portion is a good idea. As a main course, peel the avocado halves and serve with the mixture on a bed of seasoned rice.

Serves 8 as a starter, 4 as a main course

CHICK PEA ACCRA

This recipe is adapted from a West African dish using black-eyed peas which obviously found its way to the Caribbean with the West African slaves. But here I have substituted chick peas for black-eyed peas. You can use black-eyed peas if you so wish; it is well worth attempting, but it is time-consuming. The black-eyed peas should be soaked overnight, immersed in boiling water for about 10 minutes and allowed to cool. Then each pea must be skinned before being pounded in a mortar with a pestle, as of old. Today in the Caribbean, accra (or akkra) is prepared with various fishes combined with a seasoned flour paste. Salted cod is the most popular – but on the island of Dominica a very minute elver (ti-ti-oui), much smaller than a whitebait, is used.

340 g (¾ lb) chick peas, soaked overnight
1 small onion, grated
½ hot pepper, or to taste, deseeded and chopped (see Techniques)
2 tablespoons wholemeal flour, sifted
1 tablespoon chopped fresh chives
1 tablespoon chopped fresh parsley
1 clove garlic, finely chopped
¼ teaspoon freshly ground allspice
Freshly ground black pepper to taste
Sea salt to taste
1 egg, beaten
Oil for frying

1 Drain and rinse the chick peas then bring them to the boil in a pot of unsalted water and simmer covered for 1¾ hours or until almost tender. Remove from the heat and drain.
2 Pound in a mortar with a pestle or use a food processor. Transfer to a mixing bowl and beat vigorously for a few minutes.
3 Beat in all the other ingredients, except the oil, making certain that the flour is well mixed in. Leave to stand for a few minutes.
4 Form into 12–16 round balls; flatten into cakes between the palms of your hands and shallow fry in hot oil on both sides until golden brown.

A tomato and onion sauce (see page 186), with a little extra hot pepper added, is ideal as a complement to this dish.

Serves 6 as a starter, 4 as a main course

GUACAMOLE WITH RUM

4 avocados
Juice and zest of 1 lemon
1 small onion, finely chopped
1 clove garlic, finely chopped
2 tablespoons finely chopped fresh chives
Deseeded and chopped hot pepper to taste (see Techniques)
225 g (½ lb) tomatoes, peeled, deseeded and chopped
1½ tablespoons light rum
Sea salt to taste
Freshly ground black pepper to taste

1 Peel and stone the avocados then mash them with the lemon juice.
2 Combine the avocados with all the other ingredients, seasoning well with salt and pepper.
3 Serve as a dip. It can even be used as a dressing for cooked vegetables such as boiled breadfruit, christophene, potatoes and half-ripe plantains.

Serves 8

MUSHROOMS IN COCONUT CREAM

A deliciously unusual dish that can be served either as a starter with toast or as a main dish with slices of avocado and plain boiled rice.

50 g (2 oz) margarine
1 medium onion, finely chopped
2 cloves garlic, finely chopped
675 g (1½ lb) mushrooms, sliced (but not too thickly)
Pinch hot cayenne pepper
½ teaspoon turmeric
Sea salt to taste
Freshly ground black pepper to taste
300 ml (½ pint) very thick coconut cream (see Techniques)
1 teaspoon arrowroot, blended to a paste with a little water
Pinch freshly grated nutmeg
2 tablespoons chopped fresh parsley

1 Heat the margarine and sauté the onion until translucent but not brown.
2 Add the garlic and mushrooms and cook on a low heat for 8 minutes.
3 Add the cayenne, turmeric, salt and black pepper and cook for a further 2–3 minutes.
4 Stir in the coconut cream and the arrowroot paste and cook for a further 3–4 minutes, but certainly not more than 4 minutes.
5 Serve sprinkled with nutmeg and garnished with parsley. Grated cheese sprinkled over makes a delicious change.

Serves 6 as a first course, 4 as a main course

OKRA FRITTERS

Large okra tend to become stringy and fibrous with age, so be careful when choosing. You can usually tell by breaking off the pointed end.

24–30 fairly large okra
2 eggs, beaten
75 g (3 oz) wholemeal flour, sifted
Freshly ground black pepper to taste
Sea salt to taste
1 clove garlic, crushed
A little milk or water
Oil for deep frying

1 Wash and top the okra, cutting as close to the heads as possible. Cook them in boiling salted water for about 2 minutes, then remove from the heat, refresh in cold water and drain thoroughly. Set aside uncovered.
2 Make a fairly thick batter with the eggs, flour, pepper, salt, garlic, and a little milk or water.
3 Coat the okra in the batter. Drop them one at a time into hot oil and fry until crisp and brown. Do not overcrowd or they may stick together. Serve as a first course or as an accompaniment to any of the curry dishes.

Serves 4–6

Vegetables

ACKEE CURRY

Ackee, which forms part of Jamaica's favourite dish, ackee and saltfish, was introduced into the Caribbean by Captain William Bligh of *Bounty* fame. It is well worth trying, though unfortunately it can only be purchased in cans in this country.

- 50 g (2 oz) vegetable oil or ghee
- 2 medium onions, sliced
- 1 tablespoon mild curry powder (see Techniques)
- ¼ hot pepper, or to taste, deseeded and chopped (see Techniques)
- 1 teaspoon turmeric (optional)
- 450 ml (¾ pint) coconut milk (see Techniques)
- Sea salt to taste
- 2 teaspoons flour, made into a paste with a little water
- Juice of ½ lime (or to taste)
- 540 g (19 fl oz) tin ackee
- 2 teaspoons chopped fresh coriander leaves

1. Heat the oil and sauté the onions until translucent but not brown.
2. Stir in the curry powder, hot pepper and turmeric if using, and cook for a further 2 minutes.
3. Pour in the coconut milk and add salt to taste. Bring quickly to the boil, then lower the heat and thicken the sauce with the flour paste. Stir to prevent any lumps forming.
4. Add the lime juice. Stir and taste for seasoning.
5. Drain the ackee and add to the sauce together with the coriander leaves. Mix in very gently so as not to break up the ackee too much.
6. Simmer gently for about 12 minutes then serve immediately with riz creole (see page 133). It also goes well with creamed yams or breadfruit.

Serves 4

AUBERGINE AND GREEN PAWPAW IN HOT SAUCE

This is strictly for those who enjoy hot spicy foods.

4 large aubergines
1 green pawpaw, about 225 g (½ lb) in weight (or substitute marrow)
2 tablespoons vegetable oil
1 large onion, finely grated
2 cloves garlic, finely chopped
2 sweet red peppers, deseeded and neatly chopped
3 tomatoes, skinned, deseeded and chopped
1–2 teaspoons brown cane sugar
Sprig fresh parsley, chopped
1 teaspoon turmeric
Juice 1 lime or lemon
2 teaspoons malt vinegar
Sea salt to taste
1–2 deseeded and chopped hot peppers to taste (see Techniques)

1. Peel the aubergines and cut into slices 1 cm (½ inch) thick. Sprinkle with salt and leave to drain in a colander or on a towel for about an hour.
2. Peel the pawpaw and remove the seeds then cut into cubes.
3. Heat the oil in a heavy saucepan with a tight-fitting lid and fry the onion until translucent but not brown.
4. Add the garlic, sweet peppers, tomatoes, sugar, parsley, turmeric, citrus juice, vinegar and salt to taste. Simmer covered for 2–3 minutes.
5. Now add the hot peppers to taste and mix in very gently.
6. Add the pawpaw cubes to the sauce and simmer covered for a further 6 minutes or until the pawpaw becomes slightly translucent.
7. Pat dry the aubergines with a clean cloth and add to the sauce.
8. Simmer covered until the aubergines are tender, but not falling apart. Serve with riz creole (see page 133) or green plantain foo-foo (see page 158).

Serves 6

CREOLE AUBERGINE

This dish originates from the French-speaking islands.

2 medium aubergines
4 tomatoes, skinned and chopped
2 medium onions, chopped
1 clove garlic, chopped
1 small sprig fresh parsley, chopped
½ glass white wine
2 sweet peppers, deseeded and sliced into strips
Small amount deseeded and chopped hot pepper (optional – see Techniques)
1 vegetable stock cube, broken up
Freshly ground black pepper to taste
Sea salt to taste (very little if using salted stock cubes)

1 Wash and cube the aubergines (do not peel).
2 Place all the ingredients in a heavy pot and simmer for 25 minutes or until the vegetables are tender but still slightly firm. Do not overcook. Taste for seasoning and serve with riz creole (see page 133).

Serves 4–6

STUFFED AUBERGINES (1)

2 large aubergines
2 tablespoons olive oil
2 medium onions, finely chopped
1 medium sweet pepper, chopped
1 stick celery, finely chopped
1 clove garlic, chopped
1 wine glass cooked rice
1 small tin plum tomatoes, chopped
1 teaspoon fresh thyme leaves
Freshly ground black pepper to taste
Sea salt to taste
110 g (4 oz) cheese, grated
110 g (4 oz) wholemeal breadcrumbs
75 g (3 oz) butter or margarine, melted
Chopped chives or spring onions to garnish

1 Preheat the oven to 190°C (375°F/Gas 5).
2 Bring a pot of salted water to the boil and add the aubergines. Turn down the heat and simmer gently for not longer than 10–15

minutes. The aubergines must be tender but firm. Drain and leave to cool.

3 Meanwhile, heat the oil and sauté the onions, sweet pepper, celery and garlic until just brown. Remove from the heat.
4 Cut the cooled aubergines in half lengthways, then scoop out the flesh but leave enough to form a shell.
5 Add the rice, about one-third of the aubergine pulp (discard the remainder or use in another recipe), chopped tomatoes, thyme, black pepper and salt to the sautéed vegetables. Mix well and taste for seasoning.
6 Divide this mixture between the aubergine halves and sprinkle with the cheese and breadcrumbs mixed together. Trickle the butter or margarine over them.
7 Bake for about 30 minutes. Garnish with the chives or spring onions and serve with plain boiled rice, sweet potatoes and a tomato sauce.

Serves 4

STUFFED AUBERGINES (2)

I am uncertain of the exact origin of this dish – it is one of several I found among my collection of recipes. It could be French, Spanish or even East Indian. But regardless, it is delicious.

4 large aubergines
4 tablespoons vegetable oil
1 medium onion, finely chopped
110 g (4 oz) mushrooms, chopped
1 ripe but firm mango, peeled, stoned and chopped
3 tomatoes, skinned and chopped
2 cloves garlic, finely chopped
1 tablespoon finely chopped fresh basil
Sea salt to taste
Freshly ground black pepper to taste
225 g (½ lb) butter, melted
Freshly grated nutmeg

1 Preheat the oven to 190°C (375°F/Gas 5).
2 Cut each aubergine in half lengthways, sprinkle with salt and set aside on a plate to sweat for 30–35 minutes; then pat dry.

3 Heat the oil and fry the aubergines until light brown and fairly tender.
4 Remove from the oil and place cut side down on kitchen paper until cool enough to handle.
5 Carefully scoop out the flesh of the aubergines without breaking the skin – leaving a shell.
6 In the same oil in which the aubergines were fried (if there is not enough add some more), fry the onion until lightly browned. Add the aubergine pulp and all the remaining ingredients except the butter and nutmeg, and fry, mixing well, for about 5–6 minutes.
7 Grease a large baking pan or dish. Fill each aubergine half with an equal amount of the mixture and arrange in the dish. Pour melted butter over each half, sprinkle with grated nutmeg and bake for 20–30 minutes.
8 Serve with seasoned rice or a salad and bread.

Serves 4–8

AVOCADO, BANANA AND BREADFRUIT COO-COO

Coo-coo is a vegetable dish usually made with cornmeal and okra and served with stewed or steamed fish. It is very popular on the island of Barbados.

1 quantity breadfruit coo-coo (see page 147), kept warm – or substitute mashed or creamed potatoes (not sweet potatoes)
16 seedless avocados, or 2–3 medium ones
2 large or 4 medium bananas
Juice 2 lemons, or 1 lime and 1 lemon
1 onion, very finely chopped
1 tablespoon chopped fresh chives
1 tablespoon white wine vinegar
½ teaspoon West Indian pepper sauce
1 clove garlic, finely chopped
Pinch turmeric (mainly for colour)
150 ml (5 fl oz) carton natural yoghurt
Freshly ground black pepper to taste
Sea salt to taste

1 Peel the seedless avocados but leave them whole, or peel and stone the larger ones and cut into cubes. Peel the bananas and cut

into 2.5 cm (1 inch) pieces. Mix in a bowl with the juice of one lime or lemon.

2 Combine the remaining ingredients (except the breadfruit coo-coo) into a dressing. The amount of seasoning you use is strictly to your taste and that of your guests. You can even use fresh hot pepper if you wish.

3 Gently mix the dressing with the bananas and avocados and serve with the warm breadfruit coo-coo.

Serves 4–6

BANANA AND PEPPER PIE

675 g (1½ lb) green bananas
1½ limes or lemons
1 large green sweet pepper, deseeded and sliced
1 large red sweet pepper, deseeded and sliced
2 tablespoons grated onion
1 stick celery, finely chopped
½ teaspoon dried oregano
Sea salt to taste
Freshly ground black pepper to taste
4 eggs
40 g (1½ oz) butter
65 g (2½ oz) breadcrumbs

1 Preheat the oven to 190° C (375°F/Gas 5).

2 Peel and wash the bananas, scrubbing with half a citrus fruit (see Techniques). Then bring to the boil in salted water with the juice of half a lime or lemon and cook until tender.

3 When the bananas are cooked, drain, and slice into rings about 1 cm (½ inch) thick. Leave to cool, then carefully mix them with the sweet peppers, onion, celery, oregano, juice of the remaining citrus, and salt and pepper to taste. Arrange in a greased pie dish.

4 Beat the eggs with a little salt and pepper and pour over the banana and pepper mixture. Agitate slightly.

5 Rub the butter into the breadcrumbs, sprinkle over the pie and bake for 20–30 minutes.

6 Serve hot with a tomato and onion sauce (see page 186), and stewed pigeon peas (see page 123). Chopped fresh hot peppers are a must with this dish.

Serves 4–6

CURRIED GREEN BANANAS

6–8 green bananas (depending on size)
1 lime or lemon, plus extra lime or lemon juice to taste
2–3 tablespoons coconut oil (or substitute vegetable oil)
½ teaspoon fennel seeds
½ teaspoon turmeric
1 tablespoon fresh coriander leaves
1 medium onion, chopped
1 heaped tablespoon curry powder (see Techniques)
600 ml (1 pint) coconut milk (see Techniques)
1 vegetable stock cube (optional)
Deseeded and chopped hot pepper to taste (optional – see Techniques)
Sea salt to taste

1. Peel, wash and scrub the bananas with half the citrus fruit (see Techniques). Slice the bananas in half lengthways, then cut each half in two. Place in a bowl with just enough cold water to cover and squeeze the juice from the remaining citrus-half into the water. Set aside.
2. Heat the oil in a pot, add the fennel seeds, turmeric, coriander leaves and onion and fry gently for about 2 minutes. Do not allow to stick to the pot.
3. Drain the banana quarters, pat dry and add to the pot together with the curry powder. Cook for a further 2 minutes.
4. Pour in the coconut milk and add the stock cube, hot pepper if using, salt and citrus juice to taste. Simmer covered for about 25–30 minutes. Serve with pigeon peas or green lentils and an onion salad. It can also be served with riz creole (see page 133).

Serves 4–6

BREADFRUIT AND CASHEW PIE

1 medium breadfruit, fully mature or slightly ripe (see Glossary)
225 g (½ lb) salted cashew nuts, roughly chopped
2 medium onions, finely chopped
4 eggs, beaten
110 g (4 oz) wholemeal breadcrumbs
1 sprig fresh parsley, chopped
1 clove garlic, finely chopped

Pinch cayenne pepper
1–2 teaspoons sea salt (add cautiously, because of the salted nuts)
Freshly ground black pepper to taste
A little grated cheese, preferably a medium Cheddar

1 Preheat the oven to 190°C (375°F/Gas 5).
2 Peel, core and wash the breadfruit then boil in salted water until tender (see Techniques).
3 Drain and allow to cool slightly, then mash or grate using a food processor or grater.
4 Place in a bowl with all the other ingredients except the cheese and mix well. If the mixture is too dry you may need to add a little milk, depending on the size of the eggs.
5 Turn out into a buttered baking dish and bake for about 30 minutes or until brown. Sprinkle with the grated cheese and brown quickly under a hot grill – or return to the oven for about 10 minutes – then serve.

Serves 6

BREADFRUIT AND MUSHROOM PIE

900 g (2 lb) breadfruit
Juice ½ lemon or lime
50 g (2 oz) margarine
1 tablespoon wholemeal flour, sifted
300 ml (½ pint) milk
225 g (½ lb) mushrooms, chopped
2 heaped tablespoons grated onion
Deseeded and chopped hot pepper to taste (see Techniques)
2 eggs, beaten
225 g (½ lb) cheese, grated
Sea salt to taste
Freshly ground black pepper to taste
3 tablespoons wholemeal breadcrumbs
½ teaspoon freshly grated nutmeg

1 Preheat the oven to 190°C (375°F/Gas 5).
2 Peel and core the breadfruit then cut it into 4 cm (1½ inch) cubes (see Techniques). Wash thoroughly, then bring to the boil in salted water with the citrus juice. Cook on a low heat until fairly tender, then drain.

3 Meanwhile, melt the margarine. Add the flour a little at a time, stirring continuously, and cook for 4 minutes. Do not allow to burn.
4 Slowly pour in the milk, stirring until well blended. Add the mushrooms and onions. Simmer gently for a further 3 minutes, stirring occasionally.
5 Remove from the heat. Cool slightly, then thoroughly mix in the hot pepper, beaten egg and about 170 g (6 oz) of the grated cheese.
6 Return to the heat and simmer until the cheese has melted, stirring continuously. Remove from the heat once more and season with salt and black pepper to taste.
7 Arrange the breadfruit cubes in a greased baking tin, or a square or oblong dish. Pour the mixture over the breadfruit. Agitate slightly to mix.
8 Mix the breadcrumbs with the remaining cheese and the grated nutmeg. Sprinkle over the pie.
9 Bake in the oven for 30–45 minutes or until brown. Serve accompanied by stewed red beans (see page 127) and a green salad.

Serves 6

BREADFRUIT, CHEESE AND ONION FLAN

The Edam cheese left over from making a Keshy Yena (see page 129) can be used for this dish.

340 g (¾ lb) breadfruit (slightly under-ripe – try to get one piece)
Juice ½ lemon or lime
75 g (3 oz) butter
2 large onions, chopped or sliced
1 pre-baked savoury flan case (see page 231)
225 g (½ lb) Edam cheese, grated
1 sprig fresh parsley, chopped
2 eggs, beaten
300 ml (½ pint) light coconut cream (see Techniques) or single cream
1 tablespoon dill mustard (or substitute any smooth mustard)
Pinch freshly grated nutmeg
Sea salt to taste

Freshly ground black pepper to taste
110 g (4 oz) pine nuts

1 Preheat the oven to 180°C (350°F/Gas 4).
2 Wash the breadfruit (do not peel, cut or core) and bring to the boil in salted water with the lemon or lime juice. Cook until tender.
3 Drain and leave until it is cool enough to handle. Then peel, core and cut into cubes about 1 cm (½ inch) thick.
4 Melt the butter and sauté the onions until translucent but not brown. Remove from the heat.
5 Arrange half the breadfruit cubes in the flan case, sprinkle over half the cheese then half the onions and all of the parsley. Repeat the breadfruit, onion and cheese layers.
6 Combine the eggs, coconut cream, dill mustard and nutmeg. Season to taste and pour this over the filling in the flan case. Agitate slightly.
7 Bake in the preheated oven for 45 minutes or until set and brown. About halfway through the baking period, before the custard is quite set, sprinkle evenly with the pine nuts.
8 Serve hot or warm with a tomato and onion sauce (see page 186). A green salad, including watercress, is also recommended as an accompaniment.

Serves 4–6

BREADFRUIT CURRY

3 tablespoons coconut or vegetable oil
2.5 cm (1 inch) piece fresh ginger, peeled and finely chopped
25 g (1 oz) annatto seeds, freshly ground
1 level teaspoon freshly ground coriander seeds
2 cloves garlic, finely chopped
2 medium tomatoes, skinned and chopped
½ teaspoon turmeric
1 tablespoon curry powder (see Techniques)
2 sweet peppers, deseeded and sliced
Deseeded and chopped hot pepper to taste (see Techniques)
150 ml (5 fl oz) coconut milk (see Techniques) or plain yoghurt
Sea salt to taste
450 g (1 lb) breadfruit, cooked and diced (see Techniques)

1 Heat the oil in a pot and fry the ginger, annatto, coriander and garlic for no longer than 3 minutes.
2 Add the tomatoes, turmeric, curry powder, sweet peppers, hot pepper, coconut milk and salt to taste and simmer on a very low heat for about 4–5 minutes. Do not forget to stir occasionally.
3 Now add the diced breadfruit – mix in until well coated and cook for a further 10–15 minutes. Taste for seasoning and serve with stewed lentils or pigeon peas.

Serves 4

CABBAGE WITH MANGO STUFFING

SERVED WITH ONION, OLIVE AND CAPER SAUCE

This dish is derived from the cuisine of the Syrian merchants of the Caribbean.

8–12 large cabbage leaves
75 g (3 oz) margarine or butter
2 medium onions, finely chopped
3 cloves garlic, finely chopped
225 g (½ lb) minced TVP (soaked in vegetable stock for 1 hour)
110 g (4 oz) cooked rice
1 sprig fresh parsley, chopped
1 teaspoon fresh thyme leaves
Grated rind ½ lemon
½ teaspoon crushed fennel seeds
Deseeded and chopped hot pepper to taste (see Techniques)
1 sweet pepper, deseeded and chopped
1 teaspoon freshly ground allspice
1 large ripe but firm mango, peeled, stoned and sliced
Sea salt to taste
Freshly ground black pepper to taste
300 ml (½ pint) good vegetable stock (see page 179)
1 quantity onion, olive and caper sauce (see page 182)

1 Preheat the oven to 190°C (375°F/Gas 5).
2 Bring some salted water to the boil in a wide pot, add the cabbage leaves and cook until limp (1½–2 minutes). Drain and refresh in cold water immediately, being careful not to tear the leaves. Set aside on a clean cloth.

3 Melt the margarine or butter in a pot. Add the onions and garlic and fry until translucent but not brown.
4 Add the TVP, cooked rice, parsley, thyme, lemon rind, fennel seeds, hot pepper, sweet pepper and allspice and continue cooking for about 4–5 minutes. Do not allow to stick to the pot.
5 Now add the sliced mango and mix in without breaking up too much. Season with salt and pepper.
6 Remove from the heat and allow to cool enough to be handled. Place an equal amount of the mixture on each cabbage leaf, then carefully fold.
7 Pack the cabbage rolls fairly tightly in an ovenproof dish. Pour in the stock and bake uncovered for 30–45 minutes. Baste with the liquid occasionally.
8 Arrange on a heated platter. Pour over the onion, olive and caper sauce and serve at once.

Serves 4–6

RED CABBAGE WITH MANGO

I was introduced to this dish by a friend who is a chef at one of the top hotels in London. I had eaten red cabbage with apple before but this particular version of the dish is rather special and unusual.

2 tablespoons oil
75 g (3 oz) butter, plus a little extra
1 small red cabbage, shredded
2 medium onions, sliced
Sea salt to taste
Freshly ground black pepper to taste
Bouquet garni of fresh thyme, bay leaf, and parsley in a muslin bag
2 tablespoons redcurrant jelly
1 glass red wine
½ glass red wine vinegar (or whatever vinegar you have)
2 ripe but very firm mangoes (just turning)

1 Preheat the oven to 190°C (375°F/Gas 5).
2 In a pan heat the oil and the 75 g (3 oz) butter and sauté the cabbage and onions until they begin to sweat. Season with salt and pepper and add the bouquet garni. Place a lid on the pan and cook over a moderate heat, stirring occasionally.

3 When the cabbage and onions have released their own juices, make a well in the middle and add the redcurrant jelly. Cook uncovered on a moderate to high heat until the jelly has caramelized (without burning) then add the red wine and the vinegar. Stir well and cook until the liquid has reduced by a third.
4 Check the seasoning and add the extra butter. Remove from the heat.
5 Peel the mangoes and cut the flesh away from the stones in thin, even slices.
6 Grease a baking dish and arrange a layer of a third of the sliced mangoes on the bottom, cover that with half of the cabbage. Repeat – mango, cabbage, finishing with a layer of mangoes on the top.
7 Dot with butter, cover and bake for 30–45 minutes.

Serves 4–6

STUFFED CABBAGE

For the stuffing:
225 g (½ lb) soya beef cubes (TVP), soaked for 1–2 hours
8 capers, finely chopped
6 green olives, stoned and finely chopped
½ onion, grated
1 medium tomato, chopped
1 vegetable stock cube, crushed
Freshly ground black pepper to taste
½ teaspoon deseeded and finely chopped hot pepper
2 teaspoons soya sauce (optional)
Sea salt to taste (if necessary)

1 large savoy cabbage (or any similar cabbage will do)
1 onion, thinly sliced
1 clove garlic, crushed
1 celery stick, chopped
2 carrots, sliced
1 sprig fresh thyme
½ teaspoon fennel seeds
Freshly ground black pepper to taste
1 teaspoon yeast extract
Sea salt to taste
600 ml (1 pint) vegetable stock (see page 179)

2 tablespoons arrowroot
50 g (2 oz) unsalted butter

1 Drain the soya beef cubes. Reserve the liquid to add to the vegetable stock.
2 Chop up the soya cubes rather coarsely. Place in a bowl with the capers, olives, onion, tomato, crushed stock cube, black pepper, hot pepper and soya sauce. Mix well. Taste for seasoning and add salt if necessary. Set aside.
3 Remove about 6–8 outer leaves from the cabbage. Wash and set aside.
4 Wash the cabbage and check carefully for any foreign agents. Shake and pat dry, being careful not to damage the leaves.
5 Place the cabbage in a bowl and pour boiling water over to loosen the leaves. Leave for a few minutes then drain and pat dry. Have a saucepan of boiling water ready.
6 Carefully put the stuffing between the leaves of the cabbage.
7 Quickly dip the reserved outer leaves in the boiling water; drain and allow to cool slightly, then wrap them round the stuffed cabbage. Tie with string to secure.
8 Place the cabbage in a large pot with a tight-fitting lid, then surround it with the onion, garlic, celery, carrots, thyme, fennel, black pepper, yeast extract and a very little salt. Pour in the stock. Cover (do not bring to the boil) and simmer on the lowest possible heat for about 1½ hours. Do not allow the liquid to boil away. Add more stock if necessary.
9 Carefully remove the cabbage from the liquid, discarding the string, and place in a deep serving dish. Keep warm.
10 Strain the liquid, pressing through a fine sieve, and discard all the bits and pieces. Return to a medium heat.
11 Mix the arrowroot into a paste with some water or cold stock, and slowly stir it into the liquid until it thickens. Simmer for about 3 minutes, then add the butter.
12 Pour the sauce over the cabbage and serve immediately with rice and pigeon peas.

Serves 6

STEWED CALABAZA

900 g (2 lb) calabaza (or substitute any other pumpkin – see Glossary)

50 g (2 oz) butter
1 medium onion, finely chopped
2 cloves garlic, finely chopped
½ teaspoon freshly ground annatto seeds
¼ teaspoon freshly grated nutmeg
400 g (14 oz) tin plum tomatoes, chopped
Pinch cayenne pepper, or ½ teaspoon yellow pepper sauce
Juice 1 lemon
Freshly ground black pepper to taste
Sea salt to taste

1. Peel the calabaza, remove the seeds and fibre and cut the flesh into 1 cm (½ inch) pieces. Set aside.
2. Melt the butter in a pot and sauté the onion and garlic until the onions are translucent but not brown.
3. Add all the other ingredients including the pumpkin and simmer covered until the pumpkin is soft. The pumpkin should not be overcooked or mushy.
4. Taste for seasoning and serve with rice or as an accompaniment.

Serves 6

CALLALOO LOAF

675 g (1½ lb) callaloo leaves (or substitute spinach)
2 wholemeal bread rolls
1 wine glass vegetable stock
25 g (1 oz) butter
1 medium onion, thinly sliced
170 g (6 oz) pine nuts
170 g (6 oz) Edam cheese, grated
3 eggs, beaten
Freshly grated nutmeg
Sea salt to taste
Freshly ground black pepper to taste

1. Preheat the oven to 190°C (375°F/Gas 5).
2. Wash then coarsely chop the callaloo leaves and steam for about 20 minutes. Drain off any excess water and allow to cool.
3. Meanwhile break up the rolls and soak in the stock.
4. Melt the butter and sauté the onions without browning for about 2 minutes. Remove from the heat.

5 In a bowl combine all the ingredients, having squeezed any excess liquid from the rolls. Mix well and check the seasoning.
6 Turn the mixture into a greased 20 cm (8 inch) loaf tin and bake in the oven for about 1¼–1½ hours or until set. Turn out and serve with a creole sauce (see page 180).

Serves 4

CALLALOO PIE

900 g (2 lb) callaloo leaves (or substitute spinach)
1 quantity savoury shortcrust pastry (see page 231)
50 g (2 oz) unsalted butter
1 medium onion, grated
25 g (1 oz) wholemeal flour
150 ml (¼ pint) milk
1 heaped tablespoon chopped fresh parsley
¾ teaspoon freshly ground caraway seeds
110 g (4 oz) Edam cheese, grated (or substitute Gruyère or similar cheese)
4 hard-boiled eggs, chopped
Freshly ground black pepper to taste
Sea salt to taste

1 Preheat the oven to 200°C (400°F/Gas 6).
2 Wash and chop the callaloo leaves then steam them for about 30 minutes.
3 Meanwhile line a large pie dish with about two-thirds of the pastry.
4 Melt the butter and sauté the grated onion until soft, then slowly add the flour, stirring continuously. Do not allow to brown. Continue to cook on a low heat for 2 minutes.
5 Slowly pour in the milk, again stirring continuously, and cook for 8 minutes.
6 Now carefully but thoroughly mix in all the other ingredients, including the callaloo leaves, and check the seasoning.
7 Transfer to the pastry-lined dish and spread evenly. Cover with the remaining pastry and bake for 30–40 minutes or until the pastry is an even brown.

Serves 4–6

CARROT AND SWEET POTATO PIE

225 g (½ lb) carrots
225 g (½ lb) sweet potatoes
Piece of lemon
170 g (6 oz) wholemeal breadcrumbs
¼ teaspoon freshly grated nutmeg
1 teaspoon fresh marjoram
Pinch powdered saffron
Pinch allspice
75 g (3 oz) melted butter or margarine
Pinch cayenne
Sea salt to taste
2 eggs, well beaten

1. Preheat the oven to 180°C (350°F/Gas 4).
2. Scrape the carrots and peel the sweet potatoes. Wash thoroughly, scrubbing the sweet potatoes with the piece of lemon.
3. Bring the vegetables to the boil in salted water and simmer covered until tender. Remove from the heat, drain, then mash through a sieve or in a food processor.
4. Beat the mixture with a wooden fork, or use an electric whisk for about 4 minutes, or until light. Add all the remaining ingredients except the eggs and continue to whisk until well blended.
5. Now mix in the beaten eggs a little at a time, blending thoroughly. Turn into a well-greased ovenproof baking dish and bake for about 1¼ hours.

Serves 4

CUSH CUSH PATTIES

675 g (1½ lb) cooked cush cush (or substitute potatoes – not sweet)
110 g (4 oz) cooked yellow split peas
3 tablespoons clarified butter (ghee – see Techniques)
2 medium onions, finely chopped
2 cloves garlic, finely chopped
Deseeded and chopped hot pepper to taste (see Techniques)
2 teaspoons cumin seeds (fresh if possible)
1 tablespoon curry powder (see Techniques)
2–3 tablespoons chopped fresh coriander leaves

2 eggs, beaten
Freshly ground black pepper to taste
Sea salt to taste
Wholemeal flour for coating
Pinch ground ginger
Oil for frying

1 Coarsely mash the cush cush and mix with the split peas.
2 Heat the clarified butter and sauté the onions and garlic until the onions are translucent but not brown.
3 Add the hot pepper, cumin seeds, curry powder and coriander leaves. Mix well and simmer covered on a very low heat for about 3 minutes. Remove from the heat.
4 Combine with the cush cush and pea mixture. Beat in the eggs and season to taste with pepper and salt.
5 Form into 12–16 circular flat cakes. They must be fairly thick.
6 Mix together the wholemeal flour and ground ginger and coat the patties.
7 Fry them on both sides until golden brown. Can be served hot or warm, with or without a sauce.

Serves 4–6

CURRIED CUSH CUSH

900 g (2 lb) cush cush – potatoes can be used but it is worth seeking out the cush cush
1 lemon
3 tablespoons oil
1 teaspoon grated fresh ginger
3 cloves garlic, chopped
½ teaspoon freshly ground allspice
½ teaspoon freshly ground sesame seeds
1 teaspoon turmeric
1–2 teaspoons deseeded and finely chopped hot pepper (see Techniques)
1 tablespoon curry powder (see Techniques)
1 level teaspoon freshly ground annatto seeds
2 sweet peppers, deseeded and sliced
450 ml (¾ pint) thick coconut cream (see Techniques) or plain yoghurt

1 tablespoon plain chopped fresh coriander leaves
Sea salt to taste

1 Peel, wash and scrub the cush cush with half the lemon then bring to the boil in salted water with the juice of the remainder of the lemon. Cook on a medium heat until firm but tender. Drain, cool slightly then cut into cubes.
2 Heat the oil and fry together the ginger, garlic, allspice and sesame seeds for about 3 minutes. Add the turmeric, hot pepper, curry powder and annatto and fry for a further 2 minutes. Do not allow to burn.
3 Add the sweet peppers, coconut cream or yoghurt, coriander and salt to taste. Stir to mix well. Simmer half covered on a very low heat for 10 minutes. Taste for seasoning.
4 Add the cooked cush cush cubes and coat well with the sauce.
5 Remove from the heat and set aside, slightly covered, for 1½–2 hours. It can be served immediately but leaving it to stand improves the flavour.
6 Reheat on a low to medium heat. This curry must be fairly thick and is ideal as a filling for roti (see page 220).

Serves 6

OKRA, AUBERGINE AND TOMATO BAKE

A creole dish from old New Orleans.

2–3 aubergines (according to size)
450 g (1 lb) okra
3 tablespoons olive oil
2 medium onions, finely sliced into rings
2 cloves garlic, crushed
½ teaspoon dried oregano
1 tablespoon lemon juice
Sea salt to taste
Freshly ground black pepper to taste
450 g (1 lb) tomatoes, skinned, deseeded and chopped
170 g (6 oz) cheese, grated
75 g (3 oz) wholemeal breadcrumbs

1 Preheat the oven to 190°C (375°F/Gas 5).
2 Wash the aubergines and slice them into rounds approximately 0.5 cm (½ inch) thick. Arrange on a clean cloth or kitchen paper,

sprinkle both sides with salt and leave until most of the liquid has been extracted. Rinse and pat dry.

3 Top the okra and slice each one in half lengthways.

4 Heat the oil and fry the onions and garlic until translucent but not brown. Add the okra, aubergine slices, oregano and lemon juice and cook for a further 4 minutes. Season with a little salt and pepper.

5 Butter an ovenproof dish. Arrange half the tomatoes in the dish and cover with the okra and aubergine mixture.

6 Top with the remaining tomatoes and sprinkle them with salt and black pepper.

7 Combine the breadcrumbs and cheese and spread evenly over the tomatoes. Bake until brown – about 45 minutes.

Serves 4–6

OKRA OMELETTE

110 g (4 oz) butter
2 tablespoons finely chopped onions
2 cloves garlic, finely chopped
3 large tomatoes, skinned, deseeded and chopped
Juice ½ lemon
Freshly ground black pepper to taste
Sea salt to taste
340 g (¾ lb) okra
A little butter and oil for frying
6 eggs
2 tablespoons finely chopped chives
1 tablespoon finely chopped parsley

1 Melt 50 g (2 oz) of the butter in a shallow pan and sauté the onions and garlic for about 1–2 minutes.

2 Add the chopped tomatoes, lemon juice, black pepper and salt to taste.

3 Simmer uncovered for about 15 minutes. Give the occasional stir to prevent the mixture sticking to the pan.

4 Meanwhile wash, top and slice each okra into 3–4 pieces according to size.

5 Melt the remaining butter in a saucepan, add the okra with a little salt, and simmer partly covered until tender but still quite firm. Add to the tomato mixture and keep warm.

6 Put a large omelette pan, greased with a little butter and oil, on a low heat.
7 Beat the eggs with a little black pepper and salt then gradually beat in the chives and parsley. Pour the omelette mixture into the hot pan and cook as usual.
8 While the mixture is still quite moist, spoon in the okra and tomato sauce. Fold and serve immediately. A creole sauce (see page 180) and a green salad make good accompaniments.

Serves 3–4

ONION AND SWEET PEPPER CASSEROLE

50 g (2 oz) butter
1 tablespoon extra virgin olive oil
450 g (1 lb) small white onions, skinned
4 sweet peppers, red and green, deseeded and chopped
225 g (½ lb) soya beef cubes (TVP), soaked in water for about 1 hour
2 tablespoons tomato sauce (see page 184)
2 teaspoons caramel colouring (see Techniques)
8–10 stuffed olives
½ teaspoon freshly grated nutmeg
1 bay leaf
1 sprig fresh thyme
½ hot pepper, deseeded and chopped
2 vegetable cubes
1–2 teaspoons yeast extract
Freshly ground black pepper to taste
Sea salt to taste
300–450 ml (½–¾ pint) water (including the liquid from the soya beef cubes)
1 level tablespoon of flour, mixed with a little water, to thicken if necessary.

1 Preheat the oven to 190°C (375°F/Gas 5).
2 Heat the butter and oil in a heavy casserole and fry the onions until slightly brown.
3 Add the sweet peppers and continue to cook for a further 2–3 minutes.
4 Mix in all the other ingredients except the flour paste, pouring in

the water last. The water must reach only about two-thirds of the way up the mixture.

5 Cover, and transfer to the preheated oven for about 1 hour. About halfway through the cooking time you may thicken with the flour paste.

6 Serve with riz creole (see page 133), red beans and fried ripe plantains (see page 158).

Serves 4–6

STUFFED RIPE PLANTAINS

4–6 very ripe, good-sized plantains
3 tablespoons olive oil
50 g (2 oz) butter
2 medium onions, very finely chopped
1 tablespoon yeast extract
225 g (½ lb) cooked red kidney beans, slightly mashed
1 teaspoon curry powder
½ teaspoon freshly ground coriander seeds
Pinch ground cloves
Juice ½ lemon
Deseeded and chopped hot pepper to taste (optional – see Techniques)
1 vegetable stock cube, crushed
Freshly ground black pepper to taste
Sea salt to taste
1 egg and 2 yolks, beaten
A little fine cornmeal or wholemeal flour
A little grated cheese (optional)

1 Preheat the oven to 190°C (375°F/Gas 5).

2 Peel the plantains, then evenly slice each lengthways into 3 or 4 pieces, according to size (see Techniques).

3 Heat 2 tablespoons of the oil and quickly fry the plantain pieces on each side. This is simply to help loosen the flesh, so do not over fry. However, the slices can be lightly browned to give a bit of colour to the finished dish. Place each slice on absorbent kitchen paper.

4 Heat the remaining oil and the butter and fry the onions until soft and translucent but not brown.

5 Stir in the yeast extract, the cooked kidney beans, curry powder,

spices, lemon juice, hot pepper, stock cube, seasoning, and finally the beaten eggs.

6 Cook uncovered on a very low heat for about 10 minutes, stirring occasionally to prevent sticking to the pan.
7 Grease a baking tin and sprinkle in a little fine cornmeal or wholemeal flour. Form each slice of plantain into a circular band by bringing the ends together and securing with cocktail sticks.
8 Fill each plantain circle with the mixture. Pack in well, but carefully.
9 Sprinkle with grated cheese if liked, and bake for 30 minutes. Serve hot.

This dish could be served with a bowl of stewed lentils, but not too dry – or even rice.

Serves 4–6

PLANTAIN PIE

This is very much a creole recipe and very popular on many Caribbean islands. Though green musas are more commonly used, this dish also works well with ripe but firm plantains, as tested by my editor.

675 g (1½ lb) cooked green plantain – or substitute cooked green bananas (see Techniques)
75 g (3 oz) soft butter, plus a little extra for dotting
200 ml (7 fl oz) single cream
1 teaspoon fresh thyme leaves
1 medium onion, finely grated
1 tablespoon chopped fresh chives
Pinch saffron
Freshly ground black pepper to taste
Sea salt to taste
2 tablespoons wholemeal breadcrumbs

1 Preheat the oven to 220°C (425°F/Gas 7).
2 Mash the boiled green plantain with a fork. Do not pound like you would for foo-foo.
3 Mix in all the other ingredients except the extra butter and the breadcrumbs. Taste for seasoning.
4 Turn into a buttered pie dish and sprinkle with the breadcrumbs. Dot with the remaining butter and bake for 20–25 minutes. Serve

with a tomato and onion sauce (see page 186) and pigeon peas or green lentils.

Serves 3–4

CURRIED PUMPKIN

A really delicious dish from the French Caribbean island of Martinique.

675 g (1½ lb) pumpkin
2 tablespoons oil
1 medium onion, sliced
2 cloves garlic, finely chopped
1 tablespoon poudre de Colombo (see Techniques)
½ teaspoon freshly ground allspice
Deseeded and chopped hot pepper to taste (see Techniques)
2 tomatoes, deseeded and chopped
300 ml (½ pint) water
1½ vegetable stock cubes
Juice ½ lemon
Sea salt to taste

1. Peel and discard the stringy insides and seeds of the pumpkin, then wash and cut into 2.5 cm (1 inch) cubes.
2. Heat the oil in a heavy pot and sauté the onion until translucent but not brown.
3. Add the garlic, curry powder, allspice and hot pepper and cook for about 1 minute.
4. Add the pumpkin and chopped tomatoes and cook for a further 2 minutes, stirring occasionally.
5. Now add the water, stock cubes and lemon juice; stir to mix and simmer covered for about 20 minutes or until the pumpkin is tender.
6. Halfway through the cooking time taste for seasoning and add salt if needed.
7. Serve immediately accompanied by rice or roti bread (see page 220).

Serves 4

RATATOUILLE À LA CREOLE

I have cooked this dish many times for my vegetarian friends, using different varieties of tropical vegetables each time, depending on where I am and what's available. This is a basic recipe which you can alter, using your imagination.

2 large aubergines
2 tannias
½ lime or lemon
4 tablespoons extra virgin olive oil (preferably French)
2 large onions, thinly sliced
2 christophene, peeled and diced
2 large red sweet peppers, deseeded and thinly sliced
2 large green sweet peppers, deseeded and thinly sliced
3 cloves garlic, finely chopped
Freshly ground black pepper to taste
Sea salt to taste
1 sprig fresh parsley, chopped
1 whole hot pepper (see Techniques)
200 ml (7 fl oz) vegetable stock (see page 179)
6–12 okra (according to size), topped and left whole
3 large tomatoes, peeled and chopped

1 Cut the aubergines into cubes, sprinkle with salt and place in a sieve or colander. Set aside to sweat.
2 Peel the tannias and wash them in cold water, using the lime or lemon (see Techniques). Cut into cubes, rinse again and drain.
3 In a heavy pot with a tight-fitting lid, heat the oil and fry the onions until translucent but not brown.
4 Rinse the aubergines under cold running water and pat dry.
5 In the following order, add the tannias, christophene, aubergines, sweet peppers, garlic, black pepper and salt. Sprinkle the chopped parsley over and place the whole pepper on top. Add the vegetable stock. Cover and simmer gently for about 30 minutes.
6 Remove the whole hot pepper, which at no cost must be broken. Arrange the okra and chopped tomatoes on top then replace the hot pepper.
7 Cook for a further 20 minutes until the vegetables are tender but not falling apart. Cook uncovered for the last 10 minutes.
8 Remove the hot pepper carefully. Taste for seasoning. Serve hot or cold with the hot pepper, chopped, on a separate dish (see Techniques).

Serves 6–8

STUFFED SWEET PEPPERS

The following recipe was given to me by Jean Beckwith of Blockley in Gloucestershire.

4 fair-sized sweet red peppers
125 g (4½ oz) unsalted butter, plus a little extra for dotting
450 g (1 lb) mushrooms, finely chopped
1 wine glass dry white wine
110 g (4 oz) toasted unsalted cashew nuts
110 g (4 oz) sunflower seeds
2 cloves garlic, finely chopped
2 tablespoons tomato purée
Juice ½ lime or lemon
Pinch freshly grated nutmeg
Pinch cayenne or ½ teaspoon pepper sauce
1 tablespoon chopped fresh parsley
1 tablespoon chopped olives
170 g (6 oz) cooked brown rice
Freshly ground black pepper to taste
Sea salt to taste
170 g (6 oz) cooked brown rice
170 g (6 oz) cheese, grated
50 g (2 oz) breadcrumbs

1. Preheat the oven to 200°C (400°F/Gas 6).
2. Have a pot of water on the boil. Cut each pepper in half lengthways and remove the seeds and white flesh. Wash the peppers, then drop them into the boiling water. Remove the pan from the heat immediately and leave the pepper halves still immersed for about one minute.
3. Carefully remove the peppers from the hot water and place cut side down on a kitchen towel to drain and cool.
4. Heat the butter and sauté the mushrooms until limp.
5. Pour in the wine, then mix in all the other ingredients except the breadcrumbs and cheese. Simmer on a low heat for a few minutes, stirring to prevent any sticking to the pot. Remove from the heat and taste for seasoning.
6. Grease one or two ovenproof dishes. Fill the pepper halves with the mixture, sprinkle each with the cheese then the breadcrumbs. Dot with butter.

7 Arrange the stuffed peppers in the dish or dishes and bake for 20–30 minutes or until the cheese and breadcrumbs have turned brown. Serve hot or cold.

Serves 4

SWEET POTATOES AND ACKEE

A delicious, spicy dish that can be served either as a snack or as a main meal – when I would suggest it be accompanied by avocado slices and a green salad.

2–3 tablespoons oil
40 g (1½ oz) butter
2 medium onions, chopped
2 cloves garlic, chopped
1 teaspoon finely chopped fresh ginger
1 vegetable stock cube
675 g (1½ lb) sweet potatoes, cooked (not too soft), peeled and cubed (see Techniques)
Generous sprig fresh parsley, chopped
½ teaspoon fresh thyme leaves
1 teaspoon deseeded and chopped hot pepper, or to taste (see Techniques)
Juice ½ lime
Sea salt to taste
Freshly ground black pepper to taste
540 g (19 oz) tin ackee, drained

1 Heat the oil and butter and fry the onions until translucent, then add the garlic and ginger and continue to fry for a further 2 minutes.
2 Crumble in the stock cube and mix well, then add all the remaining ingredients except the ackee.
3 Simmer covered on a low to medium heat for 3 minutes. Taste for seasoning.
4 Add the drained ackee. Mix well, simmer covered for a further 3–5 minutes, then serve.

Serves 3–4

SWEET POTATO AND ONION PIE

900 g (2 lb) sweet potatoes
1 lemon

1 tablespoon olive oil
125 g (4½ oz) unsalted butter
675 g (1½ lb) onions, peeled and sliced
Freshly ground black pepper to taste
Sea salt to taste
3 medium tomatoes, skinned, deseeded and sliced
200 ml (7 fl oz) double cream
Freshly grated nutmeg to taste

1 Preheat the oven to 190°C (375°F/Gas 5).
2 Peel and wash the potatoes then scrub them with half the lemon. Cut into thin slices and set aside in water with the juice of the remaining lemon half.
3 In a heavy frying pan heat the oil and butter and gently fry the onions without browning.
4 Butter a pie dish large enough to hold all the ingredients.
5 Drain the sweet potatoes. Arrange a quarter of them in a layer in the dish, then arrange half the onions on top. Sprinkle with salt and pepper to taste and cover with another quarter of the potatoes. Arrange the tomatoes on top. Start again with sweet potatoes, then the remaining half of the onions, sprinkle with salt and pepper and finish with the remaining potatoes.
6 Pour in the cream, sprinkle with nutmeg and bake for about 1 hour or until the potatoes are tender.

This dish goes very well with red beans and a watercress and lettuce salad.

Serves 6

SWEET POTATO AND PLANTAIN WITH CARROT SAUCE

2 sweet potatoes
1 lemon, plus juice ½ lemon
4 ripe plantains
2 tablespoons olive oil
50 g (2 oz) butter
2 teaspoons Jamaican honey
1 tablespoon light brown rum

For the carrot sauce:
50 g (2 oz) butter
1 small onion, chopped

675 g (1½ lb) carrots, peeled, sliced and parboiled
Sea salt to taste
Pinch saffron
6 allspice berries, crushed
6 black peppercorns, freshly ground
½ wine glass Madeira
Juice ½ orange
2 teaspoons lemon juice
1 tablespoon Cointreau

1 Thoroughly wash the potatoes, scrubbing with half the whole lemon. Without peeling, put to the boil in a pan of salted water with the juice from the rest of the whole lemon.
2 Lower the heat and cook until tender, but still quite firm. Then drain and set aside.
3 Meanwhile, make the carrot sauce: heat the butter and lightly sauté the onion. Add the carrots, salt, saffron, allspice and peppercorns and sauté for a further 2 minutes. Remove from the heat.
4 Place in a blender with the Madeira, orange juice and lemon juice and blend to a smooth purée. Pass through a fine sieve and stir in the Cointreau. Set aside in a cool place, but do not refrigerate.
5 Heat the oil in a shallow pan. Peel the plantains and cut each one crossways in half; slice each half into 3 or 4 pieces lengthways and fry on both sides until golden brown. Remove from the pan and keep warm.
6 Peel the potatoes, cut each lengthways into quarters, and then slice each quarter lengthways in slices about 1 cm (½ inch) thick.
7 In the same oil in which the plantains were cooked, melt the butter, keeping the heat low, and mix in the honey, rum and remaining lemon juice. Glaze the potato slices in the honeyed mixture.
8 On a large serving platter, decoratively arrange the plantain and potato slices. Spoon the carrot sauce over the vegetables and serve accompanied by a salad and a nut roast.

Serves 6–8

SWEET POTATO AND PUMPKIN PIE

This is a delicious and unusual combination that is well worth trying.

450 g (1 lb) sweet potatoes (peeled weight)
675 g (1½ lb) pumpkin, deseeded and peeled
1 lemon, cut in half
50 g (2 oz) unsalted butter
2 tablespoons vegetable oil
1 large onion, chopped
2 cloves garlic, chopped
1 small christophene, peeled and finely chopped
225 g (½ lb) carrots, scraped and grated
1 small red sweet pepper, deseeded and chopped
½ teaspoon dried oregano
1 tablespoon chopped fresh parsley
Freshly ground black pepper to taste
Sea salt to taste
300 ml (½ pint) single cream
3 eggs, beaten
Freshly grated nutmeg

1 Preheat the oven to 190°C (375°F/Gas 5).
2 Cut the peeled potatoes and the pumpkin into chunks. Wash in cold water, scrubbing the potatoes with half the lemon.
3 Place the potatoes in a pot with cold salted water and the juice from the other lemon half. Bring to the boil, lower the heat and simmer covered for about 6 minutes. Add the pumpkin and continue to cook until the vegetables are soft. Drain, and either pass through a sieve or purée in a food processor, together with the butter.
4 Heat the oil and fry the onions and garlic until translucent but not brown.
5 Add the chopped christophene and grated carrots and cook for about 8 minutes. Add the sweet pepper and continue to cook for a further 6 minutes. Do not allow to stick to the pot. Add the herbs and season with black pepper and salt.
6 Raise the heat and pour in the cream. Stir until it begins to bubble, then lower the heat. Allow to thicken.
7 Remove from the heat and leave to cool, giving the mixture a stir now and then. When cool, thoroughly mix in the beaten eggs.
8 Combine the mixture with the puréed potato and pumpkin. Mix well and taste for seasoning.
9 Turn into a greased ovenproof dish and sprinkle with the nutmeg.

Bake for 30–45 minutes or until set. Serve with a tomato and onion sauce (see page 186) or any of the stewed bean dishes and a green salad.

Serves 6–8

SWEET POTATO AND SPINACH FRITTERS

225 g (½ lb) cooked, peeled and mashed sweet potatoes (see Techniques)
225 g (½ lb) cooked, drained and chopped spinach
110 g (4 oz) plain flour
1½ tablespoons grated onion
Deseeded and chopped hot pepper to taste (see Techniques)
½ teaspoon freshly ground allspice
½ teaspoon freshly grated nutmeg
½ teaspoon freshly ground cumin seed (a must)
1 tablespoon chopped fresh coriander leaves
1 teaspoon baking powder
½ teaspoon bicarbonate of soda (baking soda)
Sea salt to taste
Freshly ground black pepper to taste
2 size-3 eggs, beaten
Oil for frying

1. Mix the mashed potatoes with all the other ingredients, except the eggs and oil.
2. Knead in the egg and shape the mixture into 8 balls, then flatten into round patties, using a little wholemeal flour to help prevent them sticking to your hands.
3. Heat the oil and shallow fry on both sides until golden brown. Drain on kitchen paper towels.
4. Serve on their own or with beans, curried lentils or a salad.

Serves 4

SWEET POTATO MOULD WITH CURRIED VEGETABLES

900 g (2 lb) sweet potatoes
1 lemon, plus juice ½ lemon
3 tablespoons vegetable oil
1 teaspoon freshly grated ginger

2 medium onions, finely chopped
3 cloves garlic, finely chopped
1½–2 tablespoons mild curry powder (see Techniques)
340 g (¾ lb) carrots, cut into 1 cm (½ inch) dice
225 g (½ lb) christophene, diced
1 large sweet pepper, deseeded and cut into 1 cm (½ inch) pieces
450 ml (¾ pint) good vegetable stock (see page 179)
1 aubergine, diced, sprinkled with salt and left to sweat for 30 minutes
225 g (½ lb) cooked garden peas
Sea salt to taste
75 ml (3 fl oz) milk
2 egg yolks, lightly beaten
½ teaspoon freshly ground allspice
Pinch freshly grated nutmeg (optional)
1 teaspoon turmeric
Freshly ground black pepper to taste
Sea salt to taste
Butter

1. Peel and wash the potatoes, scrubbing with half the whole lemon. Cut them in half and put to boil in salted water with the juice from the rest of the whole lemon. Simmer until tender, then drain.
2. Meanwhile, heat the vegetable oil and gently fry the ginger for about 1 minute. Then add the onions and fry until they are lightly brown.
3. Stir in the garlic and curry powder. Keep the heat low.
4. Add the carrots, christophene and sweet pepper and pour in the stock. Simmer covered for about 10 minutes.
5. Add the aubergine, peas, remaining lemon juice and salt to taste. Continue to simmer on a low heat until the aubergine is tender.
6. Mash the potatoes with the milk. On a low heat, beat in the egg yolks, allspice, nutmeg if using, turmeric, pepper and salt. Beat until thick and smooth.
7. Lavishly butter a ring mould and tightly pack in the creamed potato mixture.
8. Place a warm large serving dish upside down over the mould. Turn over and carefully remove the ring mould to expose the potato. This can be achieved by gently tapping the mould all round.

9 Pour the curried vegetables into the centre of the mould and serve immediately. Spicy shredded spinach and a little plain boiled rice make good accompaniments.

Serves 6

SWEET POTATO OMELETTE

225 g (½ lb) sweet potatoes
vegetable oil or ghee (see Techniques) for frying
1 small onion, finely chopped
1 small sweet red pepper, deseeded and finely chopped
1 medium tomato, skinned, deseeded and chopped
5 eggs
Freshly ground black pepper
½ teaspoon fresh thyme leaves
Sea salt to taste
Chopped parsley to garnish

1 Peel and wash the potatoes then dice into small pieces.
2 Heat the oil or ghee in a heavy frying pan and gently fry the sweet potatoes until tender but still firm.
3 Add the onion and sweet pepper and continue to fry for another 2 minutes. Now add the tomato.
4 Very lightly beat the eggs with the pepper, thyme and salt (you should still be able to distinguish the yolk from the white).
5 Turn the heat up – wait a few seconds, then pour the lightly beaten eggs over the vegetables. Cook to your taste. I prefer the omelette moist.
6 Turn on to a warm plate and garnish with the parsley. Serve with a tomato and onion salad and fried ripe plantains (see page 158).

Serves 2–3

SWEET POTATOES WITH COCONUT CREAM

A peppery-hot and spicy dish best served with plain rice and stewed pigeon peas or green lentils. But the amount of pepper used is left strictly to your taste. The quantity given is what I would use.

50 g (2 oz) margarine or butter
2 medium onions, sliced
¼–½ hot pepper, or to taste, deseeded and chopped (see Techniques)

1 sweet red pepper, chopped
1 clove garlic, finely chopped
2 teaspoons annatto liquid
Pinch freshly ground mace
2 tomatoes, deseeded and chopped
1 tablespoon poudre de Colombo (see Techniques)
Sea salt to taste
450 ml (¾ pint) coconut cream (see Techniques)
900 g (2 lb) sweet potatoes, boiled, peeled and cubed (see Techniques)
1½ tablespoons chopped fresh coriander leaves
1 tablespoon chopped fresh chives to garnish

1 Heat the fat and sauté the onions until lightly brown. The flavour of the browned onions is important to this dish. Add all the other ingredients except the coconut cream, potatoes, coriander and chives. Mix well and simmer for 2 minutes.
2 Now add the coconut cream and increase the heat. Cook, stirring constantly, for about 6 minutes or until the sauce thickens. Taste for salt.
3 Add the cubed sweet potatoes and the coriander and cook for a further 3–4 minutes. Stir to prevent burning or sticking to the pan.
4 Garnish with the chives and serve immediately.

Serves 4–6

STUFFED SWEET POTATOES

4–6 large sweet potatoes (size according to appetite; try to choose ones that are as round and even as possible)
1 lime or lemon, cut in half
75–110 g (3–4 oz) butter or margarine, melted
150 ml (¼ pint) double cream
Small bunch parsley, finely chopped
1 teaspoon fresh thyme leaves
Deseeded and chopped hot pepper to taste (see Techniques)
Yolks 2 hard-boiled eggs
Freshly ground black pepper to taste
Sea salt to taste
2–3 tablespoons roasted desiccated coconut (see Techniques)

1 Preheat the oven to 190°C (375°F/Gas 5).
2 Thoroughly scrub and wash the sweet potatoes, then rub them with the citrus halves and rinse.
3 Grease a shallow baking dish and bake the potatoes in the preheated oven until tender (test with a sharp instrument), basting occasionally with the melted butter or margarine.
4 Remove from the oven and allow to cool slightly. Cut a slice off the top of each potato, and carefully scoop out the flesh, leaving reasonably thick shells. Set the shells and 'lids' aside.
5 Mix the scooped-out flesh with all the remaining ingredients, except the desiccated coconut, adding sea salt and pepper to taste. Refill the shells and return to the oven with the 'lids' until heated right through.
6 Remove from the oven, lift the lids and sprinkle each potato with the roasted desiccated coconut, replace the 'lids' and serve immediately. Can be served with grated cheese and a sauce of your choice if you wish.

Serves 4–6

TANNIA DUMPLINGS

900 g (2 lb) tannia, cooked and mashed (see Techniques)
340 g (¾ lb) flour
½ teaspoon freshly grated nutmeg
¼ teaspoon dried thyme
Freshly ground black pepper to taste
Sea salt to taste
1–2 eggs, lightly beaten
A little lemon juice
A little butter
Grated cheese

1 Pass the mashed tannia through a sieve.
2 Sift together the flour, nutmeg, thyme and seasoning then mix in the tannia.
3 Add the egg a little at a time and knead to a smooth dough. Pinch off small pieces and roll into balls about 3 cm (1¼ inches) in diameter.
4 Put a pan of water, with a little lemon juice, butter, salt and pepper to boil.
5 Using your thumb and forefinger shape each ball of dough into a flat

circle. Drop a few dumplings at a time into the water and cook for about 5–8 minutes or until they rise to the top. Do not crowd.

6 Use a perforated spoon to remove the dumplings, transfer to a heated serving dish and keep them in a low oven while you cook the remainder.

7 When all are ready, sprinkle with grated cheese and serve with sauce creole (see page 180) or tomato and onion sauce (see page 186).

Serves 6–8

TOMATO AND OKRA CURRY

This dish is based on a New Orleans creole recipe made with tomatoes, aubergines, onions, and occasionally okra. It also crops up in the cuisine of many Mediterranean countries. The difference in this recipe is the spicy ingredients and the coconut milk, which make it similar to many East Indian dishes from Trinidad and possibly Guyana.

450 g (1 lb) small okra
450 g (1 lb) ripe but firm tomatoes
4 cloves garlic, chopped
½ teaspoon mustard seeds
½ teaspoon cumin seeds
½ teaspoon allspice
½ teaspoon coriander
Deseeded and chopped hot pepper to taste (see Techniques)
3 tablespoons vegetable oil
2 medium onions, chopped
1 sprig fresh coriander, chopped
150 ml (¼ pint) coconut cream, not too thick (see Techniques)
Sea salt to taste

1 Wash and top the okra as close to the head as possible and leave whole.

2 You may skin the tomatoes if you wish, but they must be left as firm as possible. Cut them into quarters.

3 In a mortar, pound together the garlic, mustard seeds, cumin seeds, allspice, coriander and hot pepper to a paste.

4 Heat the oil in a pot and fry the onions until just lightly brown. Add the curry paste from the mortar and fry for a further 2–3 minutes. Do not allow to burn.

5 Add the tomatoes, okra and fresh coriander. Pour in the coconut cream and season with salt.
6 Simmer covered on a low heat until the okra are tender. Try not to break the okra. Taste for seasoning and serve hot with rice.

Serves 4–6

VEGETABLE AND CREAM CHEESE BAKE

Very popular with my vegetarian friends and ideal for a buffet or other party.

2 green plantains (or substitute 3–4 green bananas)
225 g (½ lb) yam
1 lemon, cut in half, plus juice ½ lemon
4 medium carrots, scraped, washed and cut into 1 cm (½ inch) lengths
225 g (½ lb) potatoes, peeled and diced
3 medium onions, chopped
3 eggs, beaten
300 ml (½ pint) single cream or milk
225 g (½ lb) cream cheese
170 g (6 oz) mature Cheddar cheese, grated
2 cloves garlic, finely chopped (optional)
1 large sprig fresh parsley, chopped
1 heaped tablespoon chopped fresh chives
Freshly ground black pepper to taste
Freshly grated nutmeg to taste
Sea salt to taste (add cautiously because of the cheese)

1 Preheat the oven to 190°C (375°F/Gas 5).
2 Peel and wash the plantain, or green bananas, and yam, scrubbing with the lemon halves (see Techniques). Cut into 1 cm (½ inch) cubes and rinse thoroughly.
3 Put the plantains, yam and carrots into a saucepan with cold salted water and the juice of half a lemon. Bring to the boil, add the potatoes after 5 minutes, and cook until tender but not disintegrating. Drain the water into another pan and use to blanch the chopped onions, i.e. add the onions to the water, bring back to the boil and drain immediately.
4 Mix together the beaten eggs, single cream or milk, cream cheese and half the grated cheese. Then add the garlic, parsley, chives,

black pepper and nutmeg to taste. You may add salt if you wish, but be careful.

5 Arrange the vegetables including the onion in a greased ovenproof dish and pour the creamed mixture over. Agitate a bit to ensure that the vegetables are well coated.

6 Sprinkle over the remaining grated cheese and bake for 40–45 minutes or until firm and lightly brown. Serve with stewed pigeon peas (see page 123) or red beans.

Serves 6

VEGETABLE SANCOCHE

225 g (½ lb) sweet potatoes, peeled and cubed
2 swedes, peeled and cubed
1 large, ripe but very firm plantain, peeled and cut into 2.5 cm (1 inch) lengths
1 lemon, cut in half
3 tablespoons vegetable oil
2 medium onions, finely chopped
Small piece of fresh ginger, peeled and chopped
2 cloves garlic, chopped
2 courgettes, cut into 2.5 cm (1 inch) pieces
1 aubergine, cubed
2 tomatoes, skinned and chopped
Deseeded and chopped hot pepper to taste (see Techniques)
1 generous sprig fresh parsley
1 sprig fresh coriander
2 vegetable stock cubes
Juice 1 lime
Freshly ground black pepper to taste
Sea salt to taste
300 ml (½ pint) coconut cream (see Techniques)

1 Having peeled and cubed the sweet potatoes, swedes and plantain, wash them in cold water with the lemon (see Techniques), then set aside in salted cold water with some lemon juice.

2 Heat the oil, sauté the onions until translucent but not brown, then add the ginger and garlic and cook for 1 minute.

3 Drain and thoroughly dry the vegetables and add to the onions – the potatoes first, then the swedes and lastly the plantain.

4 In the following order, add the courgettes, aubergines, tomatoes,

and hot pepper, then the herbs, stock cubes, lime juice, black pepper and salt to taste.

5 Pour in the coconut cream. Cover tightly and cook on a low heat for 30–40 minutes or until the vegetables are tender.

6 Taste for seasoning and serve. Stewed pigeon peas (see page 123) or red kidney beans make a good accompaniment.

Serves 4–6

VEGETABLE STEW WITH CORNMEAL DUMPLINGS

2 green bananas
3 medium tannias (or substitute potatoes)
1 lemon, cut in half
12 shallots, peeled but left whole
3 cloves garlic, chopped
8 callaloo leaves, washed and chopped (or substitute 340 g (¾ lb) spinach)
1 sprig fresh thyme
Small piece fresh ginger, peeled and chopped
8 whole cloves
2 vegetable stock cubes
Juice 1 lime
1 tablespoon yeast extract
900 ml (1½ pints) vegetable stock (see page 179)
Freshly ground black pepper to taste
Sea salt to taste
1 quantity cornmeal dumplings (see page 223)
1 whole hot pepper (must not be damaged or holed)
3 tablespoons extra virgin olive oil
Chopped fresh parsley to garnish

1 Peel the bananas and tannias, cut into pieces no bigger than about 4 cm (1½ inches), and wash thoroughly in cold water, scrubbing with the lemon (see Techniques).

2 Put into a pot with all the other ingredients except the dumplings, whole hot pepper, olive oil and parsley. Place on a high heat and bring to the boil.

3 Reduce the heat, add the dumplings to the pot and place the whole pepper on top. Cover and simmer gently for about 45–50 minutes or until the vegetables are cooked.

4 Taste for seasoning. Remove the whole pepper, being careful not to burst it. Pour the oil over the stew and serve straight from the pot. Serve the whole pepper, chopped, on a separate plate.

Serves 6

MIXED VEGETABLE CURRY

A dry curry, sweet and spicy, and ideal with roti (see page 220). Can also be served with rice and stewed lentils.

4 tablespoons vegetable oil
4 medium potatoes, peeled, washed, and each one cut into 6
1 courgette, peeled, cut in 3 crossways, then in 4 lengthways
1 large sweet green pepper, deseeded and diced
1 aubergine, diced
1 large onion, diced
4 cloves garlic, chopped
6 cardamon seeds, freshly ground
1 teaspoon freshly ground cumin seeds
1 teaspoon diced fresh ginger
½ teaspoon freshly ground cinnamon
½ teaspoon freshly ground mustard seed
2 tablespoons white wine vinegar
½–1 teaspoon powdered chilli (not too hot)
1 teaspoon brown sugar
Juice 1 lime
400 g (14 oz) tin chopped plum tomatoes
2 tomatoes, deseeded and quartered
4 tablespoons chopped fresh coriander leaves

1 In a very heavy pot, heat the oil until smoking.
2 Throw in the potatoes, courgette, sweet pepper, aubergine, onion and garlic and sauté until the vegetables are lightly browned.
3 Add all the other ingredients except the fresh tomatoes and the coriander leaves and continue to sauté on a high heat for about 3–4 minutes, being careful not to burn the mixture. Toss occasionally and use a wooden spatula to scrape the bottom of the pot.
4 On the lowest possible heat, cook, covered, until the potatoes are

tender. For the last 4 minutes cook uncovered, with the tomato quarters on top to heat through.

5 Remove from the heat. Remove the tomato quarters and set aside.
6 Turn out onto a serving dish or into a bowl, arrange the tomato quarters on top, garnish with fresh coriander leaves and serve.

Serves 4

WATERCRESS AND NUTMEG FLAN

50 g (2 oz) butter
1 medium onion, finely chopped
50 g (2 oz) wholemeal flour
2 bunches watercress, washed and trimmed
300 ml (½ pint) single cream
2 eggs, beaten
50 g (2 oz) Parmesan cheese, grated
Freshly grated nutmeg to taste (but not less than ⅓ teaspoon)
Freshly ground black pepper to taste
Sea salt to taste
1 pastry shell (see page 231)

1 Preheat the oven to 180°C (350°F/Gas 4).
2 Heat the butter and sauté the onion until transparent but not brown. Add the flour, blending to a smooth paste.
3 Add the watercress and cook, stirring, for about 3 minutes.
4 Pour in the cream and mix well. Simmer gently for a few minutes until the watercress is soft. Remove from the heat and allow to cool.
5 Beat in the eggs, then the grated cheese, and add nutmeg to taste. Season with black pepper and salt to taste.
6 Pour into the pie shell and bake for 30 minutes or until set.
7 Serve accompanied by a salad of cucumber, apples, celery and lettuce with a French dressing. You may also serve garlic bread or just hot buttered bread.

I have eaten this cold, but it is best served while still hot.

Serves 4–6

YAM MAYONNAISE

675 g (1½ lb) yam
1 lemon, cut in half

50 g (2 oz) butter
1 large onion, chopped
2 cloves garlic, crushed
2 tablespoons olive oil
2 tablespoons fresh lime juice
2 tablespoons chopped fresh chives (or substitute spring onions)
Freshly ground black pepper to taste
Sea salt to taste
5 tablespoons mayonnaise
1 tablespoon chopped fresh parsley leaves

1. Peel the yam and cut into chunks for cooking. Wash in cold water, scrubbing with half the lemon. Rinse and bring to the boil in salted water with the juice from the other half of the lemon.
2. Lower the heat and simmer covered until cooked but still quite firm. Drain and leave until cool enough to handle.
3. Melt the butter in a pot and sauté the onion with the garlic for no more than 2 minutes.
4. Cut the cooked yam into small cubes and add to the onion and garlic.
5. Add the olive oil, lime juice, chives, black pepper and salt to taste and gently mix without breaking the yam up too much. Taste for seasoning.
6. Remove from the heat and mix in the mayonnaise. Sprinkle with the chopped parsley and serve at once with stewed pigeon peas and callaloo (see page 123).

Serves 4

BAKED STUFFED YAM

2 soft yams, weighing about 900 g (2 lb) each (or substitute potatoes; sizes according to appetite)
1 lemon, cut in half
A little melted butter
225 g (½ lb) medium Cheddar cheese, grated
4 tablespoons mayonnaise
2 teaspoons lemon juice
1 tablespoon chopped fresh chives
A little chopped fresh parsley
Freshly ground black pepper to taste

Sea salt (not too much)
Unsalted butter

1 Preheat the oven to 180°C (350°F/Gas 4).
2 Peel and wash the yams, scrubbing with the lemon. Wipe dry, brush with the melted butter and bake until tender (test with a sharp instrument).
2 Meanwhile, mix together the Cheddar cheese, mayonnaise, lemon juice, chives, parsley and black pepper.
3 Cut the yams in half lengthways and scoop out the inside of each piece, leaving a reasonably firm shell. Set the shells aside but keep warm.
4 Add the scooped-out yam flesh to the cheese mixture. Mix slightly. It is essential not to overblend.
5 Taste for salt and add more black pepper if necessary.
6 Put back in the yam shells, dot each with unsalted butter and return to the oven for about 10 minutes to heat through. Serve cut into slices, with slices of avocado and a tomato and onion sauce (see page 186).

Serves 6

CHEESE-BAKED YAM PIE

675 g (1½ lb) white yam
1 lime or lemon
1 onion, grated
110 g (4 oz) hard cheese, grated
50 g (2 oz) butter
2 teaspoons Worcestershire sauce
Freshly ground black pepper to taste
Sea salt to taste
2 size-3 eggs, well beaten
A little single cream or milk

1 Preheat the oven to 190°C (375°F/Gas 5).
2 Peel the yam and cut into chunks for cooking. Wash well, scrubbing with the lime or lemon. Boil in salted water until tender, then drain and mash.
3 Mix together the mashed yam, the onion, half the grated cheese, the butter, Worcestershire sauce, black pepper and salt. Add the beaten eggs with a little cream or milk. Mix well.

4 Turn out into a greased baking dish. Sprinkle with the remainder of the cheese and bake for 35 minutes or until brown. Serve with creole sauce (see page 180), and stewed pigeon peas (see page 123).

Serves 4

Pulses, Nuts and Rice

CHILLI BEANS

The amount of pepper and the spicy hotness of this dish depends entirely on the taste of the individual cook. But do remember your guests' preferences; it is always more prudent to serve freshly chopped hot peppers or pepper sauce as an accompaniment to this dish.

225 g (½ lb) red kidney beans, soaked overnight
2 tablespoons vegetable oil
2 medium onions, chopped
4 cloves garlic, chopped
1 large red sweet pepper, deseeded and chopped
675 g (1½ lb) tomatoes, skinned and chopped
1 hot pepper, or to taste, deseeded and chopped (see Techniques)
8 cloves, freshly ground
1–2 teaspoons brown cane sugar
2 teaspoons fresh thyme leaves
1 sprig fresh parsley, chopped
2 vegetable stock cubes
Freshly ground black pepper to taste
Sea salt to taste
Grated cheese (optional)

1 Drain and rinse the beans and bring to the boil in enough fresh cold water to cover by 5 cm (2 inches). Boil on the highest heat possible for 10–12 minutes. Then lower the heat and simmer until tender but still fairly firm (about 45 minutes). Top up with boiling water during the cooking process if the beans seem to be boiling dry.
2 Meanwhile, heat the oil in another pot and sauté the onions until just lightly brown, then add all the other ingredients except the cheese and simmer covered for about 5 minutes.
3 When the beans are fairly tender combine everything, again except the cheese, into one pot and simmer until the beans are

properly cooked – maybe 30 minutes or slightly longer. There should be very little liquid at the end of the cooking time.

4 Taste for seasoning, serve with grated cheese, if using, and boiled rice. For those who really appreciate a hot dish serve with extra chopped peppers or pepper sauce on the side.

Serves 4

CURRIED BEANS WITH PAWPAW

225 g (½ lb) haricot beans, soaked overnight
2 tablespoons peanut oil
2 medium onions, chopped
4 cloves garlic, chopped
1 ripe but firm pawpaw, peeled, deseeded and diced
1 small mango, peeled, stoned and diced
Juice ½ lemon
6 whole allspice berries
6 whole cloves
¼ teaspoon freshly ground cinnamon
Pinch powdered ginger
1 level teaspoon cane sugar
1 tablespoon poudre de Colombo (see Techniques)
2 tablespoons white island rum (not Bacardi)
Sea salt to taste
150 ml (¼ pint) vegetable stock (see page 179)

1 Preheat the oven to 180°C (350°F/Gas 4).
2 Drain and rinse the beans. Bring to the boil in enough cold water to cover by about 5 cm (2 inches) and boil on a high heat for 12 minutes.
3 Transfer the beans with their water to a large, warmed casserole, cover and put into the oven for 1 hour. Do not allow them to bake dry, but only top up with boiling water, never cold.
4 When the beans are fairly tender (test by pressing one between thumb and finger) heat the oil and sauté the onions and garlic for about 1 minute.
5 Add all the other ingredients except the stock to the onions and garlic and cook for about 5 minutes. Give the mixture a gentle stir now and then.
6 Stir in the stock and add the curried mixture to the beans in the casserole. Continue to bake for another 20–25 minutes or until

the beans are completely tender and most of the liquid has been absorbed. But it must not be too dry. Taste for seasoning and serve at once.

Serves 4

PURÉE OF BEANS

Use any beans of your choice.

450 g (1 lb) beans, soaked overnight
1 onion, grated
Deseeded and chopped hot pepper to taste (see Techniques)
1 clove garlic, pressed
4 cloves, freshly ground
Freshly ground black pepper to taste
Sea salt to taste
110 g (4 oz) butter

1 Drain and rinse the beans, then put them in a saucepan with enough cold water to cover by about 5 cm (2 inches). Bring to the boil and cook at a high heat for 10 minutes. Reduce the heat and simmer for 1 hour. Drain and reserve the liquid.
2 Purée the beans with all the remaining ingredients except the butter. Use some of the water in which the beans were cooked to moisten them if necessary. It must be a very thick purée – much thicker than soup.
3 Melt the butter in a saucepan and add the purée. Stir while it is being reheated to prevent sticking to the bottom of the pan.
4 Taste for seasoning, and serve immediately with hot buttered bread. Garlic bread is ideal with this.

Serves 4–6

BLACK-EYED BEAN AND TANNIA CROQUETTES

I arrived at this recipe by chance while planning a dinner for a friend in London, where one of the dishes included the African version of accra made with black-eyed beans.

225 g (½ lb) black-eyed beans, soaked overnight
675 g (1½ lb) tannias, cooked and mashed
75 g (3 oz) ground peanuts

1 clove garlic, finely chopped (or use a garlic press)
½ teaspoon freshly ground allspice
½ teaspoon freshly ground mace
1 teaspoon fresh thyme leaves
1 tablespoon chopped fresh parsley
Freshly ground black pepper to taste
Sea salt to taste
2 eggs, beaten
Breadcrumbs for coating
Oil for frying

1. Drain and rinse the beans, then bring to the boil in a large pan of water. Boil on a high heat for 10–12 minutes, then simmer until very tender (about 45 minutes). Drain any excess liquid.
2. Mash the beans and mix in the mashed tannias, ground peanuts, garlic, spices, herbs and seasoning.
3. Shape the mixture into 12–16 croquettes. You may have to use a little flour to prevent them sticking to your hands.
4. Dip each croquette into the beaten egg and coat with breadcrumbs. Shallow fry on both sides until golden brown.

Without any doubt this requires a sauce. I found it went best with a tomato-based one. Serve with a green salad.

Serves 4

BLACK-EYED BEAN RISSOLES

225 g (½ lb) black-eyed beans, soaked overnight
2 medium onions, finely chopped
5 cloves garlic, chopped
½ hot pepper, or to taste, deseeded and chopped (see Techniques)
1 tablespoon chopped fresh parsley
1 teaspoon freshly ground allspice
1 teaspoon freshly ground coriander
½ teaspoon freshly ground mustard seeds
2 teaspoons freshly ground cumin
½ teaspoon ground ginger
½ teaspoon turmeric
1 teaspoon baking powder
Freshly ground black pepper to taste

Sea salt to taste
2 tablespoons strong white flour
Oil for frying

1 Drain the beans and wash at least twice. Cook on a high heat in boiling water to cover for 5 minutes. Drain and allow to cool. Now, if you have the time and patience, remove and discard the skins.
2 Place the beans in a mortar and pestle or a food processor and pound to a smooth paste. They should become light and fluffy.
3 Add the onions, garlic, hot pepper and parsley and mix well.
4 Add all the remaining ingredients, except the flour and oil, and mix again.
5 Turn out onto a floured surface and knead thoroughly to combine all the ingredients.
6 Roll into 12 small balls and flatten into circular shapes. Heat the oil and fry each cake on both sides until lightly brown. Great with avocados or a spicy creole sauce.

Serves 4

CURRIED BLACK-EYED BEANS

340 g (¾ lb) black-eyed beans, soaked overnight
2 tablespoons vegetable oil
1 large onion, chopped
3 cloves garlic, chopped
4 tomatoes, skinned and chopped
1 stick celery, chopped
2 carrots, scraped and chopped
1 level tablespoon mild curry powder (see Techniques)
Deseeded and chopped hot pepper to taste (see Techniques)
2 vegetable stock cubes
2 teaspoons coriander leaves
150 ml (¼ pint) vegetable stock or water
Sea salt to taste
Freshly ground black pepper to taste

1 Drain and rinse the beans and bring to the boil in cold water. Boil rapidly for 10–12 minutes then lower the heat and simmer covered for 30–45 minutes.
2 Meanwhile, heat the oil and sauté the onion until translucent but

not brown. Add the garlic, tomatoes, celery, carrots, curry powder, hot pepper, stock cubes, coriander leaves and the stock or water, and simmer covered for 5 minutes. Taste for seasoning and remove from the heat.

3 Test the beans for tenderness. At the end of the cooking period there should be very little liquid left, so you may have to cook them uncovered for the last few minutes.
4 Stir the beans and their liquid into the curry mixture, return to the heat and cook covered for 12–15 minutes. Taste for seasoning and then serve immediately with boiled rice.

Serves 4–6

CURRIED CHICK PEAS WITH OKRA

225 g (½ lb) chick peas, soaked overnight
2 tannias, washed, peeled and diced
2 tablespoons coconut or vegetable oil
1 medium onion, chopped
1 teaspoon freshly ground mustard seeds
1 teaspoon freshly ground cumin
1 teaspoon turmeric
½ teaspoon deseeded and chopped hot pepper or to taste (see Techniques)
2 tablespoons chopped fresh coriander leaves
½ teaspoon freshly ground cinnamon
2 tablespoons tomato purée
Sea salt to taste
300 ml (½ pint) coconut milk (see Techniques)
16 small okra, topped as close to the heads as possible and left whole
Juice 1 lime or lemon

1 Drain and rinse the chick peas and bring to the boil in enough cold water to cover by about 5 cm (2 inches). Cover and simmer for about 2¼–2½ hours or until tender, allowing most or all of the liquid to evaporate. Add salt only when the peas are fairly tender.
2 Parboil the diced tannia and drain thoroughly.
3 Heat the oil and fry the diced tannia until tender and lightly browned, then add the onion and continue to fry until that, too, is lightly browned. The flavour of the browned tannia and onion is important.

4 Add the ground mustard seeds, cumin, turmeric and hot pepper and toss in the pan for about 2 minutes.
5 Combine this mixture with the chick peas and their liquid, the coriander, cinnamon, tomato purée, salt to taste, and coconut milk, and simmer gently for 10 minutes.
6 Arrange the okra on top, squeeze the citrus juice over, and simmer until the okra is tender.
7 Taste for seasoning and serve. Stewed callaloo leaves or spinach go well with this dish, also creamed yams or plantain foo-foo (see page 158).

Serves 4

STEWED FLAGEOLETS

300 g (10 oz) flageolet beans, soaked overnight
1.25 litres (2 pints) water
1 medium onion, sliced in half rings
1 sprig fresh parsley, chopped
1 clove garlic, chopped
2 teaspoons chopped fresh coriander leaves
1 tablespoon vegetable oil
40 g (1½ oz) unsalted butter
Freshly ground black pepper to taste
Sea salt to taste

1 Rinse the beans several times and bring to the boil in enough water to cover by about 5 cm (2 inches). Boil on a high heat for 12 minutes, then reduce the heat and simmer covered for 30 minutes.
2 Add all the other ingredients and simmer for a further 50 minutes or until the beans are soft. Serve with rice or mashed vegetables.

Serves 4

HARICOTS À LA CREOLE

450 g (1 lb) haricot beans, soaked overnight
8 whole cloves
1 stick cinnamon
Freshly ground black pepper to taste
1 generous sprig fresh thyme
1–2 teaspoons cane sugar

2 onions, chopped
3 tomatoes, peeled and chopped
1 red sweet pepper, deseeded and diced
3 cloves garlic, chopped
2 vegetable stock cubes
1 sprig fresh parsley, chopped
3 tablespoons tomato purée
1–2 teaspoons hot pepper sauce
Sea salt to taste
2 tablespoons walnut oil

1 Drain and rinse the beans and bring to the boil in enough cold water to cover. Boil on a high heat for 10–12 minutes. Lower the heat and simmer gently for 15–20 minutes.
2 Add the cloves, cinnamon, black pepper, thyme, sugar, and onions and cook for a further 10 minutes.
3 Now add all the other ingredients except the walnut oil and cook until the beans and vegetables are tender. If there is too much liquid, cook uncovered for the last few minutes. Add the walnut oil.
4 Serve with rice, or creamed vegetables and a salad.

Serves 6–8

HARICOT BEAN AND SPINACH RISSOLES

170 g (6 oz) cooked haricot beans
675 g (1½ lb) spinach, chopped
2 teaspoons yeast extract
1 egg, beaten
1 teaspoon freshly ground allspice
Cayenne pepper to taste
1 clove garlic, finely chopped
1 small onion, finely chopped
Freshly ground black pepper to taste
Sea salt to taste
340 g (12 oz) wholemeal breadcrumbs
Oil for frying

1 Pound the beans in a mortar with a pestle – or use a food processor.

2 Steam the spinach, then while it is still hot mix it with the yeast extract in a large bowl. Leave until cool enough to handle.
3 When the spinach has cooled down a little add the mashed beans. Mix well, then blend in the beaten egg.
4 Combine the allspice, cayenne pepper, garlic, onion, seasoning and 225 g (8 oz) of the breadcrumbs with the bean and spinach mixture. Mix thoroughly.
5 Form into 12 flat cakes, coat with the remaining breadcrumbs and fry on both sides in hot oil until golden brown. Serve with a spicy sauce.

Serves 4

LENTIL AND YAM PIE

225 g (½ lb) brown lentils, soaked for at least 8 hours
50 g (2 oz) butter or margarine
2 medium onions, chopped
1 clove garlic, finely chopped
2 carrots, scraped and chopped
1 stick celery, chopped
1 teaspoon fresh thyme leaves
¼ teaspoon freshly ground cloves
½ teaspoon dried oregano
Freshly ground black pepper to taste
Sea salt to taste
2 tablespoons cassava farine (see Glossary)
560 g (1¼ lb) creamed yams
A little melted butter or 1 beaten egg yolk

1 Preheat the oven to 250°C (425°F/Gas 7).
2 Drain and rinse the lentils and bring to the boil in enough cold water to cover. Reduce the heat and simmer gently until the lentils are tender.
3 Meanwhile, heat the butter or margarine and slowly cook the onions, garlic, carrots and celery until tender.
4 Drain the lentils and add to the vegetables with the thyme, cloves, oregano, black pepper and salt to taste. Mix well on a low heat.
5 Stir in the cassava farine, mixing well. Butter a pie dish and spoon in the lentil mixture. Spread evenly with the creamed yam. Brush with butter or beaten egg yolk.

6 Bake for about 20–25 minutes or until brown. Serve hot with a brown creole sauce (see page 181).

Serves 4

PIGEON PEA AND VEGETABLE CURRY

This vegetable curry is ideal served with roti (see page 220).

170 g (6 oz) dried pigeon peas, soaked overnight
2 tablespoons oil
1 medium onion, chopped
3 cloves garlic, chopped
Deseeded and chopped hot pepper to taste (see Techniques)
Pinch turmeric
½ teaspoon freshly ground mustard seeds
½ teaspoon freshly ground ginger
1 teaspoon freshly ground coriander seeds
4 cloves, freshly ground
½ teaspoon freshly ground cumin
675 g (1½ lb) mixed vegetables: yam, dasheen, tannia, potatoes, aubergines, breadfruit – as many of these as you can manage, peeled, washed and cut into 2 cm (¾ inch) cubes (use half a lemon or lime in the water in which you wash them)
2 vegetable stock cubes
Juice 1 lime or lemon
2 tablespoons chopped fresh coriander leaves (no substitute in this dish)
Sea salt to taste

1 Drain the pigeon peas and rinse in fresh water; then place in a pan with enough cold water to cover and bring to the boil. Turn down the heat and simmer covered; do not add salt.
2 Meanwhile, heat the oil and fry the onion until lightly brown. Add the garlic and cook for 1 minute.
3 When the beans are fairly tender, add the onion and garlic mixture, the hot pepper and the spices and continue to cook on a low heat for about 10 minutes – be careful not to let the mixture get too dry; add hot water if necessary.
4 Add the vegetables, stock cubes, lime or lemon juice, coriander leaves and a little extra oil and some salt. Continue to cook until

the vegetables are tender. Taste for seasoning; cook for a few more minutes and serve with roti (see page 220).

Serves 4

PIGEON PEA CUTLETS

340 g (¾ lb) dried pigeon peas, soaked overnight (or substitute lentils)
900 ml (1½ pints) water
1 small onion, grated
50 g (2 oz) butter
A little hot pepper sauce
110 g (4 oz) cooked tannia, mashed (or substitute potatoes)
1 teaspoon fresh thyme leaves
1 teaspoon finely chopped fresh parsley
Pinch allspice
Freshly ground black pepper to taste
Sea salt to taste
2 eggs, beaten
Wholemeal breadcrumbs
Oil for frying

1 Drain and rinse the pigeon peas and bring to the boil in the water. Do not add salt. Add the grated onion.
2 Simmer until the peas are very soft. Remove from the heat, purée, then return to a low heat.
3 Add the butter, pepper sauce, tannia, thyme, parsley, allspice, black pepper and salt to taste.
4 Beat the mixture over the heat until most of the liquid has evaporated. The paste must be creamy without any lumps.
5 Beat in about two-thirds of the eggs, blending well.
6 When the mixture becomes a fairly stiff paste, remove from the heat. Leave until cool enough to handle then form into cutlets.
7 Coat with the remaining egg, sprinkle with the breadcrumbs, and fry each cutlet in the oil until golden brown.
8 Serve with creamed yams or creamed breadfruit, with a spicy sauce of your choice.

Serves 4–6

PIGEON PEA PATTIES

Dried pigeon peas (see Glossary) are available in most Asian, West Indian and other shops dealing in tropical produce – including a few supermarkets. They are also known as gunga peas, gungo peas or tuvar peas. Green lentils make a good substitute if you cannot find pigeon peas.

225 g (½ lb) pigeon peas, soaked overnight
2 tablespoons olive oil
1 medium onion, chopped
2 large cloves garlic, chopped
1 large carrot, scraped and chopped
4 cloves, freshly ground
½ teaspoon fresh thyme leaves
1 tablespoon chopped fresh parsley
2 teaspoons curry powder (see Techniques)
1 teaspoon brown sugar
1 tablespoon tomato purée (optional)
Freshly ground black pepper to taste
Sea salt to taste
110 g (4 oz) unsalted cashews, finely chopped
170 g (6 oz) wholemeal flour
Breadcrumbs for coating
Vegetable oil for frying

1 Drain and rinse the pigeon peas, place in a heavy pot with enough cold water to cover and bring to the boil. Reduce the heat and simmer until almost tender (45–50 minutes).
2 Meanwhile, heat the olive oil in a frying pan and fry the onion until a light golden brown. Add the garlic and carrot and fry for no more than another 2 minutes.
3 Now add the fried mixture to the pigeon peas together with the cloves, thyme, parsley, curry powder, sugar, tomato purée and black pepper. Do not add any salt yet.
4 Continue to simmer covered until the peas are completely tender, stirring occasionally to prevent sticking to the pot. Now add salt to taste and simmer until all the liquid has been absorbed.
5 Remove the lid and stir until the mixture is puréed, then remove from the heat and allow to cool. Stir in the cashew nuts.
6 Mix in the wholemeal flour a little at a time. Shape the mixture

into 10–12 patties, coat with breadcrumbs and shallow fry in hot oil until golden brown on both sides.

7 Serve with tomato and onion sauce (see page 186), a salad, or just by themselves with a little West Indian hot pepper sauce.

Serves 4

STEWED PIGEON PEAS

450 g (1 lb) fresh pigeon peas, or 225 g (½ lb) dried
2 tablespoons oil
1 medium onion, finely chopped
2 cloves garlic, crushed
½ teaspoon freshly ground allspice
1 sprig fresh thyme
1 sprig fresh parsley, chopped
Freshly ground black pepper to taste
Sea salt to taste

1 If using dried pigeon peas, soak them overnight.
2 Rinse the peas, and bring to the boil in enough water to cover. Do not add salt. Simmer until tender (30 minutes if fresh; 45–50 minutes if dried). Watch that they do not boil dry.
3 Heat the oil and fry the onion until lightly brown. Add the garlic and continue to fry for another minute or two.
4 Add the fried onion and garlic with all the other ingredients to the pigeon peas. Simmer for about 12–15 minutes. Do not allow to cook into a mush.
5 Taste for seasoning and serve. Remember this is being served as a vegetable and not a soup, so there should be very little liquid.

Serves 4–6

STEWED PIGEON PEAS AND CALLALOO

I originally prepared this dish to go with yam mayonnaise (see page 105) but it goes just as well with rice and curried dishes.

225 g (½ lb) fresh callaloo leaves (spinach can be substituted but the callaloo leaves are best)
1½ tablespoons olive oil (no other oil will do – preferably a virgin oil)
1 onion, finely chopped
1 large clove garlic, finely chopped

1½ vegetable stock cubes
2 teaspoons fresh thyme leaves
Juice ½ lime (or substitute lemon, but lime is better)
½ teaspoon deseeded and chopped hot pepper, or to taste (see Techniques)
400 g (14 oz) tin pigeon peas, or 225 g (½ lb) cooked fresh pigeon peas with a very little liquid (or substitute green lentils)
¼ teaspoon freshly ground cloves
Freshly ground black pepper to taste
Sea salt to taste

1 Wash and finely chop the callaloo leaves, place into a steamer or colander and steam covered for about 30 minutes. Sprinkle a very little salt over the leaves midway through the cooking.
2 Meanwhile heat the oil in a pan and fry the onion until lightly brown. Add the garlic and cook for a further minute.
3 Add the stock cubes, thyme, lime juice and hot pepper. Simmer covered on a very low heat for about 2 minutes. Stir occasionally.
4 Add the pigeon peas (drain thoroughly if using tinned), the ground cloves and black pepper. Simmer for 10 minutes then taste for salt – add if necessary and cook for a further 5 minutes.
5 Now add the steamed callaloo and continue to cook for another 8 minutes to marry the flavours. Mix well but gently.
6 Taste for seasoning – at this stage you can add more hot pepper if you wish. Cook for a further minute or two if you have added any seasoning. Serve hot.

Serves 4

RED BEAN LOAF

450 g (1 lb) red kidney beans, soaked overnight
2 medium onions, finely chopped
2 cloves garlic, finely chopped
1 teaspoon fresh thyme leaves
6 cloves, freshly ground
2 eggs, slightly beaten
110 g (4 oz) margarine or butter, melted, plus a little extra for basting
225 g (½ lb) wholemeal breadcrumbs
225 g (½ lb) Cheddar cheese, grated

Freshly ground black pepper to taste
Sea salt to taste

1 Drain and rinse the kidney beans and bring to the boil in enough cold water to cover by about 7.5 cm (3 inches). Boil on a high heat for 10–12 minutes then lower the heat and cook for 50 minutes or until tender. There should be very little liquid left at the end of the cooking time. Drain if necessary.
2 Preheat the oven to 160°C (325°F/Gas 3).
3 Purée the beans using a food processor or mortar and pestle. Turn the beans into a mixing bowl and thoroughly mix in all the other ingredients. Remember beans need a fair amount of salt to bring out the flavour.
4 Pack into a 23 cm (9 inch) greased loaf tin and bake for about 1½–1¾ hours or until firm. It is advisable to baste occasionally with melted margarine or butter. Serve hot with a fruit and vegetable salad.

Serves 6–8

RED BEAN AND PEPPER MIX STEW

3 tablespoons olive oil
1 onion, neatly diced
1 clove garlic, finely chopped
4 sweet peppers – 1 red, 1 green, 1 yellow, 1 purple – deseeded and diced
2 tomatoes, skinned, deseeded and diced
Deseeded and chopped hot pepper to taste (see Techniques)
6 cloves, freshly ground
6 allspice, freshly ground
1 teaspoon freshly ground coriander seeds
2 teaspoons fresh thyme leaves
2 teaspoons annatto liquid
1 wine glass tomato sauce (see page 184)
600 ml (1 pint) vegetable stock (see page 179)
Sea salt to taste
Freshly ground black pepper to taste
340 g (¾ lb) red beans, soaked overnight and cooked (see Techniques)
2 tablespoons chopped fresh chives

1 In a heavy casserole, heat the oil and sauté the onion for no more than 2 minutes.
2 Add the garlic and all the sweet peppers. Coat them completely with the oil and sauté for 3–4 minutes without browning.
3 Now add all the other ingredients except the beans and chives. Season well with salt and pepper, and simmer, loosely covered, for 10–15 minutes.
4 Taste for seasoning then add the beans. Mix carefully, and simmer gently until the beans are heated through. Again taste for seasoning, then garnish with the chives.
5 Serve with creamed yams, fried ripe plantains (see page 158) and a mixed fruit and vegetable salad.

Serves 6–8

CURRIED RED BEANS

450 g (1 lb) cooked red beans, soaked overnight
3 tablespoons vegetable oil
2 teaspoons peeled and chopped fresh ginger
½ teaspoon freshly ground cloves
½ teaspoon freshly ground cumin
1 tablespoon freshly ground coriander seeds
2 teaspoons turmeric
2 medium onions, chopped
4 cloves garlic, chopped
225 g (½ lb) tomatoes, chopped
1½ vegetable stock cubes, crumbled
Deseeded and chopped hot pepper to taste (see Techniques)
Sea salt to taste
3 tablespoons chopped fresh coriander leaves (or substitute parsley)

1 Drain and rinse the beans, then bring to the boil in enough cold water to cover by about 7.5 cm (3 inches). Boil on a high heat for 10–12 minutes then lower the heat and cook until tender. There should be very little liquid left.
2 In a heavy pot, heat the oil and fry the ginger for about 30 seconds, then add the cloves, cumin, coriander seeds, turmeric and onions and fry until the onions are slightly brown. Stir frequently to prevent burning.
3 Add the garlic, tomatoes, vegetable stock cubes and hot pepper

and continue to cook uncovered for about 4 minutes, stirring frequently.

4 Add the cooked beans and their liquid to the pot, stir well, and simmer covered on a low heat for 6–8 minutes. Taste for seasoning. If there is not enough liquid you may add a little boiling water or stock, but simmer for a further 5 minutes to blend the flavours.

5 Garnish with the coriander and serve with plain boiled rice.

Serves 6

STEWED RED BEANS

Possibly the most popular of all beans in the Caribbean. There are many recipes and each cook swears by his or her own – but the most important thing to remember is never to add salt until the beans are tender.

340 g (¾ lb) red beans, soaked overnight
1 medium onion, finely sliced
2 cloves garlic, finely chopped
1 level teaspoon cane sugar
4–6 whole cloves
1 generous sprig fresh thyme
1 sprig fresh parsley
Freshly ground black pepper to taste
Sea salt to taste
2 tablespoons vegetable oil or olive oil

1 Drain and rinse the beans, put them in a large saucepan, with enough water to cover by about 5 cm (2 inches), and bring them to the boil on a high heat for 10–12 minutes.

2 Reduce the heat and simmer covered for about 45 minutes or until the beans are almost tender. Beans absorb about three times their weight in water, so be careful not to let them boil dry. Always add hot water.

3 When the beans are almost tender, add all the other ingredients except the oil. Simmer covered for a further 20 minutes or until well cooked.

4 Taste for seasoning. The amount of liquid with the beans is up to you but remember it is not a soup. Remove the sprig of thyme, pour the oil over the beans and serve.

Serves 6–8 as a side dish

COCONUT AND FRUIT CURRY

A delicious, medium-hot curry that will suit most people's tastes. Not being able to secure a pawpaw I once substituted apples and a small firm melon. It was almost as delicious.

1 firm but ripe mango, peeled, stoned and cubed
1 small ripe pawpaw, peeled, deseeded and cut into small cubes
3 slices pineapple, peeled, cored and cut into small spears
2–3 ripe but firm bananas, peeled and cut into 1 cm (½ inch) slices
Juice 1½ limes or lemons
110 g (4 oz) ghee (see Techniques)
2 medium onions, sliced
1 small piece fresh ginger, peeled and grated
1½ tablespoons poudre de Colombo (see Techniques)
2 teaspoons finely chopped fresh parsley
1 teaspoon deseeded and chopped hot pepper, or to taste (see Techniques)
450 ml (¾ pint) light coconut milk (see Techniques)
Freshly ground black pepper to taste
Sea salt to taste
1 tablespoon light rum
2 tablespoons freshly grated coconut (see Techniques – or substitute desiccated coconut)

1. Mix the fruit with the lemon or lime juice in a bowl. Set aside.
2. Heat the ghee in a heavy pot and fry the onions until very slightly brown. Then add the ginger and fry for a further 2–3 minutes.
3. Add the poudre de Colombo and mix well. Stir over a low to moderate heat for 2 minutes.
4. Now add the parsley, hot pepper, coconut milk and black pepper and salt to taste. Cook on a moderate heat for about 3 minutes, stirring occasionally.
5. Add the fruit and any juice there may be. Pour in the rum and sprinkle with the coconut. Do not stir at this stage.
6. Simmer covered on a very low heat for 25–30 minutes. Do not overcook. Give one gentle stir, taste for seasoning and serve with riz creole (see page 133).

Serves 4–5

Tropical abundance:

1 Coconuts
2 Pumpkin
3 Dasheen
4 Yam
5 Sweet potatoes
6 Cush cush
7 Okra
8 Breadfruit
9 Turmeric
10 Christophenes
11 Pigeon Peas
12 Limes
13 Hot peppers
14 Cocoy or bluggoe
15 Plantains
16 Tannias and eddoes
17 Cassava
18 Banana flower
19 Bananas

A typical Caribbean breakfast. Clockwise from top: fresh orange juice; Jamaican Blue Mountain coffee; egg creole; bakes; cassava bread

Soups and hors d'oeuvres. Clockwise from top: callaloo fritters; mushrooms in coconut cream; avocado Dominique; black bean soup; Fedilia's green gumbo soup; hot pepper sauce; rum punches

A midday feast. Clockwise from top: mixed green salad; onion, olive and caper sauce; hot pepper sauce; riz creole avec banane et zaboca; pepper oil; mixed herb and spice vinegar

A warm afternoon glow.
Clockwise from top:
limeade; sweet potato
pudding (2); coconut
turnovers; banana loaf

A festive dinner. Clockwise from top: coo-coo with creamed yam; red cabbage with mango; creole sauce; Keshy Yena; spicy tropical fruit salad

Joyous conclusion.
Clockwise from top:
coconut ice-cream; baked
bananas with rum and
passion fruit sauce

Exotic fruits:

1 Passion fruit
2 Mangoes
3 Tamarillos
4 Caruba
5 Zallase
6 Kiwi fruit
7 Figs
8 Avocados
9 Pomegranate
10 Guavas
11 Pawpaw
12 Babaco
13 Soursop
14 Prickly pears
15 Sapodilla or naseberries
16 Rambutan
17 Kumquats
18 Ortaniques
19 Carambola or star fruit
20 Mangosteen
21 Persimmons

KESHY YENA

This superb dish, Dutch in origin, is very popular on the island of Curaçao in the former Dutch West Indies. It is ideal for a formal dinner party.

Whole Edam cheese
75 g (3 oz) unsalted butter
1 medium onion, finely chopped
6–8 button mushrooms, cut into pieces
½ small sweet pepper, sliced into neat small squares
2 tomatoes, peeled, deseeded and chopped
½ teaspoon cayenne, or any good powdered chilli
Freshly ground black pepper to taste
Sea salt to taste
75 g (3 oz) minced soya beef cubes (TVP), soaked for 30 minutes (do not use too much water)
8 stuffed olives, chopped
2 tablespoons chopped gherkins
2 heaped tablespoons raisins
75 g (3 oz) pine nuts
A few capers (optional – but good)
1–2 teaspoons Worcestershire sauce
1 teaspoon fresh thyme leaves
Juice ½ lemon
3 tablespoons wholemeal breadcrumbs
2 size-3 eggs, well beaten

1. Preheat the oven to 160°C (325°F/Gas 3).
2. Carefully peel away the red wax covering from the cheese. Cut a slice from the top to make a lid about 4 cm (1½ inches) thick.
3. With a spoon scoop out the inside of the cheese, leaving a shell about 1.5 cm (½ inch) thick. Scoop out the lid as well.
4. Place both the shell and lid into a bowl with enough cold water to cover and let soak for an hour.
5. Chop about 225 g (½ lb) of the scooped-out cheese. (Wrap and store the remainder to use in another dish.)
6. Melt the butter in a deep frying pan and sauté the onion until translucent but not brown. Add the mushrooms, sweet pepper, chopped tomatoes, cayenne or chilli, black pepper and a very little salt. Cook for 6–7 minutes.

7 Drain the soya beef cubes and add them to the sauce. Cook for another 3 minutes. Mix well.
8 Remove the pan from the heat and mix in the olives, gherkins, raisins, pine nuts, capers, Worcestershire sauce, thyme, lemon juice, breadcrumbs and the 225 g (½ lb) of chopped cheese. Mix thoroughly. Taste for seasoning then add the well-beaten eggs.
9 Remove the cheese shell from the water, drain and pat dry. Stuff with the mixture and replace the lid.
10 Place the stuffed cheese into a buttered deep baking dish about 1.5 cm (½ inch) larger than the cheese itself, and bake for approximately 20 minutes. During the cooking, the cheese will change shape. Transfer to a serving dish and serve cut into wedges.

Serves 8–10

MANGO, NUT AND PIGEON PEA PILAU

225 g (½ lb) long grain rice
1 tablespoon coconut oil or vegetable oil
75 g (3 oz) margarine
2 medium onions, sliced in half-rings
2 cloves garlic, finely chopped
4 cloves, freshly ground
7.5 cm (3 inch) cinnamon stick
600 ml (1 pint) vegetable stock (see page 179) or water
Sea salt to taste
Freshly ground black pepper to taste
2 large, ripe but firm mangoes, peeled, stoned and diced
Juice ½ lemon
1 red sweet pepper, deseeded and sliced
400 g (14 oz) tin green pigeon peas, drained and quickly rinsed under running water
150 g (5 oz) unsalted cashew nuts
Chopped fresh parsley to garnish

1 Wash the rice and leave to soak in clean water for 1 hour. Then drain and dry thoroughly.
2 Heat the oil and margarine in a heavy pot and sauté the onion and garlic until translucent. Add the rice, mix well and glaze until the rice is slightly translucent.
3 Now add the ground cloves, cinnamon stick and the stock or water. Season with salt and pepper. Bring to the boil, lower the

heat, stir, then simmer covered for 20–25 minutes or until all the liquid has been absorbed.

4 Add the diced mangoes, lemon juice, red pepper, pigeon peas and cashew nuts. Mix in carefully and cook for 5–6 minutes. Taste for seasoning then garnish with the chopped parsley and serve.

Serves 6

MIXED NUT AND BREADFRUIT ROAST

An ideal vegetarian dish that does not need more than a sauce and a salad to accompany it. I have tried substituting yams, tannias or potatoes (not sweet) for the breadfruit but the texture and slightly nutty flavour of the breadfruit works best.

450 g (1 lb) breadfruit, peeled and cored (see Techniques)
1 lemon, cut in half
2 tablespoons vegetable oil
1 large onion, finely chopped
2 cloves garlic (optional), finely chopped
225 g (½ lb) mixed nuts (peanuts, cashew nuts and pine nuts), finely chopped
110 g (4 oz) cooked garden peas
50 g (2 oz) roasted desiccated coconut (see Techniques)
2 tablespoons lemon juice
2 tablespoons dark rum
½ teaspoon freshly ground allspice
1½ vegetable stock cubes, dissolved in 3 tablespoons boiling water.
1 tablespoon dark soya sauce
225 g (½ lb) wholemeal breadcrumbs
Freshly ground black pepper to taste
Sea salt to taste
2 eggs, beaten

1 Preheat the oven to 190°C (375°F/Gas 5).
2 Scrub the breadfruit with half the lemon then cook in boiling salted water with the juice from the remaining lemon half until tender enough to mash.
3 Heat the oil and fry the onion and garlic, if using, until the onion is lightly browned.
4 In a mixing bowl, thoroughly mix together the mashed breadfruit,

fried onion and garlic and all the other ingredients except the eggs.

5 When well mixed add the beaten eggs. You may use your hands to combine the mixture.
6 Taste for seasoning and then turn out into a well-greased ovenproof dish; press down firmly and spread out evenly. Bake for 35–40 minutes or until set. Cool slightly in the dish before serving.

Serves 4

SIMPLE NUT ROAST

150 g (5 oz) chopped nuts
110 g (4 oz) wholemeal breadcrumbs
1 medium onion, grated
3 tomatoes, skinned, deseeded and chopped
Pinch allspice
1 teaspoon lemon zest
1 egg
150 ml (¼ pint) milk
2 teaspoons Madeira
Sea salt to taste
Freshly ground black pepper to taste
Roasted coconut (see Techniques)

1 Preheat the oven to 190°C (375°F/Gas 5).
2 Combine the nuts, breadcrumbs, onion, tomatoes, allspice and lemon zest.
3 Beat the egg, milk and Madeira together and add to the dry ingredients. Mix well and season with salt and pepper.
4 Turn into a greased baking tin or dish, sprinkle with the coconut and bake for about 30–45 minutes. Cool slightly before serving. Serve with a tomato sauce (see page 184ff.) or onion, olive and caper sauce (see page 182). This dish can also be served cold with a salad.

Serves 2–4

SWEET POTATO AND NUT BAKES

450 g (1 lb) cooked sweet potatoes, peeled and mashed (see Techniques)

110 g (4 oz) unsalted peanuts, finely chopped
110 g (4 oz) strong white flour
1½ teaspoons baking powder
2 tablespoons grated onion
1 clove garlic, finely chopped
1 egg, beaten
1 tablespoon melted butter
½ teaspoon freshly ground coriander seeds
Pinch hot cayenne pepper
Sea salt to taste
Freshly ground black pepper to taste

1. Preheat the oven to 190°C (375°F/Gas 5).
2. In a bowl combine the mashed potato and peanuts and sift in the flour and baking powder. Mix well.
3. Add all the other ingredients and knead gently for a short time.
4. Roll out on a floured surface to about 1 cm (½ inch) thick. Cut into rounds about 7.5 cm (3 inches) in diameter.
5. Place on greased baking sheets and bake for about 20–25 minutes or until crisp and brown. You may serve these on their own with a sauce or as part of a main course.

Serves 4–6

RICE

There are various ways of cooking rice and each person swears by his or her method. The two methods given are the ones I use. Rice must be cooked in a heavy pot with a tight-fitting lid – use foil if the lid does not fit properly. Unless otherwise stated, rice must not be disturbed until the end of the cooking time.

RIZ CREOLE (METHOD 1)

450 g (1 lb) long grain rice
2–3 teaspoons salt

1. Wash and rinse the rice several times until the water runs clear.
2. Place the rice and salt in a pot with enough water to cover by about 2.5 cm (1 inch). Bring to the boil and stir, scraping the bottom of the pot.
3. Cover tightly and simmer for about 15–20 minutes.
4. Remove from the heat and rinse immediately in cold water, twice.

5 Drain thoroughly, return to the heat and continue to cook uncovered over the lowest possible heat for about 10 minutes.
6 Fluff with a fork.

Serves 5–6

RICE (METHOD 2)

450 g (1 lb) rice – Basmati, Patna, or long grain
2 teaspoons sea salt
Twice the volume of water to rice

1 Wash the rice several times.
2 Place in a heavy pot with the salt and water, and bring to the boil. Stir to prevent sticking to the bottom.
3 On the lowest possible heat, simmer tightly covered for 25 minutes.
4 Uncover the rice for about 3 minutes. Remove from the heat, fluff with a fork and serve.

Serves 5–6

COCONUT RICE

I first prepared this rice dish for the staff of the old Le Caraïbe Restaurant where I once worked.

225 g (½ lb) long grain rice
Approximately 900 ml (1½ pints) coconut milk (see Techniques)
1 stick cinnamon
2 medium onions, finely chopped
2 cloves garlic, finely chopped
4 allspice berries
4 cloves
1 teaspoon turmeric
Freshly ground black pepper to taste
Sea salt to taste
1 whole hot pepper

1 Wash the rice 3–4 times or until the water is almost clear.
2 Put the rice and the coconut milk into a saucepan and bring to the boil. The milk must cover the rice by approximately 4 cm (1½ inches).
3 Lower the heat, add all the remaining ingredients except the hot pepper, and give 2 or 3 quick stirs.

4 Place the whole pepper on top. Cover tightly and simmer on the lowest heat possible for 20–25 minutes or until all the liquid has evaporated.
5 Serve with either red beans or pigeon peas, with the whole pepper chopped and on a separate plate.

Serves 3–4

SEASONED RICE

450 g (1 lb) long grain rice
2 tablespoons olive oil
50 g (2 oz) butter
1 medium onion, finely chopped
2 cloves garlic, finely chopped
2 bay leaves
2 teaspoons fresh thyme
6 allspice berries
1 stick cinnamon
2 vegetable stock cubes
Juice and zest ½ lemon
2 teaspoons Angostura bitters
Sea salt to taste
Freshly ground black pepper to taste

1 Wash the rice until the water runs clear. Drain thoroughly and dry by spreading on a clean tea towel.
2 In a heavy pot with a tight-fitting lid, heat the oil and butter and sauté the onion for about 2–3 minutes. Add the garlic and rice, and stir, coating with the fat.
3 Now, add all the other ingredients with enough water to cover by about 5 cm (1½ inches). Bring to the boil, stir, then simmer on a low heat tightly covered until the rice is tender and all the liquid has been absorbed. Remove the bay leaves and cinnamon stick before serving.

Serves 6

RICE AND PEAS

A favourite throughout the Caribbean, and just as good with or without fish or meat. The terms peas and beans are interchangeable in the community. For this recipe you can use any of the following:

fresh or dried pigeon peas, black-eyed beans, red kidney beans, haricot or black beans.

225 g (½ lb) dried peas or beans, soaked overnight (or 450 g (1 lb) shelled fresh pigeon peas, or 2 cans, rinsed and drained)
2 tablespoons olive oil
1 medium onion, finely chopped
2 cloves garlic, finely chopped
1 sprig fresh thyme
1 bay leaf
1 sprig fresh parsley
6 whole cloves
2 vegetable stock cubes
Freshly ground black pepper to taste
Sea salt to taste
340 g (12 oz) long grain rice

1. If using dried peas or beans, drain and rinse them and place in a pot with enough cold water to cover by about 7.5 cm (3 inches). Cook on a high heat for 10 minutes then simmer covered for a further 30–40 minutes. Fresh pigeon peas need only be cooked for 25–30 minutes. Simply add them to the onions and other ingredients at stage 3, as with canned pigeon peas.
2. Heat the oil and sauté the onion and garlic until they are pale golden in colour.
3. Scrape the sautéed onion and garlic with all the oil into the beans and add the thyme, bay leaf, parsley, cloves, vegetable stock cubes, black pepper and a very little salt. Simmer covered for 10 minutes. There must be enough liquid to cover the beans.
4. Wash the rice at least 4–5 times until the water runs clear. Drain and add to the pot, mix thoroughly. The liquid must cover the mixture by about 2.5 cm (1 inch).
5. Now simmer tightly covered until all the liquid has been absorbed, approximately 20–25 minutes. This must be done on the lowest possible heat.
6. Mix gently with a fork and serve.

Serves 6

RICE WITH PUMPKIN AND PIGEON PEAS

This dish is reminiscent of my childhood, when mother's purse could not reach out to greet meat or fish. It was usually served with a herb sauce with onions sautéed in a rather salty, annatto-flavoured butter, bright orange in colour, which we called cooking butter.

I have prepared this dish since but always with fresh pigeon peas, though tinned pigeon peas can be used – but they must be green, and should be so described on the label.

340 g (¾ lb) fresh pigeon peas (shelled weight) or substitute 2 cans
2 tablespoons coconut oil (or substitute vegetable oil)
2 medium onions, chopped
1 large clove garlic, finely chopped
1 sprig fresh parsley, chopped
1 celery stalk with leaves, finely chopped
300 ml (½ pint) coconut milk (optional)
Deseeded and chopped hot pepper to taste (see Techniques)
Juice ½ lime or lemon
225 g (½ lb) long grain rice, thoroughly washed
225 g (½ lb) pumpkin, peeled, deseeded and neatly cubed
1 level teaspoon turmeric
50 g (2 oz) salted butter
Sea salt to taste
Freshly ground black pepper to taste

1 Put the fresh pigeon peas to boil in a heavy pot large enough to contain all the ingredients. Cook covered for about 30–35 minutes or until tender. (If using canned peas, drain and rinse, then add at stage 3.)
2 Meanwhile, heat the oil and sauté the onions until translucent but not brown. Then add the garlic and cook for a further minute.
3 Now add the parsley, celery, coconut milk if using, and hot pepper. Cook for about 2 minutes, stirring all the time, then add to the pot containing the pigeon peas, which should by now be tender but still on the simmer.
4 Add all the remaining ingredients to the pigeon peas, mix well, and pour in enough hot water to cover by about 2.5 cm (1 inch). Cover tightly and simmer until all the liquid has been absorbed.
5 Serve with a sauce and a salad of your choice.

Serves 6

RIZ CREOLE AVEC BANANE ET ZABOCA (CREOLE RICE MOULD WITH BANANAS AND AVOCADO)

For the rice mould:
400 g (14 oz) long grain rice (Basmati is not suitable for this dish)
2 tablespoons olive oil
50 g (2 oz) margarine
1 medium onion, chopped
1 clove garlic, chopped
225 g (½ lb) spinach, cleaned and chopped
Juice and zest ½ orange
½ teaspoon turmeric
750 ml (1¼ pints) vegetable stock (see page 179)
Sea salt to taste
Freshly ground black pepper to taste

For the filling:
2 ripe but firm bananas
75 g (3 oz) margarine
1 small onion, cut into fine rings
2 cloves, freshly ground
4 allspice berries, freshly ground
1 tablespoon chopped fresh chives, plus extra to garnish
8 stuffed olives, quartered
2 avocados, peeled, stoned and cubed
3 tablespoons garlic mayonnaise

1 Wash the rice 3 or 4 times and leave to soak in clean water for about 45 minutes. Then drain and dry on a clean cloth.
2 Heat the oil and margarine in a heavy pot with a tight-fitting lid and sauté the onion until light brown, then add the garlic.
3 Add the rice to the pot and continue to sauté for a further 3 minutes. The grains of rice must be completely coated with the fat.
4 Add the chopped spinach, orange juice and zest, turmeric and stock. Season with salt and pepper and bring to the boil. Give a couple of stirs, scraping the bottom of the pot with a wooden spoon.
5 Lower the heat and simmer tightly covered until all the liquid has been absorbed (about 25 minutes).

6 Butter a ring mould and pack the rice firmly into it while still quite hot. Turn out onto a heated serving dish and keep warm.
7 Meanwhile make the filling: peel the bananas and cut into pieces about 4 cm (1½ inches) long. Melt the margarine and fry the banana until lightly browned. Transfer to a warm dish and set aside.
8 Sauté the onion in the margarine for no more than a minute. Toss in the ground spices then remove from the heat and add the chives, olives, avocados and fried bananas, and mix carefully.
9 Fill the rice mould with the mixture and spoon the mayonnaise over. More chopped chives can be sprinkled over as a garnish. Serve accompanied by a green salad with a light dressing.

Serves 4–5

RICE WITH CASHEW NUTS AND MANGO

225 g (½ lb) long grain rice, soaked for 1–2 hours
75 g (3 oz) unsalted butter
110 g (4 oz) cashew nuts
170 g (6 oz) mangoes (peeled weight), diced
Juice ½ lemon
½ teaspoon freshly ground cinnamon
4 whole allspice
4 whole cloves
1 bay leaf
A few raisins or sultanas (optional, but good)
Sea salt to taste
Water

1 Drain the rice thoroughly, spreading on a kitchen towel if necessary.
2 Melt the butter in a pot with a tight-fitting lid and gently brown the cashew nuts.
3 Add the rice and coat well with the butter, mixing in the nuts.
4 Add all the other ingredients with enough cold water to cover by about 2.5 cm (1 inch), and bring to the boil. Stir to make certain that nothing sticks to the bottom of the pot.
5 Reduce the heat to the lowest possible and simmer tightly covered for about 20–25 minutes or until all the liquid has been absorbed. Serve hot. Goes very well with curried pumpkin (see page 88).

Serves 4

Light Meals and Accompaniments

ACKEE AND CHEESE SOUFFLÉ

75 g (3 oz) margarine
3 tablespoons flour
300 ml (½ pint) milk
Pinch freshly grated nutmeg
1 teaspoon salt
Freshly ground black pepper to taste
3 egg yolks
50 g (2 oz) cheese, grated
540 g (19 oz) tin ackee, thoroughly drained and chopped
3 egg whites, stiffly beaten

1. Preheat the oven to 180°C (350°F/Gas 4).
2. Melt the margarine on a low heat and gradually add the flour, stirring continuously. Do not allow to brown.
3. Slowly pour in the milk and keep stirring until the mixture thickens. Mix in the nutmeg, salt and black pepper to taste.
4. Away from the heat beat in the egg yolks until well blended. Add the cheese and ackee. Mix well.
5. Still away from the heat carefully fold in the egg whites.
6. Transfer to a greased soufflé dish or a baking dish and bake for 25–30 minutes or until well risen and brown. Serve immediately.

Serves 4

ACKEE AU GRATIN

An excellent dish for a light lunch with avocados and garlic bread – or served on buttered toast garnished with chopped chives.

50 g (2 oz) margarine
1½ tablespoons strong white flour
300 ml (½ pint) milk or single cream
Pinch sea salt
Freshly ground black pepper to taste
1 tablespoon chopped fresh chives

170 g (6 oz) Gruyère cheese, grated
540 g (19 oz) tin ackee, well drained
75 g (3 oz) breadcrumbs

1 Preheat the oven to 200°C (400°F/Gas 6).
2 Melt the margarine in a pan on a low heat and slowly blend in the flour, stirring continuously.
3 Gradually pour in the milk or single cream. Continue to stir to avoid lumps and browning. Season with salt and pepper.
4 Away from the heat stir in the chives and 110 g (4 oz) of the cheese. Return to a low heat until the cheese has melted. If the sauce is too thick add a little more milk, stirring continuously.
5 Grease a baking dish and arrange the drained ackees in it. Now pour the cheese sauce over the ackees.
6 Mix together the remainder of the cheese with the breadcrumbs, sprinkle the mixture over the cheese sauce and bake for 20 minutes or until brown. Serve while still fairly hot.

Serves 4

AVOCADO STUFFED WITH ACKEE

40 g (1½ oz) butter
1 medium onion, finely chopped
2 tablespoons celery, finely chopped
1 small red pepper, deseeded and chopped
1 large tomato, skinned, deseeded and chopped
1 tablespoon fresh lime juice
Sea salt to taste
Freshly ground black pepper to taste
540 g (19 oz) tin ackee
2 large avocados
A little lime or lemon juice
225 g (½ lb) cooked rice (kept warm)
Chopped chives to garnish

1 Heat the butter in a pan and sauté the onion until translucent but not brown.
2 Add the celery, red pepper, tomato and lime juice. Season with salt and pepper to taste and simmer gently for 5–6 minutes.
3 Drain the ackee and stir into the pan, being careful not to break up the ackee. Simmer uncovered for a further 3 minutes.

4 Meanwhile, cut each avocado in half, peel, and discard the stone. To prevent discoloration brush each half with lime or lemon juice.
5 Place each avocado half on a bed of rice. Fill with the ackee mixture and arrange a little of the mixture on the rice. Garnish with the chives and serve at once.

Serves 4

SPICED AVOCADO TOAST WITH CHEESE AND TOMATOES

This dish is based on a kind of 'quick pizza' first prepared for me by a friend, Jane Ayshford, years ago. We have both enjoyed it on several subsequent occasions.

4 large slices wholemeal bread
A little soft margarine for spreading
1 large onion, very thinly sliced
1 red sweet pepper, very thinly sliced
12 stuffed olives, sliced
A few capers
Deseeded and chopped hot pepper (see Techniques)
2 large tomatoes, thinly sliced
Chopped fresh parsley (or substitute sweet basil)
Freshly ground black pepper to taste
Sea salt to taste
1 large or 2 medium avocados, peeled, stoned and sliced
Lemon juice
Thinly sliced cheese, enough to cover the bread

1 Toast the bread on one side until golden brown. Turn and just warm the other side of each slice. Spread each slice (not the browned side) with margarine.
2 Place a few slices of onion and sweet pepper on each slice and return to the grill simply to warm up the vegetables.
3 Remove from the grill and arrange the olives, capers, hot pepper, tomatoes and parsley on the toast in that order. Season to taste.
4 Then arrange an equal number of the avocado slices on each, splashed with a little lemon juice. Finish up with slices of cheese.
5 Grill under a moderate heat until the cheese has melted and is

golden brown, turning the heat up for the last minute. Serve at once.

Serves 4

GREEN BANANA BALLS

900 g (2 lb) green bananas, cooked and mashed (see Techniques)
2 eggs, well beaten
2 medium onions, grated or minced
1 clove garlic, crushed
50 g (2 oz) butter, melted
1 teaspoon baking powder
½ teaspoon bicarbonate of soda (baking soda)
50 ml (2 fl oz) milk
Freshly ground black pepper to taste
Sea salt to taste
Breadcrumbs, seasoned with a little salt and pepper
Oil for frying

1 Thoroughly mix together the mashed bananas, half the beaten egg, the onion, garlic, melted butter, baking powder, soda, milk, black pepper and salt to taste.
2 Flour your hands and make about 16–20 small balls of the mixture. Dip in the remaining egg, roll in the breadcrumbs and fry until golden brown.

Serves 4–6

BEAN AND BREADFRUIT ACCRA

50 g (2 oz) unsalted butter
1 medium onion, chopped
110 g (4 oz) cooked flageolets or black-eyed beans, mashed
675 g (1½ lb) breadfruit, parboiled, cored and peeled, then grated (see Techniques)
3 eggs, beaten
75 g (3 oz) wholemeal flour
½ hot pepper, or to taste, deseeded and chopped (see Techniques)
50 g (2 oz) cheese, grated
2 tablespoons chopped fresh chives
150 ml (¼ pint) milk

Sea salt to taste
Freshly ground black pepper to taste
Oil for frying

1 Heat the butter then sauté the onion until translucent.
2 Make a batter by combining the mashed beans, the breadfruit, beaten eggs, flour, hot pepper, cheese, chives and milk. Season with salt and pepper and mix in the sautéed onions. If the batter is too heavy simply add a little more milk.
3 In a large, heavy frying pan heat oil to a depth of 2.5 cm (1 inch).
4 Drop a serving spoonful of batter into the oil and fry on both sides until golden brown.
5 Drain on kitchen paper but keep fairly warm until all the batter has been used up. Serve with a creole sauce (see page 180).

Serves 6–8 as an accompaniment, or 4 as a main dish

BREADFRUIT COO-COO

50 g (2 oz) butter
1 onion, finely chopped
1 clove garlic, chopped
675 g (1½ lb) cooked breadfruit (see Techniques), mashed
1 tablespoon chopped fresh coriander leaves (or parsley)
Freshly ground black pepper to taste
Sea salt to taste
Juice ½ lemon

1 Melt the butter in a non-stick pan and sauté the onion and garlic until translucent but not brown.
2 Keeping the heat low, and using a wooden spoon, thoroughly blend in the mashed breadfruit.
3 Add the coriander leaves, black pepper and salt to taste. Squeeze in the lemon juice. Mix well.
4 Turn out into a warm buttered dish and serve. Can be served with a spicy creole sauce (see Sauces). Reheat covered in the oven if necessary.

Serves 4

CABBAGE WITH COCONUT MILK SAUCE

This is a delicious and different way of serving cabbage to accompany any dish of your choice.

1 firm cabbage, large enough to serve 4–6 people
300 ml (½ pint) coconut milk (see Techniques)
Small piece hot pepper (see Techniques), deseeded but not chopped
½ teaspoon caraway seeds
1 medium onion, cut in half and one half finely chopped
75 g (3 oz) butter
1 tablespoon wholemeal flour
Freshly ground black pepper to taste
Sea salt to taste

1. Remove and discard the outer leaves of the cabbage and wash it well. Cut into 4 or 6 lengthways then remove the core but leave enough to hold the leaves together.
2. Bring a pot of salted water to the boil. Put in the cabbage pieces and simmer uncovered for about 10 minutes, depending on the size of the pieces, then drain.
3. Meanwhile make the sauce: put the coconut milk in a saucepan with the hot pepper, caraway seeds and the half onion. Quickly bring to the boil, uncovered, then leave for about 8 minutes on the lowest possible heat. (If using electricity remove the saucepan from the ring immediately it comes to the boil and do not replace until the glow of the ring has died down.)
4. On a moderate heat melt the butter in a separate pan, and sauté the finely chopped onion until translucent. Stir in the flour, and cook, stirring, until lightly browned.
5. Strain the coconut milk and slowly add to the flour paste, stirring continuously to prevent any lumps forming. Season with salt and black pepper to taste. Remove from the heat.
6. Arrange the cabbage in a serving dish and pour the sauce over it.

Serves 4–6

CALLALOO FRITTERS

675 g (1½ lb) callaloo (or substitute spinach)
50 g (2 oz) wholemeal breadcrumbs
75 g (3 oz) fine cornmeal
Freshly grated nutmeg to taste
Freshly ground black pepper to taste
Sea salt to taste
3 size-2 eggs, beaten

75 g (3 oz) wholemeal flour, sifted (optional)
Oil for frying

1 Finely chop the callaloo and boil it in a little salted water (if using spinach remove the stalks) for 5–6 minutes.
2 Drain and press out any liquid (save the liquid to add to a soup).
3 Chop further if your discretion tells you the callaloo is not fine enough, then mix thoroughly in a bowl with the breadcrumbs, cornmeal, nutmeg, black pepper and salt to taste.
4 Pour in the eggs a little at a time and mix well, adding flour if necessary. The mixture must not be too moist. Add flour if you need to.
5 Drop by the spoonful into the frying pan, flatten with a spatula, and fry in about 1–2 cm (½–¾ inch) oil until brown.
6 Drain well on kitchen towels and serve.

Serves 4–6

BAKED CARROTS WITH RUM

Young carrots (allow 6 per person)
110 g (4 oz) brown cane sugar
2 tablespoons light rum
Fresh wholemeal breadcrumbs
Grated rind 1 lemon
Melted butter

1 Preheat the oven to 200°C (400°F/Gas 6).
2 Scrape and wash the carrots, bring to the boil in salted water and simmer until tender but still quite firm.
3 Meanwhile make a thick syrup with the sugar and a very little water. Allow to cool and add the rum.
4 Drain the carrots and put to marinate in the syrup for about an hour.
5 Mix together the breadcrumbs and lemon rind.
6 Remove the carrots from the marinade and coat each one in the melted butter then the breadcrumbs. Place in a baking pan and bake for 15 minutes or until brown.
7 Boil down any syrup there may be and pour over the carrots before serving. Goes well with christophene with cheese (see page 152) or Keshy Yena (see page 129).

Serves 4–6

CREOLE CAULIFLOWER CHEESE

As far as I know, cauliflowers have not been successfully grown in the Caribbean. Most of them are flown in from the American mainland, generally to Martinique, Guadeloupe and one or two of the more tourist-trampled islands. I have attempted to grow cauliflowers at River Claire on the island of Dominica. I harvested each time a few small heads, full of flavour, but not in a worthwhile quantity for the time and effort put in. The following is my creole version of cauliflower cheese, which I have more than once prepared with cauliflowers grown in my cottage garden in Northumberland.

1 cauliflower, separated into florets
75 g (3 oz) butter
1 medium onion, chopped
2–3 cloves garlic, finely chopped
4 cloves, freshly ground
¼ teaspoon freshly ground fennel seeds
¼ teaspoon freshly ground cinnamon
1 teaspoon West Indian hot pepper sauce
300 ml (½ pint) single cream
225 g (½ lb) Cheddar cheese, grated
A little milk (optional)
Sea salt to taste
Freshly ground black pepper to taste
4 tomatoes, sliced
50 g (2 oz) Parmesan cheese, grated
2 tablespoons breadcrumbs

1. Preheat the oven to 190° (375°F/Gas 5).
2. Parboil the cauliflower florets in salted water, drain thoroughly and set aside.
3. Melt the butter in a pot and sauté the onion until translucent but not brown.
4. Add the garlic, ground cloves, fennel seeds, cinnamon, hot pepper sauce and cream. Stir and simmer gently for about 3 minutes.
5. Now add 170 g (6 oz) of the Cheddar cheese. Mix well and cook until the cheese has melted. If in your opinion the sauce is too thick, stir in a little milk until the desired consistency is reached. Season with salt and pepper.
6. In a greased baking dish arrange the cauliflower florets. Cover

with the sauce then the sliced tomatoes. Sprinkle the tomatoes with a little salt and pepper (very little salt).

7 Mix together the rest of the grated Cheddar cheese, the Parmesan and the breadcrumbs and sprinkle over the tomatoes. Bake for about 30 minutes or until lightly browned.

Serves 4–6 as an accompaniment, 2–3 as a main course

CURRIED CAULIFLOWER

A really delicious and spicy dish, with French and Asian influences, that is well worth trying. The curry flavour is not too strong and therefore should be appreciated by most people.

1 large cauliflower
2 tablespoons vegetable oil or ghee (see Techniques)
1 teaspoon mustard seeds
1 teaspoon freshly ground annatto seeds
1 cm (½ inch) piece fresh ginger, finely chopped or grated
Deseeded and finely chopped hot pepper to taste (see Techniques)
1 teaspoon ground allspice
1 teaspoon freshly ground coriander seeds
2–3 cloves garlic, finely chopped
1 teaspoon turmeric
1 medium onion, chopped
1 wineglassful half white wine and half vegetable stock
Sea salt to taste
300 ml (½ pint) coconut cream (see Techniques) or plain yoghurt
2 tablespoons chopped fresh chives (or substitute spring onions)

1 Clean and trim the cauliflower and cut it into neat florets. Set aside.

2 Heat the oil in a pot, add the mustard seeds and fry gently until they begin to pop.

3 Add the annatto, ginger, hot pepper, allspice, coriander, garlic, turmeric and onion and continue to fry for a few more minutes, stirring continuously. Add the wine and stock. Mix well.

4 Now add the cauliflower florets, salt to taste and the coconut cream. Simmer gently until the cauliflower is tender but still quite firm.

5 Taste for seasoning, then serve garnished with the chopped chives or spring onions.

This dish can be served on its own with a little rice or as part of a meal.

Serves 2–3 as a main course

CHRISTOPHENE WITH CHEESE

675 g (1½ lb) christophenes
1 small onion, finely grated
50 g (2 oz) butter
4 tablespoons grated cheese
½ teaspoon aniseed
2 eggs, lightly beaten
3 tablespoons single cream
Freshly ground black pepper to taste
Sea salt to taste

1 Preheat the oven to 220°C (425°F/Gas 7).
2 Peel the christophenes (see Techniques) then chop them very finely.
3 Place in a saucepan with just enough water to reach about a third of the way up the christophenes. Cover and simmer until tender, turning the pieces over occasionally.
4 Drain off any excess liquid and return to the heat with the onion, half the butter, 2 tablespoons of the cheese, the aniseed, beaten eggs, cream, black pepper and salt to taste. Mix thoroughly and cook on a very low heat for about 3 minutes. Do not allow to burn.
5 Turn into a buttered baking dish. Sprinkle with the remaining cheese, dot with the remainder of the butter and bake for 15 minutes or until brown. Serve immediately.

Serves 4–6

BAKED CHRISTOPHENE IN CREAM SAUCE

3 christophenes
75 g (3 oz) margarine
1 tablespoon grated onion
2 teaspoons flour
300 ml (½ pint) single cream

Freshly ground white pepper to taste
Sea salt to taste
110 g (4 oz) Cheddar cheese, grated
50 g (2 oz) wholemeal breadcrumbs
Freshly ground black pepper to taste
½ teaspoon freshly ground fennel seeds

1 Preheat the oven to 200°C (400°F/Gas 6).
2 Peel the christophenes and cut each in half. Bring to the boil in salted water. Lower the heat and simmer covered until tender. Drain and leave to cool.
3 Meanwhile, make the sauce by melting the margarine, adding the grated onion and cooking gently for about 1 minute. Stir in the flour and cook for about 4–5 minutes without browning.
4 Pour in the cream a little at a time, stirring continuously. Simmer on a low heat for about 8–10 minutes then season to taste with the white pepper and salt. Remove from the heat and pass through a fine strainer.
5 Mix together the cheese, breadcrumbs, black pepper and ground fennel.
6 Slice the christophenes in thin segments and arrange in an ovenproof dish. Pour the cream sauce over and then sprinkle with the topping mixture.
7 Bake for 20 minutes until lightly browned. Serve hot with a green salad and more grated cheese or as an accompaniment.

Serves 4–6

STEWED CHRISTOPHENE

3 tablespoons sesame seed oil
2 medium onions, sliced
3 tomatoes, skinned and finely chopped
1 small sprig fresh thyme
1 sprig fresh parsley
1 clove garlic, crushed
2 large christophenes, peeled and cut into cubes (see Techniques)
Freshly ground black pepper to taste
Sea salt to taste
West Indian pepper sauce (optional)

1 Heat the oil in a heavy pot with a lid and fry the onions until translucent and slightly browned.

2 Add all the other ingredients, except the pepper sauce. Stir.
3 Cover and simmer gently until the christophenes are tender. Taste for seasoning and add the pepper sauce.

Serves 3–4

STIR-FRIED CHRISTOPHENE AND CUCUMBER

2 medium christophenes
1 cucumber
75 g (3 oz) unsalted butter
1 teaspoon chopped fresh basil
1 teaspoon chopped fresh parsley
1 tablespoon chopped fresh chives
Pinch freshly grated nutmeg
1 teaspoon lemon rind
Freshly ground black pepper to taste

1 Peel the christophenes and shred into a colander with the cucumber. Sprinkle with salt and leave for 1 hour or more.
2 Spread out on a clean kitchen towel and gently pat as dry as possible.
3 Melt the butter in a shallow pan and when fairly hot throw in the shredded vegetables.
4 Add the remaining ingredients and fry for 3 minutes, tossing occasionally. Serve at once. This goes well with patties, rissoles, nut roasts and similar dishes.

Serves 4

COO-COO

Originally a dish from West Africa, known as foo-foo, made from pounded green plantain or finely ground rice cooked until all the water has evaporated. Today it is made throughout the Caribbean, especially in Barbados, with ground corn and okra.

225 g (½ lb) okra
600 ml (1 pint) water
½–1 teaspoon salt
150 g (5 oz) fine cornmeal
Butter (optional)

1 Wash the okra, cut off the tops and slice into small pieces.
2 Bring the water to the boil with the salt, drop in the okra and simmer covered for 8–10 minutes.
3 Slowly pour in the cornmeal, stirring constantly, until the mixture is thick and smooth and begins to leave the sides of the pot. It should almost turn into a round ball.
4 Turn out onto a dish, spread with butter if using, and serve with a tomato and onion sauce (see page 186).

Serves 4–6

EGG CREOLE

25 g (1 oz) butter, plus a little extra for baking
2 medium onions, finely diced
1 clove garlic, chopped
1 sweet red pepper, deseeded and chopped
1 sweet green pepper, deseeded and chopped
½ small christophene (or substitute marrow or courgettes), peeled, cored, finely diced, then blanched for 2 minutes
110 g (4 oz) mushrooms, chopped
100 ml (4 fl oz) thick coconut cream (see Techniques) or single cream
½–1 teaspoon deseeded and chopped hot pepper (see Techniques)
Freshly ground black pepper to taste
Sea salt to taste
3 medium tomatoes, peeled, deseeded and chopped
4 blades chives, finely chopped
4 eggs

1 Preheat the oven to 190°C (375°F/Gas 5).
2 Melt the 25 g (1 oz) butter in a saucepan, add the onions, garlic, sweet peppers and christophene and cook for about 3–4 minutes. Do not brown.
3 Add the mushrooms, coconut cream, hot pepper, and black pepper and salt to taste. Simmer, slightly covered, for about 5 minutes.
4 Mix in very carefully the chopped tomatoes and chives. Taste for seasoning.
5 Pour the mixture into a shallow ovenproof dish large enough to contain the eggs as well.

6 Make 4 holes in the mixture. Break an egg into each hole, and place a knob of butter on each egg.
7 Bake for about 10–12 minutes or until the eggs are set. Serve with avocados and baked yams or with hot buttered bread and a creole sauce (see Sauces).

Serves 4

CREOLE MACARONI PIE

On many Caribbean islands macaroni pie is a must as part of a late Sunday lunch. It is almost always served as an accompaniment, especially in the English-speaking islands.

450 g (1 lb) macaroni
110–170 g (4–6 oz) margarine or butter
170 g (6 oz) hard cheese, grated
1 small onion, grated
Freshly ground black pepper to taste
Sea salt to taste
2 eggs, well beaten with a little milk

1 Preheat the oven to 200°C (400°F/Gas 6).
2 In a large pot bring some salted water to the boil. Add the macaroni and cook uncovered for 15 minutes. Drain thoroughly.
3 Return to the heat with the margarine or butter, then add the cheese, onion, pepper and salt. Mix well.
4 Remove from the heat and quickly mix in the beaten eggs. Turn into a buttered baking dish, cover with foil and bake for about 20 minutes or until brown and set.

Serves 6–8

OKRA IN TOMATO SAUCE

This is one of the oldest creole dishes and is very often served for breakfast.

2 tablespoons coconut oil
1 medium onion, finely chopped
2 cloves garlic, finely chopped
400 g (14 oz) tin plum tomatoes, chopped
1 small branch fresh basil, chopped
Pinch freshly grated nutmeg

Freshly ground black pepper to taste
Sea salt to taste
450 g (1 lb) okra, washed and topped

1. Heat the oil in a pan and sauté the onion and garlic until translucent but not brown.
2. Add all the other ingredients except the okra, and simmer gently for about 6 minutes, stirring occasionally to prevent burning.
3. Now add the okra, covering them with the sauce. Simmer gently for a further 15–20 minutes. Give a stir now and then to prevent the mixture sticking to the pot.
4. Taste for seasoning and serve as an accompaniment to spinach and cornmeal fritters (see page 222), plantain pie (see page 87), and of course with either coo-coo (see page 154) or foo-foo (see page 158).

Serves 2–4

CURRIED OKRA WITH NUTS

50 g (2 oz) ghee (see Techniques)
1 teaspoon freshly ground coriander seeds
1 teaspoon freshly ground cumin
1 teaspoon freshly ground mustard seeds
6 cloves, freshly ground
75 g (3 oz) cashew nuts
1 teaspoon turmeric
Deseeded and chopped hot pepper to taste (see Techniques)
450 g (1 lb) okra, topped
3 tomatoes, skinned and chopped
Sea salt to taste
150 ml (5 fl oz) carton natural yoghurt

1. Melt the ghee, add the ground coriander, cumin, mustard seeds and cloves and fry for 3 minutes. Now add the cashew nuts, turmeric and hot pepper and fry for a further 2 minutes.
2. Add the okra, tomatoes and salt to taste. Simmer covered until the okra are just about cooked.
3. Taste for seasoning and gently stir in the yoghurt. Cook for a further 3–4 minutes and serve.

Serves 4

PLANTAIN FOO-FOO

A dish from the West Coast of Africa which was brought to the West Indies during the slave trade.

3–4 large green plantains
1 lemon, cut in half
75–100 g (3–4 oz) butter
Sea salt to taste
Freshly ground black pepper

1 Peel and wash the plantains with half the lemon (see Techniques), then bring to the boil in salted water with the juice from the other lemon half. Cook until tender.
2 Place in a large mortar, with the butter, salt and black pepper, and pound into a smooth paste. You may have to dip the pestle in cold water several times to prevent sticking.
3 Taste for seasoning then serve warm with a sauce of your choice and a stewed bean dish.

Serves 2–4

FRIED RIPE PLANTAINS

The plantains must be very ripe, soft to the touch and almost black, if possible. A yellow plantain does not mean it is ideal for frying. Allow about half a plantain per person. You will also need oil for frying.

1 Wash the plantains then peel (see Techniques). Cut each one crossways in half, slice each half lengthways in 3 or 4 slices.
2 Heat the oil in a heavy frying pan and fry the slices of plantain on both sides until golden brown. Drain on kitchen paper. Ideal with curried dishes.

RIPE PLANTAINS IN CORNMEAL

A sweet-savoury dish ideal for a snack or as part of a main meal.

2 eggs
Pinch ground allspice
A little deseeded and finely chopped hot pepper (see Techniques) – optional
110 g (4 oz) fine cornmeal
Approximately 150 ml (¼ pint) milk
Sea salt to taste

2 ripe plantains
A little medium-to-coarse cornmeal
Oil for deep frying

1 In a bowl, beat the eggs, then add the allspice and hot pepper. Mix well, then gradually mix in the fine cornmeal.
2 Add sufficient milk to make a thick batter. Season with salt.
3 Peel the plantains, slice each across in half then slice each half into 3–4 pieces lengthways (see Techniques).
4 Coat each slice with batter then sprinkle well with the medium or coarse cornmeal.
5 Deep fry in hot oil until golden brown. Drain on kitchen paper and serve.

I have often used sweet potatoes, which are first cooked, as a substitute. Cooked and sliced christophenes or marrows can be used as well. All can be served with a cream or cheese sauce.

Serves 2–4

JACKET SWEET POTATOES

4 good-sized sweet potatoes
40 g (1½ oz) butter plus a little extra for dotting
2 tablespoons chopped shallots
110 g (4 oz) cream cheese
½ teaspoon deseeded and chopped hot pepper, or to taste (see Techniques)
1 tablespoon mayonnaise
Sea salt to taste
Freshly ground black pepper to taste
Chopped fresh chives to garnish

1 Preheat the oven to 190°C (375°F/Gas 5).
2 Wash and pat dry the sweet potatoes and bake until tender. Test with a skewer.
2 Allow the potatoes to cool, then carefully scoop out the flesh without damaging the skins. Mash the flesh.
3 Melt the 40 g (1½ oz) butter and sauté the shallots until softened. Allow to cool completely. Then mix together in a bowl with the potato flesh, cream cheese, hot pepper, mayonnaise, salt and black pepper.
4 Fill the potato shells with the mixture. Dot with butter and grill

until golden brown. Garnish with the chopped chives before serving.

Serves 4

SPICED SWEET POTATOES

675 g (1½ lb) sweet potatoes
4 tablespoons vegetable oil
1 large onion, finely chopped
3 cloves garlic, chopped
6 cloves, freshly ground
Pinch freshly grated nutmeg
½ teaspoon deseeded and chopped hot pepper, or to taste (see Techniques)
¼ teaspoon ground ginger
Sea salt to taste (optional)

1. Wash the sweet potatoes, but do not peel. Bring to the boil in salted water, lower the heat and cook until tender but still quite firm.
2. Allow to cool, then peel and cut into neat cubes. Set aside, but keep warm.
3. Heat the oil and fry the onion until translucent but not brown. Add the garlic and fry for another minute.
4. Now add the cloves, nutmeg, hot pepper and ginger and fry for a further 1 minute.
5. Mix in the cubed potatoes very carefully and coat with the spiced mixture. Sprinkle on some salt if you wish. Serve hot.

Serves 4

TANNIA OR YAM SOUFFLÉ

675 g (1½ lb) tannias or yam, cooked (see Techniques)
75 g (3 oz) butter
2 medium onions, finely chopped
Pinch freshly grated nutmeg
170 g (6 oz) cheese, grated
1 whole egg, beaten
Sea salt to taste
3 egg whites

1 Preheat oven to 180°C (350°F/Gas 4).
2 Mash or pass through a sieve the tannias or yam.
3 Melt the butter and sauté the onions until translucent but not brown. Add to the mashed vegetables and mix well, together with the nutmeg, grated cheese and beaten whole egg. Taste for salt.
4 Stiffly beat the egg whites with a pinch of salt, and fold into the vegetable mixture.
5 Pour into a greased soufflé dish and bake for 35–40 minutes or until brown and well risen. Serve immediately.

Serves 6

Salads and Salad Dressings

AVOCADO AND GRAPEFRUIT SALAD

This can be served either as a starter or as part of a main course.

4 tablespoons walnut oil
2 tablespoons freshly squeezed orange juice
1 tablespoon Jamaican honey
½ teaspoon freshly ground allspice
¼ teaspoon ground ginger
Juice 1 lemon
Sea salt to taste
Freshly ground white pepper to taste (or try green, which has a more delicate flavour)
1 pink grapefruit
1 other grapefruit
1 large West Indian or South American avocado (or 2–3 medium ones)

1. Combine all the ingredients, except the avocado and grapefruits, and whisk until well blended.
2. Carefully peel the grapefruits, removing all white pith and the membrane covering the segments, and carefully extract any pips. Arrange on individual dishes or plates.
3. Cut the avocado in half, discard the stones, and segment in slices similar to the grapefruit slices. Peel each slice (a well-ripened avocado should peel almost as easily as a banana; otherwise, use a sharp knife to ease the skin gently away, but do not cut too deeply).
4. Arrange the avocado slices on the plates with the grapefruit.
5. Give the dressing a final shake and spoon over the fruit. Serve as soon as possible. This salad will not keep.

Serves 4–6

BEAN SALAD OF THE ISLANDS

170 g (6 oz) cooked red kidney beans
170 g (6 oz) cooked black beans
170 g (6 oz) cooked black-eyed beans
} tinned may be used

2 tablespoons olive oil
2 cloves garlic, chopped
Deseeded and chopped hot pepper to taste (see Techniques)
Juice 1 lemon
½ teaspoon freshly ground cloves
½ teaspoon fresh thyme leaves
Freshly ground black pepper to taste
Sea salt to taste
1 teaspoon brown cane sugar (omit if using tinned beans)
6 stoned green olives, chopped
3 tablespoons chopped fresh chives (or substitute spring onions)
2 tablespoons chopped fresh coriander leaves

1 If using tinned beans, empty them into a sieve or colander and rinse under cold running water, then spread over a clean cloth to dry almost completely.
2 Combine the oil, garlic, hot pepper, lemon juice, ground cloves, fresh thyme, seasoning, and sugar, if using. Blend well with a fork or wire whisk. A swizzle stick will do a perfect job.
3 Place the beans in a bowl together with the olives, chives and coriander leaves. Toss to mix.
4 Pour the dressing over the bean mixture. Toss again. Taste for seasoning, then set aside for an hour so that the beans may absorb the combined flavours of the dressing.
5 Serve as part of a main meal or simply on its own with hot garlic bread and sliced avocado.

Serves 4–6

MIXED BEAN, TOMATO AND AVOCADO SALAD

2 tablespoons olive oil
Juice 1 lime
Grated rind ½ lime
2 cloves garlic, finely chopped
½ teaspoon deseeded and chopped hot pepper (see Techniques)
¼ teaspoon freshly ground allspice
Sea salt to taste
Freshly ground black pepper to taste
170 g (6 oz) red beans, cooked, drained and cooled slightly

170 g (6 oz) black-eyed beans, cooked, drained and cooled slightly
1 large or 2 small avocados, ripe but firm
4 large tomatoes, skinned, deseeded and diced
3 tablespoons chopped fresh chives
2 tablespoons chopped fresh parsley (or coriander)

1 Make a dressing with the oil, lime juice and rind, garlic, hot pepper, allspice, salt and black pepper to taste.
2 Mix the beans together in a bowl and pour in half the dressing. Toss, set aside and allow to cool completely.
3 Peel and stone the avocado, add with the tomatoes and chives to the beans. Pour in the balance of the dressing. Toss gently, without breaking up the avocado.
4 Garnish with the parsley or coriander and serve.

Serves 6

CARROT AND PAWPAW SALAD

1 or 2 pawpaws (weight about 450 g (1 lb) in all)
340 g (¾ lb) carrots
2 good-sized celery stalks
225 g (½ lb) cashew nuts
Juice ½ lemon
A little chopped fresh parsley (optional)
4 tablespoons mayonnaise (or more if you wish)
Sea salt to taste

1 Peel the pawpaws and discard the seeds. Then cut into neat squares and place in a salad bowl.
2 Scrape and wash the carrots then grate them and add to the pawpaw.
3 Thinly slice the celery and add to the salad bowl with the remaining ingredients. Mix well, taste then serve.

Serves 4–6

CREOLE GREEN SALAD WITH PASSION FRUIT DRESSING

For the salad:
1 lettuce, cleaned and separated into leaves
1 bunch watercress, cleaned and trimmed
1 sweet green pepper, deseeded and sliced
½ cucumber, thinly sliced

1 sprig fresh parsley, chopped
8 green Spanish olives, stoned and sliced
1 bunch fresh chives, chopped
1 large avocado

For the dressing:

3 tablespoons olive oil or vegetable oil
1 tablespoon white wine vinegar
Juice ½–1 lime
2 cloves garlic, crushed but left as whole as possible
2 teaspoons fresh orange juice
2 passion fruit, cut in half and pulp and seeds scooped out (discard skin)
Sea salt to taste
Freshly ground black pepper to taste

1 Arrange all the salad ingredients, except the avocado, in a salad bowl.
2 Combine all the dressing ingredients in a jar. Shake well and vigorously.
3 Remove the crushed garlic and pour half the dressing over the greens. Toss well.
4 Peel, stone and neatly slice the avocado lengthways, then arrange on top of the greens in the salad bowl. Pour the balance of the dressing over the avocado and serve.

Serves 6

MANGO, APPLE AND MUSHROOM SALAD

Apples are not privately or commercially grown in the West Indies. They are imported mostly from Canada and America.

2 red apples, cored and sliced, not peeled
2 ripe but firm mangoes, peeled, stoned and sliced
225 g (½ lb) mushrooms, washed and sliced
50 g (2 oz) unsalted, roasted cashew nuts (optional)
Juice ½ small orange
1 tablespoon chopped fresh chives
Juice ½ lemon
4 tablespoons cottage cheese
1 tablespoon finely chopped celery
Freshly ground black pepper to taste
Sea salt to taste

1 Place the sliced apples, mangoes and mushrooms, with the cashew nuts, if using, in a salad bowl.
2 Combine the remaining ingredients. Do not overblend. Pour over the fruit and mushroom mixture and toss lightly. Serve immediately.

Serves 6–8

MANGO AND CHEESE SALAD

4 large, ripe but firm mangoes
1 onion, finely chopped
4 tablespoons mayonnaise
Juice and rind ½ lime
4–6 green olives, chopped
2 stalks celery, thinly sliced
Freshly ground white pepper to taste
Sea salt to taste
110 g (4 oz) cheese, grated
Chopped fresh chives to garnish

1 Peel, stone and slice the mangoes.
2 Place in a bowl with all the other ingredients except the grated cheese and chives.
3 Gently mix until the mango slices are well coated.
4 Fold in the grated cheese and transfer into a salad bowl. Sprinkle the chives over and serve.

Serves 4–6

MELON AND AVOCADO SALAD

I originally thought of serving this dish as a dessert with other fruity ingredients at a large party given by my literary agent, but a vegetarian friend of mine suggested that it might be best as a starter. She was absolutely correct.

1 honeydew melon (or use water melon)
2 fairly large, ripe but firm avocados
Juice 1 lime or lemon
Rind and juice 1 small orange
2 tablespoons vegetable oil, suitable for a salad
1 tablespoon chopped fresh chives
1 clove garlic, chopped (optional)

Freshly ground white pepper to taste
Sea salt to taste

1 Peel the melon and remove the seeds (do this over a bowl so as to collect any of the juices). Cut into neat cubes.
2 Peel and stone the avocados and cut into neat cubes.
3 Combine in a salad bowl (do not use a blender) the remaining ingredients and any juice collected from the melon. Season well.
4 Very gently mix in the melon and avocado. Serve chilled.

Serves 6–8

PAWPAW AND CRISP LETTUCE SALAD

This is well worth trying and makes a good accompaniment to many of the vegetable pies or nut dishes. It is based on an Eastern Caribbean recipe I have long used.

200 ml (7 fl oz) olive oil
50 ml (2 fl oz) white wine vinegar
Juice ½ orange
2 teaspoons lemon juice
2 teaspoons cane sugar
1 small onion, minced
½ teaspoon Angostura bitters
1 clove garlic, pressed
Freshly ground white pepper to taste
A little sea salt
1 large crisp lettuce, washed and shredded
2 ripe pawpaws, peeled, deseeded and neatly cubed

1 Blend in an electric blender, or with a whisk in a bowl, the oil, vinegar, orange juice, lemon juice, sugar, onion, bitters, garlic, pepper and salt. You may adjust the proportions to your taste. I often do.
2 Arrange the shredded lettuce around the sides of a large salad bowl, leaving a well in the centre.
3 Arrange the pawpaw cubes in the well, pour the dressing over the pawpaw and serve.

Serves 6–8

PIGEON PEA SALAD

This is definitely one dish that calls for *fresh* pigeon peas.

450 g (1 lb) fresh pigeon peas, cooked (see Techniques) then drained (save the liquid for a rice and peas dish)
5 tablespoons olive oil
2 tablespoons vinegar
1 tablespoon lemon juice
½ teaspoon deseeded and chopped hot pepper (optional – but see Techniques)
1 small clove garlic, finely chopped
Freshly ground black pepper to taste
Sea salt to taste
1 medium onion, finely chopped
1–2 tablespoons finely chopped fresh parsley

1 Put the pigeon peas in a bowl and add the oil, vinegar, lemon juice, hot pepper, garlic, and black pepper and salt to taste. Mix gently but thoroughly, using a wooden spoon. Taste for seasoning.
2 Sprinkle with the chopped onion and parsley then serve.

Serves 4–6

CREOLE POTATO SALAD

Breadfruit makes a very good substitute for the potatoes, but it must be well matured – almost a rich cream in colour – but not ripe. Peel, core and cut it into roughly 2.5 cm (1 inch) pieces before cooking in salted water with a little lime and lemon juice (see Techniques).

450 g (1 lb) potatoes
Juice 1 lemon
1 sprig fresh parsley, chopped
Freshly ground black pepper
Pinch freshly grated nutmeg
Sea salt to taste
450 g (1 lb) tomatoes, neatly diced
150 ml (5 fl oz) carton yoghurt
2 tablespoons mayonnaise
Cayenne pepper to taste
1 tablespoon chopped fresh basil
2 tablespoons chopped fresh chives
2 hard-boiled eggs, chopped

1 Cook the potatoes, dice them, and while they are still slightly warm place in a bowl with the lemon juice, parsley, black pepper, nutmeg and a pinch of salt. Toss lightly to coat the potato pieces and leave to stand until cold.
2 Add the tomatoes to the potatoes and then mix in the yoghurt, mayonnaise and cayenne. Taste for salt and add if needed. Sprinkle over the basil.
3 Toss together the chives and chopped eggs, spread over the salad mixture and serve.

Serves 6

CREOLE RED BEAN SALAD

170 g (6 oz) red kidney beans, soaked overnight
5 tablespoons oil
1 teaspoon brown cane sugar
¼ teaspoon freshly ground cloves
2 cloves garlic, chopped
2 level teaspoons fresh thyme leaves
Juice ½ lemon
Freshly ground black pepper to taste
Sea salt to taste
4 shallots, chopped
2 medium tomatoes, diced
1 small, ripe but firm mango, peeled, stoned and diced
1 small stick celery, diced
1 heaped teaspoon chopped fresh chives
2 tablespoons wine vinegar

1 Drain the beans, rinse in cold water, cover by about 5 cm (2 inches) with cold water and boil on a very high heat for 10–12 minutes. Reduce the heat and simmer covered for 45 minutes.
2 When fairly tender add a little salt and cook until most or all of the liquid has evaporated. Do not allow to burn. Gently stir now and then.
3 Meanwhile, combine 2 tablespoons of the oil, the sugar, ground cloves, 1 clove of garlic, the thyme leaves, lemon juice, black pepper and a little salt. Add to the beans.
4 Remove the beans from the heat and set aside to cool, uncovered. When fairly cool add the shallots, tomatoes, mango and celery.

5 Prepare a dressing with the remaining oil and garlic, the chives, wine vinegar, and some black pepper and salt to taste.
6 Mix in with the salad and allow to cool to room temperature.

Serves 4

SPICY TROPICAL FRUIT SALAD

You can substitute other fresh tropical fruits if you wish. Though I have known friends to use tinned fruit, I personally avoid this. There is such a wide choice of fresh fruit available that it seems a shame not to take advantage of it.

2 lemons
2 tablespoons olive oil
Freshly ground black pepper to taste
Pinch salt
1–2 ripe mangoes (according to size)
1 avocado
1 pawpaw
1 grapefruit (pink, if available)
2 tablespoons chopped fresh chives
Deseeded and chopped hot pepper to taste (see Techniques)

1 Make a dressing with the juice of 1 of the lemons, the oil, black pepper and salt.
2 Over a dish, so as to collect any of the juices, peel and cube the mango, discarding the stone. Do the same with the avocado, then the pawpaw, discarding the black seeds.
3 Over a plate, with a sharp knife cut away the skin of the remaining lemon and the grapefruit, removing as much of the pith as possible. Segment and remove the pips.
4 Place all the fruits, with the chives and hot pepper, in a bowl.
5 Pour the dressing and any juice over the fruits and lightly toss.
6 Chill for 30 minutes to 1 hour and serve.

I sometimes garnish with fresh mint or dill leaves picked straight from my herb garden.

Serves 6

AVOCADO DRESSING

1 large or 2 medium avocados
50 ml (2 fl oz) extra virgin oil

Juice ½ lemon
1 tablespoon thyme and hot pepper vinegar (see page 188)
1 tablespoon finely chopped fresh chives
1 clove garlic, crushed
Sea salt to taste
Freshly ground white pepper to taste

1. Cut the avocado in half, then peel and discard the stone.
2. Place all the ingredients in a blender and mix until creamy. If a blender is unavailable, pass the avocado through a fine sieve then thoroughly mix in all the remaining ingredients.

This dressing will not keep, as the avocado tends to discolour, even with the lemon juice and vinegar included.

Makes approximately 300 ml (½ pint)

AVOCADO MAYONNAISE

Ideal as a salad dressing, especially on the firmer type of lettuce such as Cos and Iceberg, also celery, Chinese leaves, etc.

1–2 avocados (according to size), peeled and stoned
Juice 2 lemons
2 egg yolks
2 tablespoons mayonnaise
1 small clove garlic, crushed
Deseeded and chopped hot pepper to taste (see Techniques)
150 ml (¼ pint) olive or vegetable oil
2 tablespoons chopped fresh chives
Sea salt to taste
Freshly ground black pepper to taste

1. Place all the ingredients except the oil, chives and seasoning in a blender and blend at a low to moderate speed, while gradually pouring in the oil.
2. Taste for seasoning, add salt and pepper if needed and blend briefly.
3. Mix in the chives, but do not blend.

The dressing should really be used on the day it is made.

Makes approximately 300 ml (½ pint)

LIME OR LEMON DRESSING

Ideal for any green salad.

Juice 1 lime or lemon
75 ml (3 fl oz) extra virgin oil
1 clove garlic, finely chopped
1 tablespoon white wine vinegar
½ teaspoon sugar
1 tablespoon finely chopped fresh chives
Sea salt to taste
Freshly ground black pepper to taste

1 Place all the ingredients in a jar or bowl and beat with a whisk or fork, until well blended. Leave aside for about 8–10 minutes. Beat again and use.

Makes approximately 150 ml (¼ pint)

CREOLE SALAD DRESSING

A dressing from the islands of Martinique and Guadeloupe. The spiciness depends on how much hot pepper sauce you enjoy.

2 garlic cloves, crushed but left as whole as possible
Juice ½ lemon or lime
2 tablespoons wine vinegar
Hot pepper sauce to taste
1 teaspoon cane sugar, or to taste
2 tablespoons tomato purée
Worcestershire sauce (to taste, but do not overdo)
100 ml (4 fl oz) olive oil
Freshly ground black pepper to taste
Sea salt to taste

1 Thoroughly rub a deep bowl with the garlic then discard the cloves.
2 Place all the remaining ingredients in the bowl and blend thoroughly with a whisk or fork. Store in a screwtop jar in the refrigerator and use as needed. The dressing must be well shaken before use.

Makes approximately 175 ml (6 fl oz)

Stocks and Sauces

VEGETABLE STOCK

2 tablespoons oil
40 g (1½ oz) butter
340 g (¾ lb) onions, sliced
340 g (¾ lb) carrots, sliced
6 celery stalks, chopped
4 cloves garlic, crushed
2 tomatoes, chopped (optional)
2 bay leaves
1 sprig fresh parsley
1 sprig fresh thyme
4 cloves
6 peppercorns
Juice ½ lemon (optional)
1.75 litres (2 pints) water
2 teaspoons sea salt
1 glass white wine (optional)

1. In a large pot, heat the oil and butter and sauté the onions until translucent but not brown.
2. Add the carrots and celery and continue to sauté for a further 5 minutes, stirring occasionally. Do not brown.
3. Add all the other ingredients and bring to the boil. Lower the heat and skim off any scum.
4. Simmer uncovered on the lowest heat possible for 2 hours, skimming off any scum that forms. At no time must the stock be brought to the boil.
5. Sieve the stock into a clean container, using a spoon to press the vegetables. Allow to cool completely.
6. Strain through a fine muslin and refrigerate until needed. The stock must be used within 6 days or it can be kept in a freezer for 2 months.

Makes approximately 1.25–1.5 litres (2–2½ pints)

BROWN VEGETABLE STOCK

3 tablespoons vegetable oil
2 medium onions, chopped
3 large carrots, scrubbed and chopped (do not peel)
1 christophene, peeled and chopped (see Techniques) or substitute turnip or swede if christophenes are not available
3 celery stalks, chopped
110 g (4 oz) mushrooms, quartered
3 tomatoes, quartered
1–2 teaspoons caramel colouring (see Techniques)
1 sprig fresh thyme
1 sprig fresh parsley
1–2 bay leaves
5 peppercorns
4 allspice
1.5 litres (2½ pints) water
A little sea salt

1 In a large wide pot heat the oil and fry the onions and other vegetables until a rich brown. Stir in the caramel and continue to fry for about 1 minute.
2 Add the herbs and spices, pour in the water, season and bring to the boil. Lower the heat and skim off any scum, repeating when necessary.
3 Simmer covered for about 30 minutes. Remove from the heat and strain through a very fine sieve, pressing the vegetables with a wooden spoon.
4 Allow to cool and refrigerate until needed. It will keep for a few days.

Makes approximately 1.25 litres (2 pints)

CREOLE SAUCE

2 tablespoons olive oil
2 red sweet peppers, deseeded and chopped
Deseeded and chopped hot pepper to taste (see Techniques)
2 cloves garlic, crushed
1 tablespoon finely chopped fresh parsley
1 teaspoon fresh thyme leaves
1 teaspoon cane sugar (optional)

Glass white wine
1 recipe basic tomato sauce (page 184)

1 Heat the oil and gently sauté the sweet peppers without too much of the colour being lost.
2 Add all the other ingredients except the tomato sauce, mix well and cook on a moderate heat for 5–8 minutes.
3 Now add the tomato sauce and heat through without boiling. Adjust the seasoning if necessary and serve. This sauce will keep for a few days in the refrigerator.

Serves 8 or more

BROWN CREOLE SAUCE

2 tablespoons coconut oil (or substitute vegetable oil)
1 large onion, chopped
1 carrot, chopped
1 stalk celery, chopped
2 cloves garlic, finely chopped
1 sprig fresh thyme
1 sprig fresh parsley
1 bay leaf
1 tablespoon red wine vinegar
2–3 teaspoons caramel colouring (see Techniques)
1 level tablespoon tomato ketchup
½ teaspoon freshly ground allspice
6 cloves, freshly ground
1 teaspoon brown sugar (optional)
600 ml (1 pint) water
Freshly ground black pepper to taste
Sea salt to taste
2 tablespoons flour mixed to a paste with a little water
½ glass sherry or 1 tablespoon dark rum

1 Heat the oil and fry the onion, carrot and celery until a rich brown.
2 Stir in all the remaining ingredients except the flour paste and sherry or rum. Bring to the boil, then lower the heat and simmer for 10 minutes.
3 Stir in the flour paste and continue to simmer very gently for

another 20 minutes. Here you may add a little more caramel if the sauce is not rich enough in colour.

4 Remove from the heat, stir in the sherry or rum and serve.

Makes about 450–600 ml (3/4–1 pint)

HOT PEPPER SAUCE

A very hot sauce best left for 2–3 weeks before using. Will keep for months in a cool place.

225 g (½ lb) hot peppers (a mixture of green, red and yellow Scots Bonnets)
½ green pawpaw, deseeded, peeled and chopped
3 cloves garlic, finely chopped
1 medium onion, finely chopped
6 cloves, freshly ground
4 allspice, freshly ground
2 teaspoons freshly grated ginger
2 teaspoons turmeric
Juice 2 limes
300 ml (½ pint) wine vinegar
3 teaspoons salt
1½ tablespoons brown cane sugar

1 Wash the peppers and remove stalks and seeds (see Techniques). Set aside.
2 Place all the remaining ingredients in a saucepan. Bring to the boil, then cook on a moderate heat for about 4–5 minutes or until the pawpaw is tender. Stir frequently. Taste for salt.
3 Add the hot peppers and cook for a further 3 minutes.
4 Remove from the heat, transfer to a blender and blend to a purée (or pass through a sieve).
5 Return to the pan, bring quickly to the boil, and boil for about 1½ minutes, stirring constantly.
6 Pour into sterilized jars and store.

Makes approximately 750 ml (1¼ pints)

ONION, OLIVE AND CAPER SAUCE

Olives are mostly used on the Spanish-speaking islands, and to a certain extent on the French-Patois islands as well.

75 g (3 oz) butter
2 medium onions, grated
1 clove garlic, finely chopped
2 tablespoons flour
300 ml (½ pint) warm milk (a light coconut milk can be used instead – see Techniques)
8 green olives, stones and chopped
8 capers, finely chopped
2 teaspoons chopped fresh parsley
Freshly ground white pepper to taste
Sea salt to taste
Juice ½ lime or lemon
A little cayenne pepper to garnish

1 Melt the butter, add the onions and garlic and fry until translucent but not brown.
2 Gradually add the flour, stirring continuously. Slowly pour in the warm milk, again stirring continuously.
3 Now add the chopped olives, capers, parsley, lots of white pepper, and salt to taste. Mix well, and simmer gently for a few minutes.
4 Add the citrus juice (it should not curdle). Taste for seasoning, and serve with the cayenne sprinkled over.

Serves 4–6

SALAMAGUNDI SAUCE

Ideal as an accompaniment to rissoles, burgers, nut roasts and similar dishes, especially some patties.

2 tablespoons vegetable oil
4–5 tomatoes, skinned, deseeded and chopped
½ christophene, peeled and grated (see Techniques)
2 medium onions, finely chopped
1 clove garlic, finely chopped
¼ hot pepper, deseeded and chopped (see Techniques)
¼ teaspoon freshly ground allspice
1 carrot, peeled and finely chopped
2 sweet red peppers, deseeded and chopped
300 ml (½ pint) water
2 vegetable stock cubes
1 glass white wine
1 tablespoon wine vinegar

Sea salt to taste
Freshly ground black pepper to taste

1 In a heavy pot, heat the oil, add the tomatoes and cook for about 2–3 minutes.
2 Add the remaining ingredients and simmer covered for 20 minutes. Then taste for seasoning. Add if needed, and cook for a further 10–15 minutes.

This sauce can be made a day or two in advance.

Serves 6–8

BASIC TOMATO SAUCE

A very simple sauce that can be used as it is or as the base for other sauces, especially creole sauce from the French-speaking islands of the Caribbean.

675 g (1½ lb) tomatoes, skinned, deseeded and chopped
2 tablespoons olive oil
75 g (3 oz) butter
2 medium onions, chopped
Juice ½ lime or lemon
2 tablespoons finely chopped fresh basil
1 teaspoon brown sugar (optional)
300 ml (¼ pint) vegetable stock (see page 179)
Sea salt to taste
Freshly ground black pepper to taste

1 Pass the tomatoes through a fine sieve and set aside in a pan.
2 In another pan, heat the oil and butter and sauté the onions until translucent, but not brown.
3 Sieve the onions into the same pan as the tomatoes.
4 Add the remaining ingredients and place the pan on the heat. Simmer gently, uncovered, for about 8 minutes then serve.

This sauce will keep for up to 3 days in the refrigerator.

Serves 8

TOMATO SAUCE

Of Spanish origin

25 g (1 oz) butter
1 medium onion, chopped

450 g (1 lb) very ripe tomatoes, chopped
1 sprig fresh parsley
Juice ½ lemon
1 teaspoon brown cane sugar
½ teaspoon deseeded and chopped hot pepper (see Techniques)
12 capers, chopped
6 basil leaves (or 1 teaspoon dried basil)
8 stuffed olives, chopped
Sea salt to taste
450 ml (¾ pint) water
2 teaspoons annatto liquid

1. Melt the butter in a saucepan and sauté the onion until translucent but not brown.
2. Add all the remaining ingredients except the annatto liquid.
3. Bring to the boil. Reduce the heat to very low and simmer for 30–40 minutes.
4. Remove from the heat and pass through a fine sieve.
5. Taste for seasoning (you may prefer the sauce either sharp or sweet, the choice is yours) and return to the heat.
6. Heat thoroughly without boiling. Stir in the annatto liquid and serve.

This sauce will keep up to 8 days if refrigerated, or longer if frozen.

Serves 4–6

TOMATO AND MANGO SAUCE

3 tablespoons vegetable oil
2 medium onions, finely chopped
4 cloves garlic, finely chopped
1–2 ripe mangoes (weighing approximately 450 g (1 lb)), peeled, stoned and chopped
900 g (2 lb) tomatoes, peeled, deseeded and chopped (save as much of the juice as possible)
4 cloves, freshly ground
4 allspice, freshly ground
8 black peppercorns, freshly ground
½ teaspoon deseeded and chopped hot pepper (see Techniques)
3 tablespoons red wine vinegar
Juice 1 lime or lemon
1 tablespoon light brown cane sugar, or to taste

1 Heat the oil in a pot. Add the onions and garlic and cook until they are soft, without browning.
2 Add all the remaining ingredients. Mix well.
3 Simmer over a low heat until the mixture is thick and well blended. Stir occasionally to avoid burning.
4 Taste for seasoning, especially salt, and you may want to add a little extra vinegar.
5 Remove from the heat. Pass through a sterilized sieve using a spoon that has also been sterilized. Return to the heat and cook for a further 6–7 minutes. Pour into sterilized jars and store.

Makes approximately 900 ml (1½ pints)

TOMATO AND ONION SAUCE (1)

2 tablespoons olive oil
225 g (½ lb) onions, chopped
2 cloves garlic, chopped
1 small stick celery, finely chopped
½ teaspoon deseeded and chopped hot pepper (see Techniques)
1 tablespoon celery leaves, chopped
Juice ½–1 lemon
½ teaspoon freshly ground allspice
1 teaspoon Worcestershire sauce
Freshly ground black pepper to taste
Sea salt to taste
2 tomatoes, chopped
½ quantity basic tomato sauce (see page 184)

1 Heat the oil in a saucepan and sauté the onions until just about soft. They must not be too limp.
2 Add all the remaining ingredients except the chopped tomatoes and the tomato sauce and cook uncovered for about 3 minutes. Stir to prevent burning.
3 Add the chopped tomatoes. Mix in well.
4 Add the tomato sauce and simmer covered for about 5 minutes or until the flavours are well blended.

Serves 4–6

TOMATO AND ONION SAUCE (2)

225 g (½ lb) onions
50 g (2 oz) butter

2 teaspoons flour
½ teaspoon crushed dill seeds
1 teaspoon fresh thyme leaves
1 tablespoon chopped fresh parsley
340 g (¾ lb) tomatoes, deseeded and chopped
300 ml (½ pint) milk or water
Freshly ground black pepper to taste
Sea salt to taste

1 Peel the onions and chop them into large pieces. Drop them into a pan of boiling water. Lower the heat and simmer for no longer than 2 minutes. Drain thoroughly.
2 Melt the butter in a saucepan and sauté the onions for about 2 minutes over a moderate heat.
3 Stir in the flour. Mix well but do not allow to brown.
4 Add all the remaining ingredients and simmer covered for 30 minutes.
5 Taste for seasoning. Pass through a fine sieve. Reheat and serve.

Makes about 450 ml (¾ pint)

SPICY COLD SAUCE

Ideal for patties, burgers and similar eats. If refrigerated will keep for about 8–10 days.

2 small onions, finely chopped
1 clove garlic, finely chopped
400 g (14 oz) tin plum tomatoes, chopped
1 sprig fresh parsley, finely chopped
Deseeded and chopped hot pepper to taste (see Techniques)
Juice 3 limes
2 teaspoons light rum
1 tablespoon Worcestershire sauce
1 tablespoon green olives, chopped
4 capers, chopped
Sugar to taste (the sauce should not be too sweet)
Sea salt to taste

1 In a large bowl, beat together all the ingredients, then serve. If storing, place in sterilized jars and seal tightly.

Makes approximately 600 ml (1 pint)

CARIBBEAN MANGO CHUTNEY

My favourite chutney is made with green mangoes rather than ripe ones. Green mangoes are plentiful in markets and shops selling exotic fruits, as they are imported when not quite matured. This chutney will keep for months in a well-sterilized jar, and is ideal with most curried dishes and as a relish with cheese.

3–4 green mangoes, weighing approximately 1.25–1.5 kg (2½–3 lb)
4 cloves garlic, finely chopped
225 ml (8 fl oz) white wine vinegar
2 cloves, freshly ground
2 allspice, freshly ground
225 g (8 oz) brown cane sugar
Juice 1 lime
2 teaspoons freshly grated ginger
1 tablespoon sea salt

1 Using a sharp knife, peel the mangoes and cut off the flesh from the stone, chopping into small pieces.
2 Place all the ingredients in a heavy pot, bring to the boil and then simmer covered, until the mixture is thick and the mangoes soft. For the last 10 minutes, cook uncovered on a slightly higher heat. Stir occasionally.
3 Pour into a sterilized jar or jars and seal tightly. Leave for at least 2 weeks before using.

Makes approximately 900 ml (1½ pints)

VINEGARS WITH HERBS AND SPICES

It is very easy to prepare your own flavoured vinegars and the following are just a few of the many you can make. Always use the best wine vinegar available.

THYME AND HOT PEPPER VINEGAR

500 ml (17 fl oz) bottle white wine vinegar
2 large sprigs fresh thyme
5 hot peppers (the long green ones)
1 whole clove garlic

1 Pour half the vinegar into a clean measuring jug.
2 Wash the thyme under cold running water then pat dry with a clean cloth. Do the same with the peppers.
3 Now place the hot peppers and garlic into the bottle, then the thyme sprigs, stems downwards.
4 Top up the bottle with the vinegar from the jug. Any vinegar left over should be poured into a clean bottle for future use.
5 Replace the cork or cap on the bottle and set aside for at least 2–3 weeks before using.

TARRAGON VINEGAR

Follow the method for thyme and hot pepper vinegar, substituting 2 sprigs French tarragon (do not use Russian tarragon) for the thyme, peppers and garlic.

MIXED HERB AND SPICE VINEGAR

Follow the method for thyme and hot pepper vinegar, using 1 sprig fresh thyme, 1 sprig fennel leaves, 12 white peppercorns, 12 black peppercorns, 10 cm (4 inch) cinnamon stick and 2 whole cloves garlic. Ideal for using in salad dressings.

PEPPER OIL

To make a very hot peppery oil which can be used for frying and in salad dressings, wash and dry with a clean cloth about 6 whole fresh chilli peppers (if using Scots Bonnet you should only need 3 or 4), then place them in a sterilized 450 g (1 lb) jam jar, and top up with a good vegetable oil. If using olive oil use a second or third pressing. Leave aside for about a month before using.

Ice-creams, Sweets and Fruit Desserts

BASIC ICE-CREAM CUSTARD

VANILLA ICE-CREAM

900 ml (1½ pints) single cream
6 egg yolks
150 g (5 oz) caster sugar
½–¾ teaspoon natural vanilla extract (to taste)

1 Bring the cream to the boil on a medium heat, stirring constantly.
2 Remove from the heat immediately, but keep warm. Stir occasionally to prevent a skin forming.
3 Whisk the egg yolks and sugar until creamy, then gently combine with the cream. Blend well then add the vanilla extract.
4 Return to a low heat, or use a double boiler. Cook until the mixture becomes a creamy custard, thick enough to coat a spoon. Stir constantly to prevent lumps and burning. Do not allow to boil.
5 Remove from the heat and allow to cool completely before freezing. It helps to stand the pan in ice-cold water, but stir the custard frequently. For a stronger flavour the vanilla extract may be added when the ice-cream is cooling.
6 To freeze the ice-cream: either use an ice-cream maker (hand or electrically operated), the ice compartment of a refrigerator, or a freezer. If using a freezer or ice compartment the ice-cream must be taken out about every 30 minutes and beaten or whisked to prevent ice from forming and to obtain a creamy consistency. Each time, the mixture must be returned to freeze immediately.

Makes approximately 1.25 litres (2 pints)

COCONUT ICE-CREAM

The favourite ice-cream of the Caribbean.

Ingredients as for vanilla ice-cream but substituting for half the single cream 600 ml (1 pint) thick coconut cream, made from 2 coconuts (see Techniques)

1 Combine the coconut cream and the single cream.
2 Proceed as for vanilla ice-cream.

MANGO ICE-CREAM

Ingredients as for vanilla ice-cream plus:

200 g (7 oz) ripe mango pulp
50 g (2 oz) sugar (optional, depending on the sweetness of the mango)

1 Blend together the mango pulp and sugar until the sugar has dissolved.
2 Proceed as for vanilla ice-cream, adding the mango pulp after stage 5.

GUAVA ICE-CREAM

Ingredients as for vanilla ice-cream plus:

200 g (7 oz) guava pulp, sieved
75 g (3 oz) caster sugar

1 Stew the guava and sugar on a moderate heat for about 10–12 minutes. Allow to cool completely.
2 Proceed as for vanilla ice-cream, adding the guava pulp after stage 5.

PINEAPPLE ICE-CREAM

Ingredients as for vanilla ice-cream plus:

340 g (12 oz) pineapple, peeled, cored and finely chopped (a small pineapple weighing approximately 785 g (1¾ lb))
110–150 g (4–5 oz) caster sugar

1 Mix the pineapple and caster sugar together and cook for 12–15 minutes (note: uncooked pineapple will not freeze properly). Stir to prevent burning.
2 Allow to cool completely, then proceed as for vanilla ice-cream, adding the cooked pineapple after stage 5.

PEANUT ICE-CREAM

Another favourite of the Caribbean.

Ingredients as for vanilla ice-cream plus:

150 g (5 oz) roasted unsalted peanuts, finely chopped

1 Proceed as for vanilla ice-cream, adding the peanuts at the end of stage 4.

ARROWROOT PUDDING

3 tablespoons St Vincent arrowroot
600 ml (1 pint) milk (coconut milk can be used instead)
A little freshly grated nutmeg
2 tablespoons soft brown cane sugar
2 eggs, well beaten
Unsalted butter for dotting

1 Preheat the oven to 190°C (375°F/Gas 5).
2 Mix the arrowroot into a paste with about 100 ml (4 fl oz) of the milk.
3 Bring the remaining milk to the boil, lower the heat and stir in the arrowroot paste, nutmeg and sugar. Keep on a very low heat and stir continuously until it thickens, using a wooden spoon.
4 Stir in the well-beaten eggs. Do not allow lumps to form. If this does happen, press the mixture through a fine sieve.
5 Pour into a buttered baking dish and bake for 30–45 minutes or until set. Halfway through the cooking time, dot with butter. Serve hot or cold.

Serves 4

COCONUT CREAMED RICE WITH GLAZED MANGOES

170 g (6 oz) white pudding rice
750 ml (1¼ pints) coconut milk (see Techniques – freshly made is best for this recipe)
¼ teaspoon freshly grated nutmeg
110–170 g (4–6 oz) caster sugar (or substitute ⅔ tin condensed milk)
1 teaspoon natural vanilla extract
Grated rind ½ lemon
2 eggs, beaten
A little milk (optional)
2–3 ripe mangoes

2 tablespoons light brown rum
75 g (3 oz) brown cane sugar
2 teaspoons water
A little extra brown sugar and grated nutmeg for sprinkling

1. Thoroughly wash the rice, leave it to soak in clean, cold water for at least 1 hour, then drain.
2. Blend together the coconut milk, nutmeg, caster sugar or condensed milk, vanilla extract and lemon rind.
3. Pour into a saucepan and stir in the rice. Bring to the boil and lower the heat immediately. Stir a few times.
4. On the lowest heat possible, simmer tightly covered for 1¼–1½ hours, or until the rice is creamy and most of the milk has been absorbed. You may have to stir occasionally to prevent burning. It is advisable to use a heat mat if you possess one.
5. Remove from the heat and allow to cool. Stir occasionally to prevent a skin forming.
6. When reasonably cold, stir in the beaten eggs, adding a little milk if the rice mixture seems too thick.
7. Transfer the mixture to a well-greased baking dish, and keep warm in a low oven.
8. Peel the mangoes and cut away the flesh in neat slices. Set aside.
9. Mix together the rum, brown sugar and water, and caramelize on a low heat.
10. Arrange the mango slices over the creamed rice and glaze with the caramel.
11. Sprinkle with a little brown sugar and grated nutmeg, and place under a hot grill until the sugar bubbles. This should not take more than a few minutes. Do not allow to burn or catch fire.
12. Serve when cool.

Serves 6

COCONUT PANCAKES

A variation on coconut turnovers (see page 226).

For the filling:
6 tablespoons water
1 stick cinnamon
225 g (½ lb) brown cane sugar
Drop or two natural vanilla extract
1 coconut, freshly grated (or substitute 300 g (10 oz) desiccated coconut)

For the pancakes:
170 g (6 oz) sifted wholemeal (weight *after* the coarse bran has been sieved out)
Pinch cinnamon
¼ teaspoon fine sea salt
2 eggs, beaten
300 ml (½ pint) milk
unsalted butter for greasing

1 Bring to the boil the 6 tablespoons of water with the cinnamon stick. Reduce the heat until the water is just about bubbling. Simmer covered until most of the flavour has been extracted from the cinnamon (about 10–12 minutes).
2 Add the sugar, vanilla extract and coconut and cook on a low heat until the sugar has completely dissolved. Stir as often as possible to prevent burning. Continue to cook for about another 4–5 minutes after the sugar has dissolved. Remove from the heat.
3 To make the pancake batter, sift together the flour, cinnamon and salt. Slowly whisk the sifted ingredients into the beaten eggs, then gradually beat in the milk until a smooth batter is arrived at.
4 Preheat a shallow frying pan, rubbed well with unsalted butter, over a low heat until it is very hot.
5 Pour in enough batter to cover the bottom of the pan in a thin layer. Agitate until the mixture is no longer runny. It is not necessary to cook on both sides.
6 Transfer each pancake as it is made to a large plate. Place a tablespoon of coconut mixture on each, and roll. Keep warm until ready to serve.

Makes 10–12 pancakes

COCONUT PUDDING

3 eggs
600 ml (1 pint) coconut milk (see Techniques)
½ teaspoon freshly grated nutmeg
Grated rind ½ lemon
3–4 level tablespoons caster sugar (to taste)
3 tablespoons breadcrumbs
25 g (1 oz) desiccated coconut

1 Preheat the oven to 190°C (375°F/Gas 5).
2 Beat the eggs well, then beat in the coconut milk.

3 Stir in the nutmeg, lemon rind, caster sugar and breadcrumbs. Mix well.
4 Pour into a buttered pie dish, sprinkle with the desiccated coconut and bake for about 1 hour or until set. Serve immediately.

Serves 4

COCONUT SORBET

300 ml (½ pint) freshly made coconut milk (see Techniques)
110 g (4 oz) caster sugar
½ teaspoon natural vanilla extract
2 tablespoons light brown rum
Pinch freshly grated nutmeg
2 egg whites, stiffly whipped

1 Whisk together the coconut milk, sugar, vanilla extract, rum and nutmeg until the sugar has dissolved.
2 Fold in the egg whites and put in the freezer.
3 Remove the mixture from the freezer every 30 minutes until frozen and beat with a wooden fork or whisk with a hand whisk.

Serves 4

SWEET POTATO CUSTARD

This is a delicious dessert, with a texture and flavour similar to that of puréed chestnuts.

8 tablespoons water
5 cm (2 inch) cinnamon stick
1 vanilla pod or ¼ teaspoon natural vanilla extract
Dried peel ½ lemon (see Herbs, Spices and Other Condiments)
300 g (10 oz) cooked sweet potatoes
170 g (6 oz) caster sugar (or substitute vanilla sugar and dispense with the pod or extract)
8 egg yolks, lightly beaten
Freshly grated nutmeg (optional)

1 Bring the water to the boil with the cinnamon stick, vanilla pod and lemon peel. Reduce the heat and simmer covered until the spices have released their flavours – about 5 minutes. If using vanilla extract do not add yet.
2 Meanwhile, thoroughly mash the potatoes and pass through a fine sieve. There must be absolutely no lumps whatsoever.

3 Strain the flavoured liquid into a container through a cloth or very fine sieve. Discard the cinnamon stick and lemon peel but retain the vanilla pod for future use (see Herbs, Spices and Other Condiments).
4 Measure the liquid back into the saucepan – there should be 3–4 tablespoons; if less, make up with water; if more, reduce rapidly on a high heat.
5 Combine the sugar with the liquid and cook until syrupy. It need not be too thick.
6 Keeping the heat low, gradually beat in the creamed potatoes. Cook for 10 minutes, stirring constantly.
7 Remove from the heat and allow to cool. If necessary sieve again.
8 Off the heat, thoroughly blend in the beaten egg yolks a little at a time. If using vanilla extract, add now.
9 Return to a very low heat and cook until a rich custard is produced. Stir continuously to prevent any lumps forming. It must be as creamy as possible.
10 Pour into individual bowls, sprinkle with grated nutmeg if using and refrigerate until cold.

Serves 4–6

BANANA AND COCONUT CREAM SPONGE

1 lemon sponge base (see page 228)
2 tablespoons light brown island rum (preferably from Martinique)
Juice ½ small orange
450 g (1 lb) ripe bananas
Juice ½ lemon
110 g (4 oz) caster sugar
6 eggs, beaten
600 ml (1 pint) thick coconut cream (see Techniques)
50 g (2 oz) freshly grated coconut (see Techniques) – desiccated coconut can be used, but fresh gives a much better flavour
Few drops natural vanilla extract

1 Preheat the oven to 160°C (325°F/Gas 3).
2 Line a well-greased ovenproof dish with the sponge.
3 Mix together the rum and orange juice and pour over the sponge.
4 Lightly mash the bananas with the lemon juice.

5 Thoroughly blend together the caster sugar, eggs, coconut cream, coconut and vanilla extract.
6 Spread the mashed bananas over the sponge then pour in the egg and milk mixture. Bake for about an hour or until set. Serve hot or cold.

Serves 6–8

BANANA AND MANGO MERINGUE

300 ml (½ pint) mango pulp
110 g (4 oz) brown cane sugar
½ teaspoon freshly ground allspice
Juice 2 limes or lemons
6 large ripe bananas
2 teaspoons light brown or white rum (optional)
2 egg whites
Pinch salt
1 tablespoon icing sugar
Grated rind 1 lemon

1 Preheat the oven to 200°C (400°F/Gas 6).
2 Place the mango pulp, brown sugar, allspice and the juice of 1 lime or lemon in a saucepan and cook on a medium to low heat until the mixture is the consistency of jam. Allow to cool.
3 Peel the bananas and then mash them with the rum and the juice of the remaining lime or lemon.
4 Butter a baking dish deep enough to hold all the ingredients and pack in the mashed bananas. Spread the mango jam over them.
5 Beat the egg whites with a little salt until stiff; lightly fold in the icing sugar and lemon rind and spread over the mango jam.
6 Bake for 30–40 minutes or until brown. Serve immediately.

Serves 6–8

BANANAS AND ORANGES BAKED WITH RUM

110 g (4 oz) butter
200 ml (7 fl oz) fresh orange juice
110 g (4 oz) brown cane sugar
Pinch freshly grated nutmeg
Grated rind 1 orange
6 ripe bananas

Juice 1 lemon
4 oranges, peeled and sliced into rounds
3 tablespoons dark island rum (not Navy)

1. Preheat the oven to 180°C (350°F/Gas 4).
2. Make a syrup with the butter, orange juice, sugar, nutmeg and orange rind. It must be fairly thick.
3. Meanwhile peel the bananas and divide each into quarters, first cutting lengthways and then across.
4. Arrange the sliced bananas in a buttered baking dish large enough to hold them in one layer. Pour the lemon juice over.
5. Arrange the orange slices on top of the bananas. Cover with the syrup and bake for about 30 minutes. The bananas must not be overcooked.
6. Flambé with the rum and serve. Always warm the rum first.

Serves 6

BANANA AND ORANGE SALAD

3 ripe but firm bananas
Juice ½ lemon
2 oranges
Juice 1 small orange
2–3 teaspoons cane sugar
Handful of raisins
2 teaspoons brandy (optional)

1. Peel the bananas and cut them into thin slices. Place in a bowl, pour in the lemon juice and mix gently.
2. Peel the oranges and remove the pips. Cut up into neat pieces.
3. Mix together all the ingredients and serve.

Serves 4

BANANA AND RAISIN PUDDING

900 g (2 lb) ripe bananas
Juice 1 lemon
110 g (4 oz) demerara sugar
75 g (3 oz) unsalted butter, melted
170 g (6 oz) breadcrumbs
1 teaspoon baking powder
3 eggs, well beaten

75 g (3 oz) raisins
½ teaspoon freshly ground cinnamon
2 drops vanilla extract
Pinch salt
1 tablespoon light brown or dark rum (not navy)

1 Preheat the oven to 180°C (350°F/Gas 4).
2 Peel and mash the bananas. Add the lemon juice, sugar and melted butter and beat until creamy.
3 Mix the breadcrumbs with the baking powder and stir into the banana mixture. Blend well.
4 Stir in the beaten eggs, then add the remaining ingredients. Pour into a buttered dish. Cover loosely with foil.
5 Place the baking dish into another pan containing about 2.5 cm (1 inch) water. Bake for 1½–2 hours or until set. Cool slightly then serve.

Serves 6–8

BANANA FLAMBÉ

Only the best rum should be used for this wonderful but simple dessert. This is possibly one of the most popular dishes I have prepared for friends over the years.

50 g (2 oz) unsalted butter
110 g (4 oz) brown cane sugar
Juice 3 oranges
Juice 1 lime
Rind 1 orange, cut into thin slivers
4 ripe bananas
2 oranges, peeled and sliced into rounds
2 tablespoons rum
Freshly grated nutmeg to taste

1 Melt the butter in a frying pan and add the sugar, orange juice, lime juice and orange rind. Cook until a syrup is formed.
2 Peel the bananas and add them to the pan, turning over to coat all sides with the syrup. Cook until the bananas are slightly tender but still quite whole.
3 Add the orange slices and warm through.
4 Pour in the rum and flambé very briefly. Blow out the flames before all the alcohol evaporates and the bananas discolour.

5 Sprinkle the nutmeg over and serve while still warm. This goes well with double cream and is wonderful with a vanilla and coconut ice-cream.

Serves 4–6

BANANA OMELETTE

2 tablespoons Rose's lemon and lime marmalade
1 tablespoon water
4 eggs
1 large, ripe banana
Juice ½ lemon
2 teaspoons caster sugar
40 g (1½ oz) butter, softened
Pinch cinnamon
1 tablespoon island rum (preferably Dominican)
A little caster sugar for sprinkling

1 Gently heat the marmalade in a small saucepan with the water. Mix well. Remove from the heat but keep warm.
2 Beat the eggs until slightly frothy.
3 Pass the marmalade through a fine sieve and beat into the eggs.
4 Have your omelette pan on a low to moderate heat, greased with a very little unsalted butter.
5 Peel and very lightly mash the banana. Mix with the lemon juice, sugar, softened butter and cinnamon.
6 Pour the beaten eggs into the hot omelette pan and cook in the usual way. The omelette should not be runny.
7 Quickly stir the rum into the banana mixture, then place the mixture on half the omelette and fold over. Serve immediately, sprinkled with a little caster sugar.

Serves 2–3

BANANA PANCAKES

A simple but tasty dish, using up bananas that are overripe.

3 bananas
2 tablespoons soft brown cane sugar
1 egg, beaten
4 tablespoons self-raising flour
½ teaspoon freshly ground cinnamon

Zest ½ lime or lemon
Oil and butter for frying
A little sugar for sprinkling

1 Peel and mash the bananas in a bowl, add the sugar and blend well with a fork.
2 Beat in the egg, then beat in the flour, cinnamon and lime or lemon zest and mix thoroughly.
3 Heat the oil and butter in a frying pan on a medium to low heat. Make 4 or 6 pancakes, frying gently on both sides until golden brown.
4 Serve hot, with a very little sugar sprinkled on each if you wish.

Serves 4–6

BAKED BANANAS WITH RUM AND PASSION FRUIT SAUCE

Juice 3 passion fruit (see Techniques)
Juice 1 lemon
Grated rind and juice 1 large orange
Pinch ground cinnamon
75 g (3 oz) cane sugar
4 large or 8 small bananas – ripe but firm
2 tablespoons island rum, preferably dark
2 passion fruit, washed and cut in half, to garnish

1 Preheat the oven to 160°C (325°F/Gas 3).
2 Blend together in a small saucepan the passion fruit juice, lemon juice, orange rind and juice, cinnamon and sugar.
3 Quickly bring to the boil, lower the heat and cook until it reaches the consistency of a syrup. Then remove from the heat and allow to cool.
4 Peel the bananas, then slice each in half lengthways and arrange in one layer in a baking dish.
5 Blend the rum with the cool syrup and pour over the bananas.
6 Bake for 25 minutes, basting with the syrup in the baking dish. Arrange on separate dishes with half a passion fruit on each dish. Delicious on its own or with vanilla and coconut ice-cream.

Serves 4

CARIBBEAN HIGHLIGHT

Expensive but well worth it for a special occasion. The sauce can be made in advance.

1 large pineapple, with leaves intact
8 sapodillas, peeled and halved
3 mangosteens, peeled and carefully deseeded
2 tree tomatoes (tamarillos), peeled and sliced
2 mangoes, skinned, stoned and diced
1 large orange, segmented
2 guavas, peeled, deseeded and sliced
6 passion fruit
Juice 1 lemon
3 tablespoons Jamaican honey
Pinch grated cinnamon
2 tablespoons rum

1 Wash the pineapple and pat dry. Cut lengthways in half from the bottom towards the leaf fronds.
2 Carefully scoop out the flesh, leaving a shell of each half. Cut about a third of the pineapple flesh into cubes, retaining the balance for future use.
3 Letting loose your artistic flair, arrange all the fruit except the passion fruit in the pineapple shells.
4 Cut the passion fruit in half and scoop out the flesh and seeds into a small saucepan. Add to that the lemon juice, Jamaican honey, 2 tablespoons water, and cinnamon. Simmer, stirring, for 1–2 minutes.
5 Remove from the heat and leave until cold.
6 Add the rum and pour over the fruit in the pineapple shells.

Serves 10–12

MANGO AND GINGER SALAD

Allow 1–2 ripe but firm mangoes per person, according to size
170 g (6 oz) preserved ginger
8–10 cocktail cherries
1–2 tablespoons simple syrup (see page 241)
½ teaspoon freshly ground cinnamon
1 tablespoon island rum

Juice ½ lime or lemon
1 teaspoon grated lime or lemon rind

1. Peel and stone the mangoes and cut into cubes.
2. Place in a bowl and mix with all the other ingredients. Chill for 15–20 minutes.
3. Serve with cream if desired.

Serves 4

MANGO AND RUM SORBET

300 ml (½ pint) water
75 g (3 oz) caster sugar
2.5 cm (1 inch) cinnamon stick
3 allspice
Rind ½ lime
200–225 ml (7–8 fl oz) mango purée
Juice ½ lemon
3 tablespoons white rum (see Glossary)
2 size-3 egg whites, stiffly beaten

1. Bring the water to the boil with the sugar, cinnamon, allspice and lime rind. Lower the heat and simmer very gently for 3–5 minutes.
2. Remove from the heat and set aside for about 15 minutes, then strain through a fine strainer pressing the spices with your fingers to extract as much of the flavour as possible.
3. When completely cool stir in the mango purée, lemon juice and rum. Mix well.
4. Carefully fold in the stiffly beaten egg whites and then freeze. The sorbet should be taken out of the freezer and beaten with a wooden fork or whisked with a hand whisk every 20 minutes until creamy.

Serves 4–6

MANGO PUDDING

340 g (¾ lb) ripe mangoes (peeled and stoned weight)
Grated rind and juice 1 lemon
3 egg yolks
75 g (3 oz) caster sugar
50 g (2 oz) very fine cornmeal

½ teaspoon freshly grated nutmeg
2–3 drops natural almond essence
4 egg whites
Fine sea salt

1 Preheat the oven to 180°C (350°F/Gas 4).
2 Dice the mangoes into small pieces and put into a bowl with the lemon juice and rind.
3 Beat the egg yolks with the sugar until the sugar has almost dissolved.
4 Gradually pour in the fine cornmeal, blending well.
5 Add the nutmeg and the almond essence, then combine with the diced mango.
6 Whisk the egg whites with a pinch of salt until stiff and fold into the mixture.
7 Turn into a greased baking dish and bake for about 1¼–1½ hours or until set and lightly browned.

Serves 4–6

MANGO SAUCE

2 mangoes, peeled, stoned and chopped
75 g (3 oz) light brown cane sugar
1 tablespoon water
Piece vanilla pod or 3 drops natural vanilla essence
1 tablespoon West Indian rum or brandy

1 Thoroughly mash the mangoes to a pulp.
2 In a saucepan dissolve the sugar with the water over a medium heat, then add the mango pulp and the vanilla. Cook until fairly thick.
3 Remove from the heat and strain through a fine sieve, pressing with a wooden spoon. Return to the saucepan with the rum and cook for about 2 minutes, stirring.
4 Allow to cool before serving with a fruit salad of your choice or poured over ice-cream.

Serves 4–6

MANGO SOUFFLÉ

75 g (3 oz) unsalted butter
50 g (2 oz) fresh wholemeal breadcrumbs

900 g (2 lb) mango pulp, mixed with a little lime or lemon juice
110–170 g (4–6 oz) soft brown sugar (according to the sweetness of the mangoes)
Rind 1 lemon
1–2 drops natural vanilla extract
3 egg yolks, beaten
1 tablespoon dark island rum
5 egg whites, stiffly beaten

1 Preheat the oven to 190°C (375°F/Gas 5).
2 Melt the butter and gently brown the breadcrumbs.
3 Add the mango pulp, sugar, lemon rind, vanilla extract and lastly the beaten egg yolks. Mix well, keeping the heat as low as possible.
4 Remove from the heat, allow to cool slightly then add the rum.
5 Fold in the stiffly beaten egg whites and bake for about 30 minutes. Serve immediately.

Serves 6–8

MANGOSTEEN SORBET

An expensive dessert, but possibly one of the finest.

75 g (3 oz) caster sugar
2 teaspoons water
170 g (6 oz) puréed mangosteen (from about 10 fruits, peeled, stoned and sieved)
1 glass dry white wine
Juice ½ lemon
1 egg white, whisked until stiff

1 Heat the sugar and water to make a syrup, not too thick. Allow to cool.
2 Add to the syrup the puréed mangosteen, white wine and lemon juice. Mix thoroughly.
3 Fold in the whisked egg white. Combine well but carefully.
4 Freeze. Remove the mixture from the freezer every 30 minutes and beat with a wooden fork or whisk with a hard whisk.

Serves 4–6

ORANGE FRITTERS

1 quantity batter (see page 232)
6 oranges (of a reasonable size)
Oil for deep frying
Caster sugar for sprinkling
Grated rind 1 orange

1. Have your batter ready.
2. Peel the oranges, discarding as much of the white pith as possible, then slice into 1 cm (½ inch) circles. Carefully remove all the pips.
3. Heat the oil until almost boiling.
4. Dip each orange slice into the batter and fry until golden brown.
5. Drain on kitchen towels. Sprinkle with the caster sugar and orange rind and serve immediately.

Try serving with cream whipped with a little rum and caster sugar.

Serves 6

PAPAYA SARA

WITH TAMARILLO AND PASSION FRUIT SAUCE

A delightful and refreshing dessert. The following recipe is for two but will serve four with an extra pawpaw, an extra kiwi fruit, a passion fruit and a whole mango.

1 large ripe pawpaw
2 sapodillas
½ small mango, peeled and stoned
1 kiwi fruit
1 tamarillo
2 tablespoons Jamaican honey
Pinch cinnamon (a very small amount)
1 tablespoon port (the best you can afford)
1 passion fruit

1. Cut the pawpaw in half lengthways. Carefully scoop out the seeds into a bowl, but do not discard. Scoop out a little of the flesh into the same bowl.
2. Peel the sapodillas, cut each in half crossways and discard the stones. Cut each half again in two and place in a bowl.

3 Dice the mango into small pieces and add to the sapodillas.
4 Peel the kiwi fruit and slice it in thin rounds, then cut each round into 4 spear shapes. Set aside.
5 Peel the tamarillo, cut in half and scoop out the seeds into the same bowl as the pawpaw seeds. Finely chop half the tamarillo and add to the seeds. Dice the other half and add to the bowl with the sapodilla and mango.
6 Mix together the sapodilla, mango and the tamarillo pieces and fill each pawpaw half with an equal amount of the mixture. Place the pawpaw halves on individual serving plates.
7 Extracting as much of the juice as possible, sieve together the pawpaw flesh and seeds and the tamarillo flesh and seeds. Stir the honey, cinnamon and port into the sieved juice.
8 Cut the passion fruit in half and scoop out the flesh and seeds into the juice and honey mixture. Mix well.
9 Spoon an equal amount over each pawpaw half. Decorate with the kiwi fruit spears. Chill for 30 minutes before serving.

Serves 2

PEARS IN RUM AND ORANGE SAUCE

Juice 6 large oranges
1 stick cinnamon
6 cloves
Rind and juice 1 lemon
170 g (6 oz) brown sugar
6 ripe but firm pears
2 teaspoons arrowroot
3 tablespoons light brown rum
1 tablespoon orange liqueur

1 Bring the orange juice to the boil with the cinnamon, cloves, lemon juice and rind.
2 Reduce the heat and add the sugar. Stir over a low heat until dissolved.
3 Peel the pears, leaving on the stalks. Add them to the pan and simmer slightly covered for about 30 minutes. Keep turning the pears in the syrup.
4 Carefully remove the pears from the syrup and keep them warm.
5 Rapidly boil the syrup down by about a third if you think there is too much. Remove and discard the cinnamon and lemon peel.

6 Mix the arrowroot into a paste with a little orange juice and use to thicken the liquid in the pan. Stir in well to avoid any lumps.
7 Return the pears to the syrup. Baste them to coat evenly on all sides. Simmer for 2–3 minutes.
8 Pour in the rum and the orange liqueur. Remove from the heat and allow to cool slightly before serving.

Serves 6

PINEAPPLE AND ORTANIQUE SALAD

1 small ripe pineapple
5 ortaniques (or substitute mandarins)
2 teaspoons Cointreau
2 teaspoons caster sugar (optional)
1 teaspoon Angostura bitters
12 maraschino cherries

1 Peel and core the pineapple then cut the flesh into small cubes.
2 Peel, segment and deseed the ortaniques.
3 Place all the ingredients except the cherries into a salad bowl. Gently mix together.
4 Garnish with the cherries and serve chilled.

Serves 6

PINEAPPLE WITH MANGO AND BLACK PEPPER

75 g (3 oz) unsalted butter
8 slices (rounds) from a small pineapple
3 tablespoons cane sugar
Juice 1 orange
Juice ½ lemon
8–10 black peppercorns, freshly ground (or substitute allspice berries)
2 mangoes, peeled, stoned and sliced
Rum to flambé

1 Melt the butter and brown the pineapple slices on both sides. Be careful not to burn the butter.
2 Add the sugar and allow to dissolve.
3 Carefully remove the pineapple slices to a dish and keep warm.

4 Add the orange juice, lemon juice and ground peppercorns to the pan to make a sauce. Cook until the sauce is thick and syrupy.
5 Add the mango slices to the sauce and cook for 3 minutes.
6 Return the pineapple slices to the pan and warm through for a couple of minutes.
7 Arrange on a serving dish. Heat the rum, flambé and serve immediately.

Serves 4–6

BAKED TROPICAL FRUITS

For a large dinner party.

3 ripe but firm mangoes, peeled, stoned and cubed
3–4 bananas, cut into 2.5 cm (1 inch) lengths
1 small pineapple, peeled, cored and cubed
2 pawpaws, peeled and cubed
4 guavas, peeled, deseeded and quartered
4 tablespoons dark rum
110 g (4 oz) breadcrumbs
150 g (5 oz) brown sugar
2 tablespoons farine, roasted
Vanilla essence
50 g (2 oz) unsalted butter

1 Preheat the oven to 180°C (350°F/Gas 4).
2 Arrange the fruits in a shallow, buttered baking dish. Pour half the rum over.
3 Mix together the breadcrumbs, sugar, roasted farine, vanilla essence, remaining rum, and butter. Spread the mixture over the fruit.
4 Bake in a preheated oven for 20 minutes. This can be served hot or cold – serve with cream if cold.

Serves 12

TROPICAL FRUIT SALAD WITH CUSTARD APPLE PURÉE

You may wish to substitute whatever exotic fruits are available.

1–2 ripe custard apples (or substitute 175 ml (6 fl oz) soursop juice)

Juice ½ lemon
2 tablespoons simple syrup (see page 241)
1 small ripe pawpaw, peeled, deseeded and sliced
1 guava, peeled and thinly sliced
1 banana, peeled and sliced
1 kiwi fruit, peeled and sliced

1 Peel and deseed the custard apples then pass the white flesh through a sieve and combine with the lemon juice and simple syrup.
2 Arrange the prepared fruit on a serving dish and cover with the custard apple purée.
3 Chill for 30 minutes before serving with any ice-cream of your choice.

Serves 4–6

Breads, Cakes and Puddings

BAKES

Bakes are possibly one of the most popular forms of bread in the Caribbean. They are basically a fried flour and yeast dough, though they may also be gently roasted on a charcoal fire or baked in the oven. I have, in this recipe, omitted the lard, and indeed many Caribbean cooks prefer not to use lard in the preparation of the dough.

225 g (½ lb) flour
2 teaspoons baking powder
1 teaspoon sugar
½ teaspoon fine sea salt
Water
Oil for frying

1. Sift together all the dry ingredients into a bowl.
2. Add water a little at a time to make a soft dough. Turn on to a floured surface and knead.
3. Tear off pieces of dough the size of a large lemon or small orange. Roll into balls then form into flat circles.
4. Heat a little oil in a heavy frying pan and fry the bakes on both sides until golden brown.
5. Keep them warm in a low oven while you fry the remainder. Serve while still warm.

Serves 4–5

CORNMEAL BAKES

An unusual but excellent 'bread' for breakfast with scrambled eggs. Goes well with marmalade when still hot.

75 g (3 oz) fine to medium cornmeal
150 g (5 oz) plain flour
2½ teaspoons baking powder
¼ teaspoon bicarbonate of soda (baking soda)
1½ teaspoons fine sea salt

2 teaspoons sugar
50 g (2 oz) butter
Approximately 150 ml (¼ pint) water

1 Preheat the oven to 180°C (350°F/Gas 4).
2 In a bowl combine the cornmeal, flour, baking powder, bicarbonate of soda, salt and sugar. Using a fork or fingers, mix well.
3 Thoroughly rub in the butter.
4 Add enough water to make a firm but smooth dough. Set aside for 5–10 minutes.
5 Divide into 10 equal pieces, knead each piece into a ball between your hands and set aside for another 10 minutes.
6 Flatten each ball into circles about 0.5–1 cm (¼–½ inch) thick. Place on greased baking sheets and bake for 25–30 minutes.

CASSAVA BREAD

Cassava, like 'boucan' meat (meat which has been preserved to take on journeys), was handed down to us by the Carib Indians.

There is nothing like the aroma, first thing in the morning, of freshly roasted coffee and cassava bread drifting on the breeze of a tropical dawn in some small village.

The juice is extracted from the grated flesh of the cassava, which is then dried in the sun, shaped into flat large breads, and slowly baked over an open wood fire or charcoal.

The cassava used in this book is the sweet variety and not the bitter kind (see Glossary).

110 g (4 oz) lard or margarine
340 g (¾ lb) cassava root, grated, then wrung in a cloth to extract the juice
150 g (5 oz) coconut, freshly grated (see Techniques)
50 g (2 oz) wholemeal flour
Sea salt to taste (possibly never used by the Caribs)
Milk or water to bind if necessary

1 Preheat the oven to 220°C (425°F/Gas 7).
2 In a large bowl, mix all the ingredients into a dough, using a little liquid to bind if necessary.
3 Turn out onto a floured surface and knead until fairly firm.
4 Divide into four and roll each piece into a ball, then flatten out into disks about 0.5 cm (¼ inch) thick.
5 Bake for about 25–30 minutes or until slightly brown.

Great in the morning with black coffee – Blue Mountain or Café Noir, of course!

Serves 8

CORNMEAL BREAD

170 g (6 oz) fine or medium cornmeal
150 g (5 oz) plain flour
2 teaspoons baking powder
Pinch fine sea salt
25 g (1 oz) caster sugar
2 eggs
75 g (3 oz) unsalted butter, melted
Approximately 150 ml (¼ pint) milk

1 Preheat the oven to 190° (375°F/Gas 5).
2 Sift the dry ingredients into a mixing bowl.
3 In another bowl, beat the eggs then thoroughly blend in the melted butter. Gradually pour in the milk, whisking all the time.
4 Next beat the egg and milk mixture into the dry ingredients. Blend thoroughly.
5 Transfer the mixture to a well-greased 23 cm (9 inch) loaf tin and bake for about 1 hour or until a sharp instrument inserted in the centre comes out clean.

Delicious hot with jam or marmalade.

FLOATS

A recipe from the island of Trinidad for one of the most popular yeast breads in the Caribbean.

2 heaped teaspoons dried yeast
1 teaspoon brown sugar
400 g (14 oz) plain flour (or sifted wholemeal)
1½ teaspoons salt
110 g (4 oz) lard
Oil for frying

1 Mix the yeast and sugar in a bowl with 3 tablespoons warm water and leave to stand in a warm place until the mixture bubbles and almost doubles in quantity.
2 Sift the flour and salt into a mixing bowl and with your fingers rub in the lard.

3 Pour in the yeast mixture with sufficient warm water to make a smooth, stiff dough.
4 Turn the dough out onto a floured surface and knead for a good 12 minutes, or until the dough is smooth without being too elastic. You may need to flour your hands or the surface occasionally but do not use too much flour.
5 Cover with a clean dry cloth and set aside until the dough doubles in size.
6 Separate the dough and roll into at least 18 balls (roughly the size of a small orange). Set aside on greaseproof paper or a floured board in a warm place until doubled in size.
7 In a heavy, large frying pan, heat the oil until smoking.
8 On a floured surface, using your fingers, flatten each ball into a flat circle and fry on both sides until golden brown.
9 Drain on kitchen paper but keep warm until all the balls have been fried and you are ready to serve.

Makes 18

MASTIFF BREAD

Another popular West Indian bread; each island has its own recipe. This one is from the island of Dominica – with slight alterations.

25 g (1 oz) fresh yeast or 15 g (½ oz) dried yeast
Approximately 900 ml (1½ pints) warm water
2 teaspoons cane sugar
1.5 kg (3 lb) strong white flour
1 level tablespoon salt
110 g (4 oz) butter or margarine

1 Follow the method for wheatmeal bread (see page 222) up to the end of stage 5, adding the sugar with the flour and salt.
2 Instead of using loaf tins, shape the dough into two loaves. Place them on a large greased baking sheet about 5–7.5 cm (2–3 inches) apart.
3 Proceed as from stage 7 of wheatmeal bread.

ROTI

A flat dough bread of Indian origin, similar to parathas, which was introduced to the Caribbean by the East Indians transported to the area as indentured labour. The flat bread is filled with curried mixtures, folded, and eaten either as a main meal or snack – it is also very suitable for parties and carnival jump-up. The greatest fun is to eat it with thumb and fingers.

The following recipe was given to me by a friend.

450 g (1 lb) self-raising flour (wholemeal can be used)
1 teaspoon sea salt
1½ teaspoons baking powder
25 g (1 oz) lard
25 g (1 oz) margarine
Vegetable oil for frying

1. Sift all the dry ingredients into a large bowl and rub in the fats.
2. Knead into a firm dough with a little water. Cover with a cloth and leave in a warm place for 45 minutes.
3. Knead again for a good 5 minutes then divide into 12 balls. Cover these and leave for a further 30 minutes.
4. Roll or shape each ball into a disk about 25–30 cm (10–12 inches) in diameter. They must be as thin as possible without tearing.
5. Heat a roti pan or a very shallow, flat-bottomed, heavy frying pan over a medium heat. Water dropped on the surface should splutter.
6. Using a clean cloth, spread a very thin layer of oil on the pan, leave for about 30 seconds.
7. Now fry your roti one at a time. Place the first roti into the greased pan and cook for 1 minute on one side without turning.
8. Spread a thin layer of oil on the upper side – then turn, using a wooden spatula. Avoid tearing the dough.
9. Cook on the second side for 1–1½ minutes without browning.
10. You may need to turn the roti to cook it on the first side again, but spread it with a little oil before doing so and cook it for no longer than 1 minute.
11. As you take the roti from the pan wrap them in a clean cloth; one on top of the other in the same cloth until they are all cooked. They will keep in the cloth until they are needed but try to eat them on the same day.
12. Roti can be heated up quickly in a flat pan or a moderately heated oven but they must be covered in the oven if they are not to become too crusty and dried-up.

Makes 12

WHEATMEAL BREAD

For the most successful breads I have made, I have always used fresh yeast, as in this recipe, but you can substitute 20 g (¾ oz) dried yeast. If you want a crusty surface brush with saltwash.

Approximately 450–600 ml (¾–1 pint) warm water
40 g (1½ oz) fresh yeast
1 level tablespoon salt
675 g (1½ lb) wholemeal flour
675 g (1½ lb) strong white flour
50 g (2 oz) margarine

1 Dissolve the yeast in 300 ml (½ pint) of the warm water and set aside in a warm place for about 15–20 minutes or until it bubbles.
2 Add the flour and salt to the yeast mixture then rub in the margarine.
3 Knead into a dough, adding a little warm water as necessary, until a tight dough is formed.
4 Turn out onto a lightly floured surface and continue to knead until the dough is firm and pliable but not too stiff or sticky.
5 Return the dough to the bowl, cover and set aside in a warm place until doubled in size. Knead again on a lightly floured surface.
6 Divide into two and place in two warm, greased 23 cm (9 inch) loaf tins.
7 Cover with a clean cloth, put in a warm place and allow to rise again. Meanwhile preheat the oven to 230°C (450°F/Gas 8).
8 Place the loaf tins on the centre shelf of the oven and bake for 25 minutes. Then reduce the temperature to 220°C (425°F/Gas 7) and bake for a further 15–20 minutes.
9 Test the loaves by tapping the underside – if the bread has a hollow ring it is done. Turn out of the tins and cool on a wire tray.

CORNMEAL FRITTERS

150 g (5 oz) fine cornmeal
300 ml (½ pint) milk
2 size-3 eggs, beaten
Freshly ground black pepper to taste
Sea salt to taste
Oil for frying

1 Slowly pour the cornmeal into the milk, beating continuously.
2 Beat in the eggs, black pepper and salt. Beat until smooth.
3 Heat the oil almost to boiling.
4 Drop the cornmeal batter a spoonful at a time into the oil and fry until golden brown.
5 Remove each fritter individually with a perforated spoon. Drain well and serve immediately.
6 Can be served with jam or as an accompaniment to a savoury dish.

Serves 4

CORNMEAL DUMPLINGS

110 g (4 oz) fine cornmeal
150 g (5 oz) plain flour, sifted (or use wholemeal flour)
1½ teaspoons baking powder
1½ teaspoons fine sea salt
½ teaspoon freshly ground black pepper
75 g (3 oz) butter
1 egg, beaten
Milk or water to bind

1 In a bowl, mix together the cornmeal, flour, baking powder, salt and pepper.
2 Rub in the butter then mix in the egg.
3 Add enough milk or water to make a pliable dough.
4 Flour your hands and separate the dough into several pieces – any shape you wish. Cook in a stew or sauce of your choice.

Serves 6–8

PLAIN FLOUR DUMPLINGS

225 g (½ lb) plain flour
Sea salt to taste (roughly 1–1½ teaspoons)
Water to bind

1 Put the salt and flour in a bowl.
2 Make into a dough with some water, without making it too sticky.
3 Shape into small balls or whatever creative shapes take your fancy.
4 Cook in any stew or soup which requires dumplings.

Serves 4–6

BANANA LOAF

And there is nothing like it, spread with either marmalade or hot guava jam, or served on its own.

225 g (½ lb) plain flour
½ teaspoon salt
1½ teaspoons baking powder
½ teaspoon bicarbonate of soda (baking soda)
110 g (4 oz) butter
170 g (6 oz) caster sugar
2 size-3 eggs
500 g (1 lb 2 oz) ripe bananas (weight with skin on)
50 g (2 oz) walnuts, chopped
Few drops vanilla extract (optional)

1 Preheat the oven to 180°C (350°F/Gas 4).
2 Sift together all the dry ingredients, except the sugar and walnuts.
3 Cream together the butter and sugar, then beat in the eggs one at a time.
4 Peel and mash the bananas, add to the mixture and stir well.
5 Add the sifted ingredients a little at a time. Blend well.
6 Mix in the walnuts and the vanilla extract, if using.
7 Pour into a well-greased 23 cm (9 inch) loaf tin and bake for about 50–60 minutes or until a sharp instrument inserted into the loaf comes out clean. Leave in the tin for 5–10 minutes then turn on to a rack to cool.

CHOCOLATE, RUM AND NUT CAKE

50 g (2 oz) fresh breadcrumbs
2 tablespoons island rum
110 g (4 oz) caster sugar
110 g (4 oz) unsalted butter
4 egg yolks
4 level tablespoons grated bitter chocolate (Menier or similar)
170 g (6 oz) unsalted cashew nuts, chopped
Pinch freshly grated nutmeg
3 tablespoons plain flour
1 teaspoon baking powder
5 egg whites, stiffly beaten

1 Preheat the oven to 180°C (350°F/Gas 4).
2 Put the breadcrumbs to soak in the rum.
3 Meanwhile, cream the sugar and butter together, then beat in the egg yolks one at a time.
4 Add the grated chocolate. Mix thoroughly.
5 Add the cashew nuts, then the breadcrumbs and rum mixture and the nutmeg.
6 Sift together the flour and baking powder and mix in.
7 Finally fold in the stiffly whipped egg whites.
8 Turn into a greased, deep 20 cm (8 inch) round cake tin and bake for 50–60 minutes or until well risen. Test with a skewer or similar implement. Leave in the tin for 5–10 minutes then turn out on to a rack to cool.

If you wish you may serve with a mixture of finely chopped nuts and chocolate sprinkled on the cake.

COCONUT AND SWEET POTATO CAKE

225 g (½ lb) sweet potatoes, peeled, scrubbed with lime or lemon and grated (see Techniques)
Juice and rind ½ lemon
110 g (4 oz) desiccated coconut
75 g (3 oz) sultanas
3 eggs
110 g (4 oz) caster sugar
170 g (6 oz) butter, melted
225 g (½ lb) wholemeal flour
1½ teaspoons baking powder
½ teaspoon bicarbonate of soda
Pinch nutmeg
Pinch cinnamon
½ teaspoon natural almond essence
50g (2 oz) pistachio nuts, finely chopped

1 Preheat the oven to 180°C (350°F/Gas 4).
2 Mix together the grated sweet potatoes and the lemon juice then add the desiccated coconut and the sultanas.
3 Beat the eggs with the sugar and melted butter. When well beaten add the desiccated coconut and potato mixture.
4 Sift together the dry ingredients, including the lemon rind, and combine with the other mixture. Add the almond essence and finely chopped nuts.

5 Transfer to a deep, 20 cm (8 inch) round cake tin lined with greaseproof paper and bake for about 1¼–1½ hours or until a sharp instrument inserted in the middle comes out clean. Leave in the tin for 5–10 minutes then turn out on to a rack to cool.

COCONUT COOKIES

I could never get enough of these as a child and I believe most children who like coconut will love them.

110 g (4 oz) butter
110 g (4 oz) caster sugar
3 eggs
1 coconut, freshly grated (see Techniques) or substitute 340 g (¾ lb) desiccated coconut
225 g (½ lb) wholemeal flour
2 teaspoons baking powder
1 teaspoon bicarbonate of soda (baking soda)
1 level teaspoon salt
A little milk if necessary

1 Preheat the oven to 200°C (400°F/Gas 6).
2 Cream the butter and sugar together until light and fluffy. Beat in the eggs one at a time.
3 Sift together the dry ingredients and add a little at a time, mixing well. If too dry add a little milk.
4 Turn out onto a floured surface, knead briefly then roll out to about 0.5 cm (¼ inch) thick.
5 Cut in rounds, place on a greased baking sheet and bake for about 20–30 minutes or until lightly coloured.

Makes approximately 30

COCONUT TURNOVERS

One of the several little cakes and pastries sold in small shops, or by street vendors from their wooden trays or wicker baskets on street corners and in the market places of the Caribbean.

For the filling:
White or light brown sugar, equal in weight to the grated coconut
100 ml (4 fl oz) water
1 coconut, freshly grated (see Techniques)

1 teaspoon natural almond or vanilla essence
1 teaspoon grated lemon peel
Pinch powdered cinnamon

For the casing:
50 g (2 oz) caster sugar
110 g (4 oz) unsalted butter
1 egg
450 g (1 lb) plain flour
1 teaspoon salt
25 g (1 oz) fresh yeast or 15 g (½ oz) dried yeast
175 ml (6 fl oz) lukewarm milk
A little caster sugar for sprinkling

1 In a heavy saucepan, over a medium heat, mix the sugar and water and bring to the boil. Mix in the coconut thoroughly.
2 Lower the heat and cook to a thick consistency, stirring often. (This is very similar to a coconut jam or sweet made on the islands and could be served as such with hot bread.)
3 Remove from the heat and stir in the essence, lemon peel and cinnamon, then set aside to cool.
4 Meanwhile, in a bowl, cream the sugar with 75 g (3 oz) of the unsalted butter, then beat in the eggs one at a time, blending well.
5 Thoroughly mix in the flour and salt.
6 Mix the yeast with about two tablespoons of tepid water, add to it the lukewarm milk and mix in with the dough mixture. Now knead until smooth.
7 Cover and set aside to rise in a warm place for 30–40 minutes.
8 Preheat the oven to 200°C (400°F/Gas 6).
9 Divide the dough into about 20 equal pieces. Shape each piece quickly into a ball and roll out as thinly as possible on a floured surface. Avoid using too much flour. Each piece should be rolled out in a circular shape.
10 Place an equal amount of coconut filling on each, fold to form a semi-circle, and pinch the edges to close them, using the thumb and first finger or a fork.
11 Melt the remaining butter and use to brush the turnovers (or you may prefer to use a beaten egg).
12 Arrange on one or two greased baking sheets, and bake for 30–40 minutes or until golden brown. For the last few minutes of baking sprinkle a little caster sugar over each turnover.

Very ripe plantains or bananas can equally well be used as a filling for turnovers. Plantains or bananas should be quartered by being cut lengthwise and then crosswise (see Techniques).

Makes 20

GINGERBREAD

340 g (¾ lb) strong white flour
2 teaspoons baking powder
½ teaspoon bicarbonate of soda (baking soda)
1 teaspoon freshly ground allspice
⅓ teaspoon freshly grated nutmeg
½ teaspoon salt
225 g (½ lb) butter
110 g (4 oz) soft brown cane sugar
100 g (4 fl oz) cane molasses
100 ml (4 fl oz) evaporated milk
2 eggs, well beaten
60 g (2¼ oz) fresh ginger, grated (weight with any fibrous bits discarded)

1 Preheat the oven to 180°C (350°F/Gas 4).
2 Sift together the flour, baking powder, bicarbonate, allspice, nutmeg and salt into a large mixing bowl.
3 Melt the butter in a saucepan and blend in the sugar, molasses and evaporated milk. Remove from the heat and allow to cool.
4 Blend in the beaten eggs.
5 Combine together the sifted ingredients, molasses mixture and ginger. Mix well.
6 Pour into a greased 23 cm (9 inch) loaf tin and bake for about 1 hour or until a sharp instrument inserted into the loaf comes out dry. Leave in the tin for 5–10 minutes then turn on to a rack to cool.

LEMON SPONGE BASE

110 g (4 oz) wholemeal flour
2 level teaspoons baking powder
4 eggs, separated
Juice and finely grated rind ½ lemon
75 g (3 oz) caster sugar
Few drops natural vanilla extract

1 Preheat the oven to 180°C (350°F/Gas 4).
2 Sift the flour and baking powder into a bowl, emptying any bran left in the sieve into the bowl.
3 Whisk together the egg yolks, lemon rind and caster sugar until creamy, then add the lemon juice and vanilla extract. Mix well.
4 Gradually mix the sifted ingredients into the beaten egg yolks.
5 Beat the egg whites until stiff and fold into the mixture.
6 Bake in a greased and lined 25 cm (10 inch) sponge cake tin for 30 minutes or until well risen and lightly browned.

MANGO AND GINGER CAKE

110 g (4 oz) caster sugar
110 g (4 oz) butter, melted
2 eggs, beaten
½ teaspoon ground ginger
¼ teaspoon freshly ground allspice
¼ teaspoon freshly grated nutmeg
Pinch salt
225 g (½ lb) strong white flour (or sifted wholemeal)
2 teaspoons baking powder
½ teaspoon bicarbonate of soda (baking soda)
3 small, ripe mangoes, peeled, stoned and chopped
50 g (2 oz) crystallized ginger, finely chopped

1 Preheat the oven to 190°C (375°F/Gas 5).
2 Beat together the sugar and butter until creamy. Beat in the eggs.
3 Sift together the ground ginger, allspice, nutmeg, salt, flour, baking powder and soda.
4 Add to the creamed mixture. Mix well, then add the mangoes and crystallized ginger.
5 Pour into a deep, 20 cm (8 inch) cake tin, which has been lined with greaseproof paper.
6 Bake in the oven until a sharp instrument inserted into the centre of the cake comes out dry (about 1¼–1½ hours). Leave in the tin for 5–10 minutes then turn out on to a rack to cool.

NUT AND RAISIN LOAF

225 g (½ lb) plain flour
2 teaspoons baking powder
½ teaspoon bicarbonate of soda (baking soda)

¼ teaspoon salt
75 g (3 oz) caster sugar
Approximately 100 ml (4 fl oz) milk
2 eggs, beaten
75 g (3 oz) mixed nuts, chopped
110 g (4 oz) raisins
½ teaspoon natural almond extract

1 Preheat the oven to 160°C (325°F/Gas 3).
2 Sift together the flour, baking powder, soda and salt into a bowl. Mix in the sugar.
3 Stir in a little milk at a time. Blend well, then mix in the eggs.
4 Now mix in the nuts, raisins and almond extract.
5 Pour into a greased 23 cm (9 inch) tin.
6 Bake in the centre of the oven for 1¼–1½ hours or until a skewer inserted in the centre comes out dry. Leave in the tin for 5–10 minutes then turn out onto a rack to cool. Delicious served hot with jam.

RUM AND CARROT LOAF

3 eggs, separated
50 g (2 oz) vanilla sugar (see Techniques)
50 g (2 oz) wholemeal breadcrumbs
110 g (4 oz) almonds, finely chopped or ground
1 teaspoon freshly ground allspice
2 tablespoons rum (preferably a dark rum from the Caribbean)
225 g (½ lb) carrots, scraped and grated
1 tablespoon dried orange peel, finely chopped (see Techniques)
¼ teaspoon freshly grated nutmeg (optional)

1 Preheat the oven to 190°C (375°F/Gas 5).
2 Beat the egg yolks with the sugar until creamy.
3 Mix in the breadcrumbs, almonds, allspice and rum.
4 Now mix in the grated carrots and orange peel.
5 Beat the egg whites stiffly to form peaks, and fold them into the mixture.
6 Pour into a greased 20 cm (8 inch) loaf tin, sprinkle with the nutmeg if using, and bake for 45–60 minutes or until a skewer inserted in the centre comes out dry. Leave in the tin for 5–10 minutes then turn onto a rack to cool.

RICH SHORTCRUST PASTRY

170 g (6 oz) plain or wholemeal flour
½ teaspoon freshly ground cinnamon
1 egg, beaten
½ teaspoon freshly ground mace
40 g (1½ oz) caster sugar
50 g (2 oz) butter

1. Sift together the flour and cinnamon onto a wooden board or work surface.
2. Make a hollow in the centre and put in the egg, mace and sugar.
3. Cut the butter into small pieces and scatter over the flour.
4. Mix thoroughly with your fingers.
5. Form into a ball, refrigerate for about 1 hour, then roll out.
6. Use to line a pie dish and bake as directed in the recipe.

SAVOURY SHORTCRUST PASTRY

225 g (½ lb) plain or wholemeal flour
½ teaspoon freshly ground allspice
¼–½ teaspoon freshly ground black pepper
Pinch freshly ground cinnamon
½ teaspoon salt
110 g (4 oz) lard, butter or margarine
Iced water to bind

1. Sift the flour, spices and salt into a bowl.
2. Cut the fat into pieces and work into the flour with a knife or fork until it makes a finely crumbled mixture.
3. Add water a little at a time, still using the fork or knife to work thoroughly, until the dough is well mixed, but not sticky.
4. Form into a ball, refrigerate for about 1 hour, then roll out. One of the secrets of making successful pastry is to avoid handling the dough with warm hands, so work in a cool part of the kitchen.
5. Bake as directed in the recipe or pre-bake as directed below.

Makes sufficient for 1 double-crust pie or 2 pie shells

BAKED PIE SHELL

170 g (6 oz) plain flour
Pinch salt

25 g (1 oz) caster sugar
25 g (1 oz) lard
50 g (2 oz) butter
1 small egg yolk
2–3 tablespoons iced water
(A pinch of grated nutmeg or powdered cinnamon can be sifted with the flour)

1. Sift the flour and salt into a large, chilled mixing bowl. Add the sugar.
2. Cut the lard and butter into small pieces and scatter over the flour. Make a well in the centre and drop in the egg yolk. Mix with the finger tips.
3. Add 2 tablespoons of iced water and mix to form a dough. If the mixture is still slightly crumbly add a little more.
4. Form into a ball, sprinkle all over with a little flour, and wrap in waxed paper, strong cellophane or greaseproof paper. Refrigerate for 45–60 minutes.
5. Grease a 23 cm (9 inch) pie tin or dish.
6. Remove the dough from the refrigerator. Unwrap, place on a lightly floured board or marble slab, sprinkle with a little flour and roll out into a circle about 30–32 cm (12–13 inches) in diameter.
7. Carefully lift the dough and place over the pie dish. Gently press into place. Cut off any excess dough, but leave about 1–1.5 cm (½–¾ inch) hanging over the rim to allow for slight shrinkage during cooking.
8. Refrigerate again for 45–60 minutes, and preheat the oven to 190°C (375°F/Gas 5).
9. Remove the pie shell from the refrigerator, carefully mould a sheet of greaseproof paper over it and fill with dried beans. Place in the oven and bake for about 12–14 minutes.
10. Remove the beans and greaseproof paper (save the beans to use again). Continue to bake for a further 8–10 minutes. (Watch for excessive browning, especially round the rim, since you may be cooking the shell further with its contents.)
11. Remove from the oven and allow to cool before filling.

BATTER

FOR PANCAKES AND FRITTERS

110 g (4 oz) plain flour
Pinch salt

A little powdered cinnamon
1 egg, beaten
150 ml (¼ pint) milk

1 Sift the flour and salt into a bowl and form a well in the centre.
2 Stir into the well the cinnamon, egg and milk then mix thoroughly, using a wire whisk.
3 Place on the lower shelf of a refrigerator for about 30 minutes before using.

Makes 6–8 pancakes

BREAD AND BANANA PUDDING

A delicious dish, well worth trying, which is best served slightly warm.

5 slices wholemeal bread
450 ml (¾ pint) coconut cream (see Techniques)
3 eggs
110–170 g (4–6 oz) caster sugar
½ teaspoon natural vanilla essence
50 g (2 oz) unsalted butter, melted
2 tablespoons dark rum
10 cocktail cherries, chopped
50 g (2 oz) raisins
50 g (2 oz) walnuts, chopped
Pinch of salt
2 ripe bananas
Freshly grated nutmeg
Roasted coconut (see Techniques)

1 Preheat the oven to 180°C (350°F/Gas 4).
2 Soak the bread in the coconut cream.
3 Meanwhile, whisk together the eggs and sugar until the sugar has almost dissolved.
4 Beat in the essence, melted butter and rum. Mix in the cherries, raisins, walnuts and a little salt.
5 Stir the soaked bread and remaining coconut milk into the egg mixture. Pour half the mixture into a greased baking dish.
6 Peel and thinly slice the bananas and arrange evenly in the baking

dish. Cover with the remainder of the mixture. Sprinkle with grated nutmeg and roasted coconut.

7 Bake for approximately 1½ hours or until set.

Serves 4–6

SWEET BREADFRUIT PUDDING

An excellent way to use up ripe breadfruit, when they are much cheaper to buy.

110 g (4 oz) butter
170 g (6 oz) soft brown sugar
2 eggs, beaten
1 ripe breadfruit (about 900 g (2 lb)), peeled, cored and pounded
150 ml (¼ pint) single cream (or coconut milk – see Techniques)
Grated rind 1 lemon
1 teaspoon natural vanilla extract
150 g (5 oz) flour
1 teaspoon baking powder
Pinch of salt
Freshly grated nutmeg

1 Preheat the oven to 160°C (325°F/Gas 3).
2 Beat together the butter and sugar until creamy then gradually pour in the beaten eggs.
3 Gradually blend the pounded ripe breadfruit with the egg and butter mixture. Stir in the cream. Add the lemon rind and vanilla extract.
4 Sift together the dry ingredients and fold into the mixture. Blend well.
5 Transfer to a greased shallow dish. Bake for approximately 1 hour or until firm. Allow to cool before serving.

CORNMEAL AND FARINE PUDDING

450 ml (¾ pint) milk
150 ml (¼ pint) single cream
1 vanilla pod
7.5 cm (3 inch) cinnamon stick
Rind 1 lime or lemon
110 g (4 oz) farine
50 g (2 oz) fine cornmeal

150 g (5 oz) caster sugar
5 egg yolks, beaten
Freshly grated nutmeg

1 Preheat the oven to 160°C (325°F/Gas 3).
2 In a non-stick pan over a very low heat bring the milk, cream, vanilla, cinnamon stick and citrus rind to the boil. Simmer on the lowest heat possible for about 15 minutes to extract the flavours of the spices.
3 Whilst still on the heat, remove the vanilla pod, cinnamon stick and citrus rind. (The vanilla pod may be left to dry and used at least once more.)
4 Gradually stir in the farine, cornmeal and caster sugar and cook for a further 15 minutes, stirring occasionally.
5 Remove from the heat and slowly add the beaten eggs to the farine mixture. Blend thoroughly.
6 Pour into a buttered baking dish, sprinkle with grated nutmeg and place the dish in a baking tin which is two-thirds full of water.
7 Bake for 20–30 minutes or until set. Allow to cool then cut into squares. This could also be served hot as a dessert after a light meal.

Serves 4–6

FARINE AND BANANA PUDDING

225 g (½ lb) farine
150 g (5 oz) caster sugar
½ teaspoon freshly ground allspice
¼ teaspoon freshly ground cinnamon
¼ teaspoon freshly grated nutmeg
½ teaspoon salt
Grated rind 1 lemon
Grated rind ½ orange
2 large ripe bananas
300 ml (½ pint) milk or coconut milk (see Techniques)
2 eggs
½ teaspoon vanilla extract

1 Preheat the oven to 180°C (350°F/Gas 4).
2 In a bowl mix together the farine, sugar, allspice, cinnamon, nutmeg, salt and citrus rinds.

3 Peel and slice the bananas and then add them to the farine mixture.
4 Beat together the milk, eggs and vanilla extract. Pour over the dry ingredients and mix thoroughly.
5 Pour the mixture into a well-greased baking dish and bake for 50 minutes or until golden brown and set. Serve hot or cold. A good teatime pudding.

Serves 4–6

CREAMY RICE AND COCONUT MILK PUDDING

Approximately 750–900 ml (1¼–1½ pints) milk
5 cm (2 inch) cinnamon stick
7.5 cm (3 inch) strip lemon rind
75 g (3 oz) coconut cream (from a block)
50 g (2 oz) pudding rice
50 g (2 oz) caster sugar
Freshly grated nutmeg
Pinch of salt
Butter for dotting

1 Preheat the oven to 140°C (275°F/Gas 1).
2 Put half the milk, the cinnamon and the lemon rind into a saucepan and simmer gently for about 12 minutes.
3 Add the piece of coconut cream. Stir continuously until it melts. Remove from the heat and discard the cinnamon and lemon peel.
4 Stir in enough remaining milk to make the mixture up to 750 ml (1¼ pints).
5 Put the rice into a baking dish with the sugar, nutmeg and salt. Stir in the milk and coconut mixture.
6 Bake for 20–30 minutes then remove from the oven and stir well. Dot with butter and sprinkle with a little nutmeg.
7 Bake for another 1–1¼ hours (I personally prefer it creamy rather than firm). Serve with cream if you so wish.

Serves 4

SWEET POTATO PUDDING (1)

2 eggs, well beaten
225 g (½ lb) soft brown sugar

1 large and 1 small tin evaporated milk
75 g (3 oz) self-raising flour
50 g (2 oz) unsalted butter, melted
110 g (4 oz) currants
¼ teaspoon freshly grated nutmeg
½ teaspoon powdered cinnamon
¾ teaspoon natural vanilla extract
675 g (1½ lb) sweet potatoes, grated
50 g (2 oz) desiccated coconut (optional)

1 Heat the oven to 190°C (375°F/Gas 5).
2 Beat together the eggs and brown sugar. Whip in the evaporated milk. Continue to beat until the sugar dissolves.
3 Mix in the flour, butter and currants. Mix thoroughly. Add the nutmeg, cinnamon and vanilla extract.
4 Now add the grated potatoes and mix thoroughly.
5 Pour into a buttered baking dish and bake for 45–50 minutes or until brown. After about 15 minutes in the oven sprinkle with the desiccated coconut if using.

Serves 6

SWEET POTATO PUDDING (2)

6 medium sweet potatoes approximately 900 g (2 lb)
4 eggs, separated
225 g (½ lb) brown sugar, pounded in a mortar
110 g (4 oz) butter, melted
175 ml (6 fl oz) milk or evaporated milk
Pinch of salt
½ teaspoon powdered cinnamon
Freshly grated nutmeg, mixed with a little brown sugar

1 Preheat the oven to 180°C (350°F/Gas 4).
2 Wash the potatoes and boil them in their skins until cooked. Test with a sharp instrument. Drain and peel, then rub through a sieve into a bowl.
3 Lightly beat the egg yolks and add to the sieved potato, together with the sugar, melted butter, milk, salt and cinnamon. Mix well.
4 Beat the egg whites until stiff then fold in.
5 Pour the mixture into a buttered roasting tin. Sprinkle the nutmeg and sugar over it and bake for about 1¼ hours or until brown on top. Serve hot or warm, or leave until cold and cut into squares.

Fruit Beverages and Rum Punches

Drinking is part of the joy of the Caribbean: from sparkling fresh spring water in rainforests, freshly roasted black coffee in the mornings followed by freshly squeezed citrus fruit picked in mountain valleys, to lime and lemon squash in a bar or hotel, or rum drunk at any time, any place in little rum shops – at marriage, birth, confirmation and death, or at jump-up carnival time. Here are some of those drinks for all occasions.

SIMPLE SYRUP

450 g (1 lb) very light brown cane sugar
600 ml (1 pint) water
2.5 cm (1 inch) cinnamon stick
Rind 1 lime

1. Combine the sugar and water in a saucepan and bring to the boil.
2. Reduce the heat immediately before the liquid boils over. Add the cinnamon stick and lime rind, then simmer uncovered for 10 minutes.
3. Allow to cool, then bottle. Store at room temperature.

Makes approximately 2 70 cl bottles

PASSION FRUIT DRINK

450 ml (¾ pint) water
8 passion fruit
3–4 tablespoons white sugar (or to taste)
Juice 1½ lemons
A little rum (optional)

1. Pour the water into a bowl or jug.
2. Cut each passion fruit in half and scoop out the seeds and flesh into the water.
3. Wash the seeds between your fingers in the water until you have extracted as much of the flesh from the seeds as possible.
4. Pass through a sieve into another jug.

5 Add the sugar and lemon juice and blend until the sugar has dissolved.
6 Pour over ice in 4 glasses and serve. A little rum may be added if you wish.

Serves 4

SOURSOP MILK

1 soursop or a piece (about 340 g (¾ lb))
300 ml (½ pint) water
600 ml (1 pint) milk
Sugar to taste
Drop vanilla extract
1 egg yolk
½ teaspoon Angostura bitters
1 tumbler crushed ice

1 Remove and discard the skin and core of the soursop. Put the white pulp in a bowl and mix well with the water.
2 Pass through a sieve, rubbing with your fingers. Discard the black seeds. Pour the milk through the same sieve.
3 Place all the ingredients in a blender and blend at high speed.
4 If too thick, add some more milk and blend again after tasting for sweetness.
5 Serve in tumblers with more ice if you wish.

Serves 6–8

GUAVA SQUASH

400 g (14 oz) tin guavas, or 5 fresh guavas
900 ml (1½ pints) water
Rind ½ lime
Juice 2 limes
White sugar to taste
¼ teaspoon freshly ground cloves
¼ teaspoon freshly grated nutmeg

1 Scoop out the seeds from the guavas into a sieve and rub through into the bowl of a blender.
2 Add the guava flesh and all the other ingredients and blend at high speed. Taste.
3 Serve on crushed ice.

Serves 6–8

GINGER BEER

110 g (4 oz) fresh ginger (or to taste)
4.5 litres (1 gallon) water
675–900 g (1½–2 lb) granulated sugar
Juice and rind 1 lime
A few grains white rice

1. Wash and scrape the ginger then crush or pound it. Place it in a large bowl or a stoneware ginger jar.
2. Bring the water to the boil. Add the sugar, lime juice and rind to the ginger, then pour the boiling water over.
3. Add the rice. Cover and allow to stand for a week in a cool place. Stir at least 4 times during this period.
4. At the end of the week strain and bottle the ginger beer.
5. Refrigerate or store in a cool place, where it should keep for a week or two.
6. Serve with ice. A little rum may be added to each glass.

Makes 6–7 70 cl bottles

SORREL

450 g (1 lb) sorrel petals
1 generous cinnamon stick
Dried peel 1 orange (see Herbs, Spices and Other Condiments)
6 whole cloves
Small piece ginger, crushed
4.5 litres (1 gallon) boiling water
900 g–1.25 kg (2–2½ lb) granulated sugar (or to taste)
1–2 wine glasses rum

1. Quickly rinse the sorrel petals under cold running water. Put into a large bowl or jar together with the cinnamon stick, dried orange peel, cloves and crushed ginger.
2. Pour the boiling water over. Allow to cool, cover, then leave in the refrigerator for 2–3 days.
3. Strain, using a wooden spoon to press the petals. Pass through a fine cloth or strainer again.
4. Add the sugar and the rum (most Caribbean people like their sorrel very sweet), then bottle.
5. The sorrel can be served at this stage but it is best left for another

2–3 days. Serve chilled or with ice. More rum can be added when drinking. The sorrel should be a beautiful clear, red colour.

Makes approximately 6–7 70 cl bottles

PAWPAW SQUASH

2 ripe pawpaws, peeled
1.25 litres (2 pints) water
225 g (½ lb) sugar
Juice 3 lemons or limes

1. Place all the ingredients in a blender and process until smooth.
2. Strain and serve on ice. A few measures of rum may be added for those who indulge; I do, but the squash is very refreshing without.

Serves 8–10

LIMEADE

900 ml (1½ pints) soda water (or water)
Juice 4 limes
Sugar to taste
Rind 1½ limes
A few drops Angostura bitters
Freshly grated nutmeg

1. Combine all the ingredients except the nutmeg and blend well.
2. Strain into tumblers filled with crushed ice, sprinkle with nutmeg and serve.

Serves 4–6

PARTY FRUIT PUNCH (for children)

1 very large pineapple, peeled, cored and chopped (or 2 400 g (14 oz) tins)
Juice 1 lemon
1 large bottle lemonade
1 mango, peeled, stoned and chopped
Juice 6 oranges
½ pawpaw, peeled and chopped
2 ripe bananas, peeled and chopped
1 medium bottle ginger ale
Crushed ice

1 Put all the ingredients into a large bowl and mix.

Serves 12–15

PINEAPPLE AND ORANGE DRINK

2 thick slices pineapple, chopped
Juice 6 large oranges
Rind 1 orange
Sugar to taste
Angostura bitters (optional)
Small piece mace, freshly ground
½ teaspoon freshly ground cinnamon

1 Liquidize all the ingredients.
2 Pour the mixture over ice cubes and serve. A scoop of vanilla ice-cream in each glass makes this a wonderful treat.

Serves 2–3

SOURSOP AND PAWPAW

150 ml (5 fl oz) soursop juice (fresh or tinned)
225 g (½ lb) ripe pawpaw, peeled, deseeded and chopped
2 tablespoons sweetened condensed milk
300 ml (½ pint) milk
½ teaspoon Angostura bitters
Freshly grated nutmeg
Sugar to taste
Rum or cognac (optional)

1 Combine all the ingredients in a blender at high speed.
2 Taste for sweetness, add sugar if necessary and blend again.
3 Pour into glasses filled with crushed ice. You may add rum or cognac if you wish. The quantity depends on you.

Serves 2

GUAVA CUP

225 g (½ lb) guavas, deseeded and puréed
Simple syrup or sugar to taste
Juice ½ lemon
Pinch freshly grated nutmeg

750 ml (1½ pints) water
Guava slices to garnish

1 Blend all the ingredients in a liquidizer or mix well in a jug.
2 Strain and chill.
3 Serve in cups or tumblers filled with crushed ice. Garnish each with a slice of guava.

Serves 4–6

CREOLE FRUIT PUNCH

NON-ALCOHOLIC

Juice 4 oranges
Juice 3 grapefruits
Juice 2 limes
Juice 2 lemons
Juice extracted from 2 tablespoons maraschino cherries
2 teaspoons Angostura bitters
6 slices orange
6 slices lemon
Seeds and pulp of 2 passion fruit
Simple syrup to taste (see page 241)
Crushed ice
150 ml (¼ pint) water

1 Mix together the first five ingredients and then add the remaining seven.
2 Serve in large tumblers with straws and garnish with slices of any of the fruits used.

Serves 4–6

BARBADOS RUM PUNCH

These are the correct proportions for making rum punch – the quantity is up to you. The measure can be anything from a tablespoon upwards.

1 of lime juice
2 of simple syrup (see page 241)
3 of rum
4 of water
Dash Angostura bitters

Crushed ice
Freshly grated nutmeg

1 Put the lime juice, syrup, rum, water, Angostura and ice into a cocktail shaker.
2 Shake vigorously.
3 Serve with a little grated nutmeg.

PLANTER'S FRUIT PUNCH

3 tablespoons rum (matured)
2 tablespoons water
2 tablespoons simple syrup (see page 241)
1 tablespoon fresh lime juice
Tropical fruit, cut into chunks – banana, pineapple, orange, mango, etc.
Dash Angostura bitters
Crushed ice
Freshly grated nutmeg

1 Mix all the ingredients in a tall glass with the grated nutmeg sprinkled on top and serve.

Serves 1

BANANA DAIQUIRI

150 ml (5 fl oz) light rum
1 small banana, peeled and chopped
3 tablespoons banana liqueur
1½ wine glasses crushed ice
Banana and lime slices to garnish

1 Place all the ingredients (except the garnish) in an electric blender and whisk at high speed until smooth.
2 Serve garnished with a slice of banana and a slice of lime on a cocktail stick.

Serves 2

PINEAPPLE DAIQUIRI

150 ml (5 fl oz) finely crushed pineapple
100 ml (4 fl oz) light island rum
Juice ½ lime

25 ml (1 fl oz) orange liqueur
Caster sugar to taste

1 Place all the ingredients except the sugar in a blender.
2 Blend quickly, then add a little sugar to taste.
3 Blend very quickly again, and pour into glasses over ice.

Serves 2–3

RUM SOUR

3 tablespoons light brown island rum
2 tablespoons fresh lime juice
1 teaspoon simple syrup (see page 241)
1 tablespoon fresh orange juice
Crushed ice

1 Put all the ingredients into a cocktail shaker.
2 Shake vigorously, strain into a glass and serve.

Serves 1

COCONUT PUNCH

This is one of the favourites on the island of Dominica.

225 ml (8 fl oz) light rum
150 ml (5 fl oz) thick coconut milk (see Techniques)
75 ml (3 fl oz) sweetened condensed milk
Freshly grated nutmeg
Freshly ground cinnamon
Vanilla extract

1 Combine all the ingredients in an electric blender at high speed.
2 Pour over ice cubes in small tumblers. Stir once and serve sprinkled with extra nutmeg.

Serves 4

COCONUT MILK PUNCH

1 bottle white rum
1.1 litres (2 pints) coconut milk (see Techniques)
½ bottle gin
1 teaspoon natural vanilla essence
2 teaspoons Angostura bitters

Freshly grated nutmeg
1 tin sweetened condensed milk

1 Put all the ingredients into a large jug or bowl and whisk until well blended.
2 Decant into bottles and place in the lowest part of the refrigerator until needed. Coconut milk tends to thicken the colder it gets, so you may have to allow the bottles to stand at room temperature before serving.
3 Each bottle must be shaken vigorously before use, or poured into a cocktail shaker.
4 Serve with ice cubes. A little grated nutmeg may be sprinkled on top.

Serves 15 generously

Nutritional Tables*

KEY	
g	gram
k cal	kilocalorie
kJ	kiloJoule
mg	1 milligram (1,000th gram)
μg	1 microgram, also denoted by 'mcg' (1,000,000th gram)
Na	Sodium
K	Potassium
Ca	Calcium
Mg	Magnesium
Fe	Iron
Cu	Copper
Zn	Zinc

Carotene – Provitamin A

B1, B2, Niacin, Folic Acid – members of the 'B complex' of vitamins

C	Vitamin C (Ascorbic Acid)
N	Negligible
Tr	Trace

*Data adapted from *Immigrant Foods*, second supplement to *The Composition of Foods*, with the permission of the Controller of Her Majesty's Stationary Office.

Vegetables: Composition, Vitamins and Minerals per 100g

	Energy value		Protein	Fat	Carbo-hydrate	Minerals (mg)	
Food	k cal	kJ	g	g	g	Na	K
Ackee canned	151	625	2.9	15.2	0.8	240	270
Aubergine/brinjal/ eggplant raw	14	62	0.7	Tr	3.1	3	240
Cassava							
fresh, raw	135	565	1.0	0.2	31.4	2	394
frozen, raw	139	591	0.6	N	36.3	9	360
Chinese leaves/ amaranth raw	26	109	3.6	0.1	3.5	N	N
Cho cho/chayote/ vegetable pear raw	19	79	0.7	0.1	4.0	2	108
Courgettes/zucchini/ squash raw	25	105	1.6	0.4	4.5	1	202
Garlic raw	117	490	3.5	0.3	26.7	18	373
Ginger roots raw	46	192	1.6	0.8	7.9	7	316
Green banana/ Plantain raw	89	379	1.2	N	22.4	2	400
Lettuce raw	12	51	1.0	0.4	1.2	9	240
Mushroom raw	13	53	1.8	0.6	0	9	470
Okra/lady's fingers							
fresh raw	17	71	2.0	Tr	2.3	7	190
canned, drained solids only	15	64	1.4	N	2.5	440	105
Olives in brine, flesh and skin only	103	422	0.9	11.0	Tr	2250	91
Pepper, green raw	15	65	0.9	0.4	2.2	2	210
red/chilli raw	116	485	6.3	1.4	9.8	23	1286
Pumpkin raw	15	65	0.6	Tr	3.4	1	310
Shallot raw	48	201	1.9	0.3	9.6	8	297
Spinach fresh, raw	26	109	3.2	0.3	3.7	71	470
canned, drained solids only	24	100	2.7	0.6	2.7	236	250
Spring onion flesh of							
bulb only, raw	35	151	0.9	Tr	8.5	13	230
bulbs and tops, raw	28	117	1.6	0.4	4.8	4	178
Sweetcorn, on the cob							
kernels only, raw	127	538	4.1	2.4	23.7	1	300
canned, kernels only	76	325	2.9	0.5	16.1	310	200
canned, immature baby corn, drained solids only	21	88	2.9	0.4	2.4	1140	183
Sweet potatoes raw	91	387	1.2	0.6	21.5	19	320
Taro tuber raw	94	393	2.2	0.4	20.2	10	448
Tomato fresh, raw	14	60	0.9	Tr	2.8	3	290
canned, drained solids only	12	51	1.1	Tr	2.0	29	270
paste in tube	67	286	6.1	Tr	11.4	420	1540
Watercress raw	14	61	2.9	Tr	0.7	60	310
Yam raw	131	560	2.0	0.2	32.4	N	500

Mg	Fe	Cu	Zn	Vitamins: Carotene µg	B1 mg	B2 mg	Niacin mg	C mg	Total folic acid µg
40	0.7	0.27	0.6	N	0.03	0.07	1.1	30	41
10	0.4	0.08	N	Tr	0.05	0.03	0.9	5	20
4	0.9	N	N	0	0.05	0.04	0.6	0	24
21	0.1	0.09	0.3	0	0.02	0.01	0.4	18	13
160	2.9	0.37	N	6540	0.04	0.22	0.7	23	85
N	0.4	N	N	15	0.01	0.02	0.4	14	N
6	2.4	N	N	350	0.05	0.09	0.4	16	48
8	1.5	N	0.9	Tr	0.24	0.05	0.4	10	6
N	1.3	N	N	55	0.01	0.03	1.7	4	N
33	0.2	0.11	0.2	73	0.03	0.02	0.4	14	6
8	0.9	0.03	0.2	1000	0.07	0.08	0.4	15	34
13	1.0	0.64	0.1	0	0.10	0.40	4.6	3	23
60	1.0	0.19	N	90	0.10	0.10	1.3	25	100
32	5.4	0.36	0.5	N	0.07	0.04	0.2	1	12
22	1.0	0.23	N	180	Tr	Tr	0.1	0	N
11	0.4	0.07	0.2	200	Tr	0.03	0.9	100	11
19	3.6	0.10	0.3	6600	0.37	0.51	2.5	96	16
8	0.4	0.08	0.2	1500	0.04	0.04	0.5	5	13
N	0.7	N	N	0	0.04	0.05	1.0	6	N
88	3.1	0.16	N	4860	0.10	0.20	1.1	51	123
63	2.6	N	N	4800	0.02	0.12	0.3	14	N
11	1.2	0.13	N	Tr	0.03	0.05	0.4	25	40
N	1.2	N	N	890	0.06	0.11	0.5	29	N
46	11	0.16	1.2	240	0.15	0.08	2.2	12	52
23	0.6	0.05	0.6	210	0.05	0.08	1.5	5	32
N	1.2	N	N	140	0.02	0.04	0.6	14	N
13	0.7	0.16	N	4000(a)	0.10	0.06	1.2	25	52
33	1.2	N	N	Tr	0.12	0.04	1.4	8	N
11	0.4	0.10	0.2	600	0.06	0.04	0.8	20	28
11	0.9	0.11	0.3	500	0.06	0.03	0.8	18	25
66	5.1	0.63	1.7	2860	0.34	0.17	4.8	100	140
17	1.6	0.14	0.2	3000	0.10	0.10	1.1	60	N
40	0.3	0.16	0.4	12	0.10	0.03	0.8	10	N

Fruits: Composition, Vitamins and Minerals per 100g

Food	Energy value		Protein	Fat	Carbo-hydrate	Minerals (mg)		
	k cal	kJ	g	g	g	Na	K	Ca
Avocado fresh, raw	223	922	4.2	22.2	1.8	2	400	15
Banana raw	79	337	1.1	0.3	19.2	1	350	7
Breadfruit canned, drained solids only	64	273	0.6	N	16.4	255	125	14
Custard apple raw	92	385	2.1	0.5	15.7	N	N	26
Guava fresh, raw	62	259	0.8	0.6	9.4	4	289	23
canned in syrup, whole contents	60	258	0.4	Tr	15.7	7	120	8
Jackfruit canned, drained solids only	101	429	0.5	N	26.3	4	130	10
Kumquats canned	138	577	0.4	0.5	35.4	111	156	16
Lime fresh, raw	36	151	0.5	2.4	5.6	2	82	13
Loquats/Japanese medlar canned	84	351	0.3	0.1	22.2	N	N	22
Mangoes fresh, raw	59	253	0.5	Tr	15.3	7	190	10
canned in syrup, whole contents	77	330	0.3	Tr	20.3	3	100	10
juice canned	44	184	0.1	0.2	11.7	9	18	2
Melon, honeydew raw	21	90	0.6	Tr	5.0	20	220	14
musk, cantaloupe raw	24	102	1.0	Tr	5.3	14	320	19
water melon raw	21	92	0.4	Tr	5.3	4	120	5
Ortaniques raw	49	205	1.0	0.2	11.7	N	N	41
Passion fruit raw	34	147	2.8	Tr	6.2	28	350	16
Pawpaw/papaya fresh, raw	45	188	0.5	0.1	11.3	4	221	24
canned, whole contents	65	275	0.2	Tr	17.0	8	110	23
Pineapple fresh, raw	46	194	0.5	Tr	11.6	2	250	12
whole contents canned in syrup	77	328	0.3	Tr	20.2	1	94	13
Pomegranate, fruit fresh, raw	72	301	1.0	0.6	16.6	1	379	13
juice fresh	44	189	0.2	Tr	11.6	1	200	3
Sapota/sapodilla/ Nase berry fruits raw	76	318	0.4	0.7	16.9	3	181	27

(a) Value for ripe, orange-coloured mangoes. The carotene content varies according to the colou
orange flesh.

				Vitamins					Total folic acid
Mg	Fe	Cu	Zn	Carotene µg	B_1 mg	B_2 mg	Niacin mg	C mg	µg
29	1.5	0.21	N	100	0.1	0.1	1.8	15	66
42	0.4	0.16	0.2	200	0.04	0.07	0.8	10	22
9	0.3	0.05	0.2	N	0.04	0.02	0.2	10	32
N	0.9	N	N	Tr	0.08	0.10	0.5	22	N
13	0.9	N	N	168	0.05	0.05	1.2	242	N
6	0.5	0.10	0.4	100	0.04	0.03	1.0	180	N
10	0.6	0.10	0.4	N	0.02	0.12	0.2	2	N
N	0.8	N	N	25	0.09	0.06	0.5	40	N
N	Tr	N	N	10	0.03	0.02	0.1	46	N
N	0.1	N	N	120	0.01	0	0.5	0	N
18	0.5	0.12	N	1200(a)	0.03	0.04	0.4	30	N
7	0.4	0.09	0.3	1200	0.02	0.03	0.2	10	N
N	1.5	N	N	210	Tr	Tr	0.9	25	N
13	0.2	0.04	0.1.	100(b)	0.05	0.03	0.5	25	30
20	0.8	0.04	0.1	2000(c)	0.05	0.03	0.5	25	30
11	0.3	0.03	0.1	20	0.02	0.02	0.3	5	3
N	0.4	N	N	120	0.10	0.04	0.4	50	N
39	1.1	0.12	N	10	Tr	0.10	1.9	20	N
8	0.7	0.01	0.4	710	0.03	0.05	0.4	73	1
8	0.4	0.10	0.3	500	0.02	0.02	0.3	15	N
17	0.4	0.08	0.1	60	0.08	0.02	0.3	25	11
8	0.4	0.05	N	40	0.05	0.02	0.2	12	N
12	0.7	0.17	N	0	0.07	0.01	0.3	7	N
3	0.2	0.07	N	0	0.02	0.03	0.2	8	N
N	0.6	N	N	25	Tr	Tr	0.2	13	N

nd unripe mangoes contain one-tenth of this amount. (b) Value for green flesh. (c) Value for

Index